Spatial Statistics & Geostatistics

Geographic Information Science and Technology (GIST) is enjoying profound innovation in its research and development. *SAGE Advances in GIST* will provide students with learning resources to support and enrich their interest in the workings of Geographic Information Science and Technology. These highly visual and highly applied texts will promote curiosity about developments in the field, as well as provide focussed and up-to-date tools for doing GIS research.

Series edited by Mei-Po Kwan, Department of Geography, University of California, Berkeley

Titles forthcoming:

Spatial Modelling
Antonio Paez

GIS Algorithms
Ningchuan Xiao

Titles in development:

Geovisual Analytics

Spatial Databases

Spatial Analysis

GIST

Spatial Statistics & Geostatistics

Theory and Applications for Geographic Information Science & Technology

Yongwan Chun & Daniel A. Griffith

SAGE

Los Angeles | London | New Delhi
Singapore | Washington DC

Los Angeles | London | New Delhi
Singapore | Washington DC

SAGE Publications Ltd
1 Oliver's Yard
55 City Road
London EC1Y 1SP

SAGE Publications Inc.
2455 Teller Road
Thousand Oaks, California 91320

SAGE Publications India Pvt Ltd
B 1/I 1 Mohan Cooperative Industrial Area
Mathura Road
New Delhi 110 044

SAGE Publications Asia-Pacific Pte Ltd
3 Church Street
#10-04 Samsung Hub
Singapore 049483

Editor: Robert Rojek
Editorial assistant: Alana Clogan
Production editor: Katherine Haw
Copyeditor: Richard Leigh
Marketing manager: Michael Ainsley
Cover design: Francis Kenney
Typeset by: C&M Digitals (P) Ltd, Chennai, India
Printed by: Ashford Colour Press, Gosport, Hants

© Yongwan Chun and Daniel A. Griffith 2013

First published 2013

Library of Congress Control Number: 2012938996

British Library Cataloguing in Publication data

A catalogue record for this book is available from
the British Library

MIX
Paper from
responsible sources
FSC
www.fsc.org FSC® C011748

ISBN 978-1-4462-0173-2
ISBN 978-1-4462-0174-9 (pbk)

This book is dedicated to our wives, Hyunju Lee and
Diane Griffith, and our good friend Heja Kim

Table of Contents

About the Authors

Yongwan Chun is an Assistant Professor of Geospatial Information Sciences at The University of Texas at Dallas. He earned a PhD in geography and a master's degree in statistics from the Ohio State University. His research aims at developing quantitative methods for spatial analysis and modeling. Particularly, his research interests lie in spatial statistics and GIS focusing on urban and economic issues including population migration, commuting, and urban crime. His papers have been published in *Annals of the Association of American Geographers*, *Cartography and Geographic Information Science*, *Journal of Geographical Systems*, and *Journal of Urban Affairs* among others.

Daniel A. Griffith, an Ashbel Smith Professor of Geospatial Information Sciences at The University of Texas at Dallas, has published 17 books and over 200 scholarly pieces appearing in geography, statistics, mathematics, economics, and regional science journals and other outlets. He served as editor of *Geographical Analysis* from 2009 to 2014. He is a Fellow of the American Association for the Advancement of Science, the Guggenheim Foundation, the Regional Science Association International, the Spatial Econometrics Association, and the New York Academy of Sciences. His current research interests include spatial statistics, spatial epidemiology, urban public health, and economic geography.

Preface

Matheron began formal theoretical developments for geostatistics as early as the mid-1960s at the École Normale Supérieure des Mines de Paris, expanding on research by Krige, a South African mining engineer. Cliff and Ord began formal theoretical developments for spatial autoregression in the late 1960s, extending work by Geary, Moran, Whittle, and Meade. These two academic endeavors developed in parallel for about two decades, primarily because geostatistics research was being published in French, and spatial autoregression research was being published in English. Interaction between these two communities of scholars finally began to occur in the 1970s, with considerable expansion of geostatistics into the English academic community in the 1980s. Cressie's *Statistics for Spatial Data* capped this development as the 1990s began. Today, geostatistics and spatial autoregression coexist in spatial statistics courses and research.

Meanwhile, the principal breakthrough for eigenvector spatial filtering (ESF) occurred in 1996, with *The Canadian Geographer* publication entitled "Spatial autocorrelation and eigenfunctions of the geographic weights matrix accompanying geo-referenced data." Tiefelsdorf and Boots's 1995 *Environment and Planning A* paper, entitled "The exact distribution of Moran's *I*," established the foundation for ESF that allowed this breakthrough. Formal theoretical ESF developments occurred during the next fifteen years. The publication of *Spatial Autocorrelation and Spatial Filtering* (2003) promoted this endeavor, which in turn resulted in a US National Science Foundation–funded workshop in 2008, held at the University of Texas at Dallas, whose purpose was to disseminate the ESF methodology. This workshop introduced a group of emerging academics and established professionals, who are engaged in spatial analysis, demography, epidemiology, ecology, or econometrics, to the novel methodology of ESF. In its non-parametric and semi-parametric forms, ESF belongs to a developing family of techniques that is geared toward analyzing geo-referenced datasets in an exploratory and confirmatory framework. The dissemination of this methodology via the 2008 summer workshop focused on: (1) the conceptual simplicity of ESF that makes spatial statistics more accessible to a very wide user group; (2) the increasing appearance of ESF approaches in methodological and applied literatures from a broad disciplinary scope; (3) how ESF dramatically simplifies the implementation of linear, nonlinear, generalized linear, as well as mixed models for spatially autocorrelated data; (4) juxtaposing ESF with geostatistics and spatial autoregression; and (5) software tools that prototype ESF within the widely available R computing platform.

This last point is critical. Although the ESF methodology has been adopted in various fields – including economics (Möller and Soltwedel, 2007; Pecci and Pontarollo, 2010; Cuaresma and Feldkircher, 2012), regional science (Grimpe and Patuelli, 2011), epidemiology (Jacob et al., 2008), and ecology (Diniz-Filho and Bini, 2005; Dormann et al., 2007; De Marco et al., 2008; Diniz-Filho et al., 2009; Ficetola and Padoa-Schioppa, 2009) – a lack of implementation software tends to hamper its dissemination. This book is an outgrowth of the workshop and this need for a better understanding of how to implement ESF methodology. Accordingly, this book includes comparisons between geostatistics, spatial autoregression, and ESF analyses. It also includes R code for implementing the analyses. All of the R code results were confirmed with SAS implementations. Digital versions of the R code are available from us upon request.

Yongwan Chun and Dan Griffith
Richardson, TX
August 2011

1

Introduction

1.1. Spatial statistics and geostatistics

As its title indicates, the theme of this book is spatial statistics and geostatistics, with emphasis on selected classical topics from these two subdisciplines in order to highlight theory and applications for geographic information science and technology. Computer code windows in almost all chapters report R code for implementing many of the techniques discussed – the criteria employed to select this software are as follows: it is free; and it contains modules for most techniques as well as geographic information system (GIS) capabilities. Computer code windows in Section 9.1 are the exception; these windows report WinBUGS code because this software package is free and is widely used for Bayesian analysis. When possible, analyses were verified with SAS and ArcGIS implementations. A sizable amount of human and physical geography data was assembled for the main island of Puerto Rico and used to formulate the empirical examples. These include remotely sensed (Landsat 7 ETM+) data, digital elevation model (DEM) data, climatological station precipitation and temperature data, United States socio–economic/demographic and agricultural census data, and computer-generated pseudo-random number data. Each chapter ends with a set of relevant references.

The set of eight chapters surveys a wide range of techniques, all of which have spatial autocorrelation as their common factor. Probability models range from conventional (bell–shaped) normal curve theory to generalized linear models (e.g., Poisson and binomial probability models). Techniques range from graphically portraying spatial autocorrelation, through spatial autoregression and semi–variogram analysis, to eigenvector spatial filtering. Selected special topics, such as determining effective geographic sample size and multiple testing for local spatial autocorrelation statistics, are interspersed with these standard topics. One goal in many chapters is to uncover, illustrate, and exploit impacts of spatial autocorrelation in georeferenced data analysis. Perhaps missing-value imputation, albeit via kriging or regression-based predicted values, best underscores the importance and utility of spatial autocorrelation.

Chapter 2 reviews the foundation indices quantifying the nature and degree of spatial autocorrelation. One unique feature of this chapter is its summary of simulation experiment results exemplifying the relationship between the join count statistics and the Moran coefficient. This chapter also presents the basic graphical portrayals and illustrates salient impacts of spatial autocorrelation. Foremost is variance inflation, a long-recognized property for the bell-shaped curve, which is extended here to Poisson and binomial random variables. Inclusion of an empirical comparison between a semi-variogram and a Geary ratio-based correlogram is another distinctive feature of this chapter. It concludes with an overview of the well-known statistical distribution theory for linear regression residual spatial autocorrelation.

Chapter 3 reviews the basic random sampling designs for collecting spatial data: unconstrained, systematic, geographic stratified, and cluster. Each of these is applied to the Puerto Rico DEM, which has a population comprising nearly 10,000 elevation locations. Sample results are compared with those for the non-probability sample of existing climatological weather station locations. A summary of simulation experiment results calls attention to selected properties of these sampling designs. One original feature of this chapter is its implementation of the hexagon tessellation stratified random sampling design: partial hexagons materializing along the boundary of the island are treated in a way that merges subsets of them for sampling purposes into comparable single hexagons. This chapter also describes how to implement the bootstrap and jackknife resampling techniques. It concludes by outlining the concept of effective geographic sample size, with special reference to its Puerto Rico DEM elevation sampling exercise.

Chapter 4 presents differentiations between homogeneity and heterogeneity in spatial data, in terms of both a mean response and its variance. This chapter's discussion is couched in terms of Box–Cox power transformations to normality, as well as their accompanying back-transformations, analysis of variance (ANOVA), and model-based inference. One innovative feature of this chapter is its inclusion of the extremely accurate approximate back-transformation equation. This chapter also describes common ways to quantify geographic contiguity, and then introduces the eigenvector spatial filtering methodology, differentiating between static geographic distributions and spatial interaction cases. It concludes with a discussion of anisotropy.

The focus of Chapter 5 is on converting the specifications of conventional statistical models into ones that take spatial autocorrelation into account. It begins by presenting a reformulation of linear regression models to spatial autoregressive and eigenvector spatial filter versions; in doing so, this chapter extends the discussion of eigenvector spatial filtering methodology initiated in Chapter 4. Eigenvector spatial filtering conceptualizations enable respecifications of binomial/logistic and Poisson regression models to account for spatial autocorrelation. One original feature of this chapter is a detailed presentation of how to implement eigenvector spatial filtering with the R package. Comparisons between results obtained with conventional and spatial model specifications corroborate the importance of accounting for spatial autocorrelation in georeferenced data analyses. This chapter concludes with a further differentiation between static geographic distributions and spatial interaction cases, with specific reference to a journey-to-work example.

Global statistics and global analyses establish the foundation for Chapters 2–5. Chapter 6 shifts attention to local geographic statistics. Its unique feature is an innovative treatment of multiple testing based upon effective sample size. Quantification of small-scale spatial clustering is achieved with both local indices of spatial association and the Getis–Ord statistics. A presentation of spatially varying coefficients extends this perspective, helping to relate local to global measures of spatial autocorrelation, and illustrating how bivariate relationships can vary across geographic space.

Geostatistics constitutes the theme of Chapter 7. The presentation casts semi-variogram models as a tool to quantify spatial variance, and co-kriging as a tool to quantify spatial covariance. One special feature of this chapter is a comparison of co-kriging results with increasing resolution of a covariate: first 112 weather stations; then 9,181 DEM rasters; and, finally, 8,987,017 satellite pixels. The next presentation is of techniques (e.g., Cochrane–Orcutt type spatial filtering) that differentiate between spatial and aspatial variance, followed by techniques that differentiate between spatial and aspatial covariance. Treatment of these latter topics includes comparisons between data analyses ignoring and accounting for spatial autocorrelation. The product moment correlation coefficient decomposition is a novel feature of this chapter. Overall, this chapter allows spatial scientists to answer the following two questions: What is special about spatial data? Do spatial autocorrelation/dependency effects matter? Model diagnostic statistics can change, statistical decisions can change, correlation coefficients (including their signs) can change, and factor structure can change.

Chapter 8 reviews the principal use of geostatistics, which is to predict unknown values of an attribute at some locations from known values of the same attribute at other locations; in other words, interpolation. Kriging is the best linear unbiased predictor (BLUP), exploiting the sufficient statistics of a sample, and hence is equivalent to an expectation–maximization (EM) solution.

The importance of this chapter lies in many spatial analysts being interested in filling holes/gaps in their maps created by incomplete data (i.e., small-area estimation). This chapter reviews the equivalence between the kriging and the spatial autoregressive missing-value imputation solutions. It also presents connections between imputation and regression prediction of new observation values. In either case, the techniques discussed support map generalization, especially from a small sample of locationally tagged values (i.e., a massive number of imputations). An innovative feature of this chapter is the extension of eigenvector spatial filtering methodology to calculate imputations for missing georeferenced values. In all cases, techniques are presented for calculating the accompanying uncertainty for mean response imputation. Although this chapter focuses on imputations, mathematical spatial statistics often dismisses this problem. Rather, the theoretical problem of interest is to estimate parameters in the presence of missing values. Chapter 8 addresses this topic, too.

Chapter 9, the final chapter, introduces three additional, more advanced topics in spatial statistics. Although many additional topics could be selected for treatment in a final chapter, this chapter spotlights three that currently possess very high profiles. Foremost is Bayesian map analysis. WinBUGS, and more specifically its GeoBUGS module, are used to present this methodology. Of note is that SAS increasingly supports this type of analysis. The R package contains modules, such as MCMC, necessary for this type of analysis, and can be used to interface with WinBUGS. Another prominent topic outlined and demonstrated in this chapter is the designing of Monte Carlo spatial simulation experiments. This tool is particularly useful in spatial statistics, where many problems defy analytical solution. This discussion complements the bootstrap and jackknife discussions appearing in Chapter 3. The Monte Carlo experiment investigating eigenvector selection from a restricted candidate set of vectors to construct a spatial filter is an exclusive feature of this chapter. The final section of the chapter presents an overview of spatial error and uncertainty, in order to raise awareness of these contemporary topics.

1.2. R basics

R is a free software environment for statistical computing and graphics. Because R is an implementation of the S programming language developed by Bell Laboratories, it is similar to S-Plus marketed by TIBCO Software Inc., which is a commercialized implementation of the S language. R is available free of charge from the R project website (www.r-project.org) under the GNU public license terms, and its installation file can be downloaded from this site. Also, R source codes are open to the public as an open-source environment.

R comprises *packages*. The R core system includes about eight packages. One of these, the *base* package, supports basic procedures. Many more R packages are available from the Comprehensive R Archive Network (CRAN) mirror sites. Specific procedures require additional packages to be installed and loaded. For example, the *spdep* package contains functions for spatial data analysis, such as spatial weights management, spatial autocorrelation quantifications, and spatial regression. R can be further extended with packages; new packages are developed, and old packages are upgraded regularly and then provided through CRAN. The great popularity of R among members of academic societies promotes its development with new functions and packages from researchers in various fields.

A user needs to know selected basics to start working with R. First, because R is mostly command line driven, the user needs to type or pass R functions to the R console. The greater than symbol '>' also is used as the prompt in the R console. For an example, a user can conduct arithmetic operations as a calculator:

```
> 2 * 3
[1] 6
```

Non-graphical output such as this also appears in the R console.

Second, R supports selected common data structures, including vector, matrix, list, and data frame. A vector is an ordered container of primitive elements. It can have multiple elements of a certain data type or class. For example, a numeric vector can be created as follows:

```
> x <- c(1, 2, 3, 4)
> x
[1] 1 2 3 4
> y <- x > 2
> y
[1] FALSE FALSE TRUE TRUE
```

The function c() is used to combine values, and '<-' is an assignment operator. Consequently, the numeric vector x contains 1, 2, 3, and 4 as its elements. Other types of vectors include logical, character, and factor. In the preceding example, a logical vector y is created by evaluating if each element of x is greater than 2 with the greater than operator (>). A matrix is a collection of homogeneous elements in a two-dimensional space. The matrix() function can be used to create a matrix. The following example creates a 2×2 matrix from the vector x:

```
> matrix(x,2,2)
   [,1] [,2]
[1,] 1 3
[2,] 2 4
```

R has functions and operators that can be performed on a matrix. For example, the matrix multiplication operator (%*%) should be distinguished from the element multiplication operator (*). A list is a collection of elements that are often vectors. It allows the combining of different types and lengths of data. The following example illustrates how to create a list from two vectors:

```
> child.names <- c("Greg", "Sally", "Chris")
> child.ages <- c(10, 8, 5)
> my.list <- list(name=child.names, age=child.ages)
> my.list
$name
[1] "Greg" "Sally" "Chris"
$age
[1] 10 8 5
```

The my.list object contains two elements. Each element can be referred to by its corresponding number, with the double squared bracket sign, or by its name. For example, my.list[[1]] and my.list$name will return the same vector, namely ("Greg", "Sally", "Chris"). A data frame is similar to a list, but it can contain only vectors with the same length. A data frame can be created with the data.frame() function as follows:

```
> my.df <- data.frame(name=child.names, age=child.ages)
> my.df
 name age
1 Greg 10
2 Sally 8
3 Chris 5
```

Third, R has functions to read external data files. For example, the read.csv() function creates a data frame from a CSV file, and the scan() function reads data into a vector or list. A package called *foreign* supports reading different types of files, including SPSS, Stata, and DBF, into an R workspace.

R provides a number of functions, from basic descriptive statistics to more advanced data analysis techniques, through packages. Graphics such as histograms, scatterplots, and boxplots can be created with R functions, although complex graphics may require multiple steps. Graphical output appears in a graphics window, and can be saved as an image file. Furthermore, a user can define a custom function with `function()`.

Finally, because this section provides very limited information about R, interested readers should consult other sources for further information. The R help system provides useful information for functions, packages, and other features of R, including descriptions, syntax, arguments, and other detailed information. R manuals are available on the R project website (http://cran.r-project.org/manuals.html). Users may also get help from other developers and users of R through the R-help list. This mailing list's information can also be found on the R project website (http://www.r-project.org/mail.html).

## 2

Spatial Autocorrelation

LEARNING OBJECTIVES:

- To review the basic quantifications of spatial autocorrelation
- To describe the basic graphical portrayals of spatial autocorrelation
- To illustrate salient impacts of spatial autocorrelation
- To outline the standard test for residual spatial autocorrelation

Much of classical statistical theory and practice assume that observations are independent and identically distributed (iid), often conforming to a bell-shaped curve (i.e., normal distribution). This assumption allows covariation terms to be set to 0, dramatically simplifying mathematical statistical theory. Correlated samples theory emerged as one of the first deviations from this iid assumption, in the form of repeated measures, leading to multivariate statistical theory: observations are paired, with the distribution of pairs being iid while the pairs themselves are correlated. Examples include pre- and post-tests, siblings as observations, and other matchings. In other words, $2n$ data values actually are treated as n data values, with covariances being weighted by the correlation between the data value pairs such that variation ranges from twice the variance (a correlation of 0) to 0 (a correlation of 1).

Repeated measures naturally led to time series analysis, for which a single time series of data values can be viewed as a sample of size 1 with repeated, sequentially correlated measures. These measures are treated as observations, such that n is the number of data values in a time series. Because the correlation is within a single observation, the prefix "auto-" was attached to "correlation" to differentiate this situation from conventional-correlated-samples situations.

The next extension was to spatial series analysis, pioneered by Moran (1948) and Geary (1954), among others, and popularized by Cliff and Ord (see *Geographical Analysis*, Issue 4, 2009). This conceptualization extends the simple linear structure of time series to a more general topological geographical structure, resulting in the adjective "spatial" being attached to autocorrelation to differentiate it from other types of correlated samples. Here a map of data values can be viewed as a sample of size 1 with repeated, nearby correlated measures. These measures are treated as observations, such that n is the number of locations on a map. Because of its tractability, the bell-shaped curve furnished the initial preferred probability model for this specification (Ripley, 1990: 8–10).

The general topological geographical structure may be operationalized by constructing an $n \times n$ table (e.g., Excel spreadsheet) of binary 0–1 indicator variables, one for each location on a map. The cell entries in this table are 1 when the row and column locations are designated as neighbors, and 0 otherwise. A recurring definition of "neighbor" is when two areal units in a surface partitioning share a common non-zero-length border. Frequently this table is denoted by the $n \times n$ matrix $\mathbf{C}$, with its cells being denoted by c_{ij}. Figure 2.1a illustrates this concept. It is part of the matrix for the Puerto Rico surface partitioning.

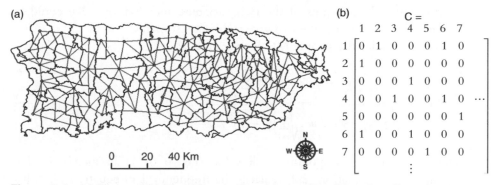

Figure 2.1   (a) The partitioning of Puerto Rico into municipalities. Gray lines denote the topological network, which connects the centroids of municipalities with common boundaries. (b) The initial part of the 73 × 73 connectivity matrix for Puerto Rico.

2.1. Indices measuring spatial dependency

Moran (1948) and Geary (1954) furnish the two most widely used indices of spatial autocorrelation. The Moran coefficient (MC) is a covariation measure that relates directly to the Pearson product moment correlation coefficient, whereas the Geary ratio (GR) is a paired comparisons measure that relates directly to the semi-variogram plot utilized in geostatistics (and discussed in the next section). The join count statistics constitute another set of spatial autocorrelation indices that deal with binary 0–1 nominal measurements. And Sen and Sööt (1977) address the case of ranked georeferenced data. Just as the point biserial and Spearman rank correlation coefficients are special cases of the Pearson product moment correlation coefficient (e.g., see Griffith and Amrhein, 1991: 109–11), the MC is capable of indexing data across all four measurement scales (i.e., nominal, ordinal, interval, and ratio; Griffith, 2010c).

Consider the sample Pearson product moment correlation coefficient, r, calculated for two variables, X and Y:

$$r = \frac{\sum_{i=1}^{n} 1\,(x_i - \bar{x})(y_i - \bar{y})\,/\,n}{\sqrt{\sum_{i=1}^{n}(x_i - \bar{x})^2\,/\,n}\ \sqrt{\sum_{i=1}^{n}(y_i - \bar{y})^2\,/\,n}}, \tag{2.1}$$

where 1 is the frequency of observation i; x_i and y_i are the paired values of two variables for observation i; $\bar{x}$ and $\bar{y}$ are the respective means of these two variables; the numerator is a covariation term; the denominator is the product of the standard deviations of the two variables; and division by n could be replaced by division by $n - 1$ to give unbiased estimates.

Next, consider the sample MC for variable Y:

$$MC = \frac{\sum_{i=1}^{n}\sum_{j=1}^{n} c_{ij}\,(y_i - \bar{y})(y_j - \bar{y})\,/\,\sum_{i=1}^{n}\sum_{j=1}^{n} c_{ij}}{\sqrt{\sum_{i=1}^{n}(y_i - \bar{y})^2\,/\,n}\ \sqrt{\sum_{i=1}^{n}(y_i - \bar{y})^2\,/\,n}}, \tag{2.2}$$

where c_{ij} is the corresponding cell value (i.e., 0 or 1) in matrix $\mathbf{C}$. The frequency c_{ij} in equation (2.2) replaces the frequency 1 in equation (2.1). Just as n counts the number of 1s in the numerator of equation (2.1), $\sum_{i=1}^{n}\sum_{j=1}^{n} c_{ij}$ counts the number of 1s in the numerator of equation (2.2). Values y_i and $\bar{y}$ in equation (2.2) respectively replace x_i and $\bar{x}$ in equation (2.1); autocorrelation refers to correlation within a single variable. Equation (2.2) often appears as its simplified form:

$$MC = \frac{n}{\sum_{i=1}^{n}\sum_{j=1}^{n} c_{ij}}\ \frac{\sum_{i=1}^{n}\sum_{j=1}^{n} c_{ij}\,(y_i - \bar{y})(y_j - \bar{y})}{\sum_{i=1}^{n}(y_i - \bar{y})^2}, \tag{2.3}$$

whose relationship with equation (2.1) is less conspicuous.

2.1.1. Important properties of MC

The most immediate noteworthy property of the MC arises from the substitutions converting equation (2.1) into (2.2): the range of the MC no longer is [−1, 1] − this interval can shrink, but usually expands − and the midpoint, denoting zero spatial autocorrelation, becomes $-1/(n-1)$ rather than 0. The MC for a regular square tessellation (e.g., the pixels of a remotely sensed image) asymptotically converges on the interval [−1, 1] with an increasing number of squares; irregular surface partitionings (e.g., the counties of the United States) do not necessarily have this convergence property. The midpoint asymptotically converges on 0 with an increasing number of locations.

Cliff and Ord (1981, p. 21) furnish complicated expressions for the variance of the MC, one based upon the iid normal assumption, and the other based upon permutations. Griffith (2010c) shows that values rendered by these expressions are very well approximated for $n \geq 25$ by

$$\frac{2}{\sum\limits_{i=1}^{n}\sum\limits_{j=1}^{n} c_{ij}}, \tag{2.4}$$

which is a dramatic simplification. This finding is analogous to the variance of the transformed Pearson product moment correlation coefficient being $1/(n-3)$. The 2 appears in the numerator here because the MC calculation involves both c_{ij} and c_{ji}. The number 2 appears in the formula for the GR for this same reason.

Griffith (2010c) shows that the preceding distributional properties (e.g., the mean and the variance) of the MC also hold for non–normal variables. Independence is the critical distributional assumption when computing the mean and the standard error for the MC under a null hypothesis of zero spatial autocorrelation. The second critical property is n. If Y is a normally distributed variable, n can be as small as 2. For non–normal variables that mimic a normally distributed one, n depends upon when the two distributions become indistinguishable, which often is by $n = 25$; sometimes parameter values reduce this threshold value of n. These distributional properties also hold for non–normally distributed variables that are symmetric, beginning with $n = 2$. When non–normally distributed variables are skewed, the threshold value of n becomes somewhat larger. In practice, evidence presented by Griffith (2010c) suggests that n should be at least 25, and preferably at least 100, depending upon the type of attribute variable being studied, in order for the standard distributional properties for the MC to hold.

2.1.2. Relationships between MC and GR, and MC and join count statistics

The GR may be rewritten in terms of the MC as follows:

$$ GR = \frac{n-1}{2\sum\limits_{i=1}^{n}\sum\limits_{j=1}^{n} c_{ij}} \frac{\sum\limits_{i=1}^{n}(x_i - \bar{x})^2 \left(\sum\limits_{j=1}^{n} c_{ij} \right)}{\sum\limits_{i=1}^{n}(x_i - \bar{x})^2} - \frac{n-1}{n} MC, \tag{2.5} $$

which emphasizes the inverse relationship between the two indices (Figure 2.2), and underscores that the GR is impacted more by attribute and configurational outliers – via the numerator term $\sum\limits_{i=1}^{n}(x_i - \bar{x})^2 (\sum\limits_{j=1}^{n} c_{ij})$ – because it accentuates large deviations (which are squared) and large numbers of neighbors. One implication of this equation furnishes an intuitive check for data behavior: if MC + GR ≈ 1, then the data are well behaved (e.g., no extreme outliers). The first term in equation (2.5) indicates that the GR is more variable than the MC. Meanwhile, the approximate standard error for the GR that is equivalent to the square root of equation (2.4) is

$$ \sqrt{\frac{2}{\sum\limits_{i=1}^{n}\sum\limits_{j=1}^{n} c_{ij}} + 2\frac{\sum\limits_{i=1}^{n}\left(\sum\limits_{j=1}^{n} c_{ij}\right)^2}{\left(\sum\limits_{i=1}^{n}\sum\limits_{j=1}^{n} c_{ij}\right)^2}}, $$

indicating that the sampling distribution for the GR also is more variable than that for the MC. For these and other reasons, the MC is the preferred index of spatial autocorrelation.

A principal drawback of the join count statistics is that a set of three measures must be interpreted: one for adjacent 1s, one for adjacent 0s, and one for

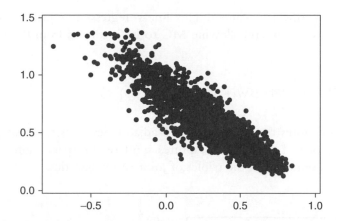

Figure 2.2 Relationship between GR (vertical axis) and MC (horizontal axis) presented in Griffith et al. (2003).

0s adjacent to 1s. The MC overcomes this weakness by furnishing a single summary index. The numerator of equation (2.3) may be rewritten as

$$\sum_{i=1}^{n}\sum_{j=1}^{n} c_{ij}\ (y_i - \overline{y})(y_j - \overline{y}) = \sum_{i=1}^{n}\sum_{j=1}^{n} c_{ij}\ y_i y_j - \overline{y}\left(\sum_{i=1}^{n}\sum_{j=1}^{n} c_{ij} y_i + \sum_{i=1}^{n}\sum_{j=1}^{n} c_{ij} y_j \right)$$
$$+ \overline{y}^2 \sum_{i=1}^{n}\sum_{j=1}^{n} c_{ij};$$

the first term captures the number of adjacent 1s, the second term captures the number of 0s adjacent to 1s, and the third term indirectly captures the number of adjacent 0s ($\sum_{i=1}^{n}\sum_{j=1}^{n} c_{ij}$ counts the total number of join counts).

An experiment was conducted to illustrate the relationship between the join count statistics and the MC. The map configuration used was a 3 × 3 regular square tessellation (Figure 2.3). All possible maps (i.e., 510) were constructed involving one 1 (9), two 1s (36), three 1s (84), four 1s (126), five 1s (126), six 1s (84), seven 1s (36), and eight 1s (9). Both the join count statistics and the MC were calculated for each map. The range of the MC values here is [−1, 0.375]. A stepwise linear regression analysis of these data reveals that the 0–1 adjacency counts account for roughly 67%, and the standard deviation of the Bernoulli variable accounts for an additional 28% of the variance in the MC values (a total of 95%). Figure 2.3 shows the observed versus predicted scatterplot for this experiment. The linear regression equation trend line describing this scatter, and allowing MC to be predicted from the join count statistics, is

$$-0.93460 - 0.16964 \text{ BW} + 3.89169\sqrt{p(1-p)},$$

where BW denotes the number of 0–1 adjacencies. This result suggests that the number of 0–1 adjacencies captures most of the spatial autocorrelation information contained in the triplet of joint count statistics.

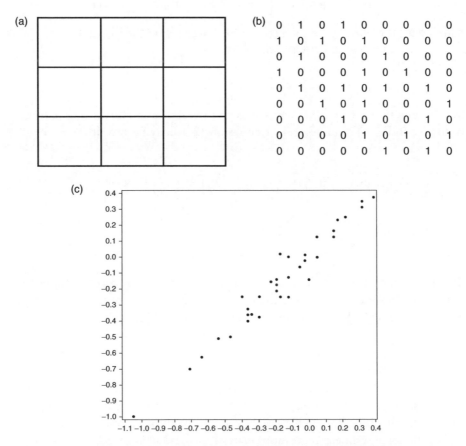

Figure 2.3   (a) The 3 × 3 regular square tessellation. (b) 9 × 9 connectivity matrix C. (c) Relationship between the MC (vertical axis) and the linear combination of 0–1 adjacency counts and the Bernoulli standard error (horizontal axis).

2.2. Graphic portrayals: the Moran scatterplot and the semi-variogram plot

Statistical graphics allow the visualization of bivariate relationships in a convincing, informative, and insightful way, supplementing and clarifying quantitative measures like the MC and the GR. They furnish a tool for communicating the underlying message that is present in, for example, a geo-referenced dataset. The Moran scatterplot and the semi-variogram plot are two such tools extensively employed in spatial data analyses.

The Moran scatterplot is a two-dimensional diagram using Cartesian coordinates to display pairs of values in a manner that summarizes the relationship between the observations comprising a univariate georeferenced dataset. Its construction can be gleaned from the following rewriting of equation (2.3):

$$
MC = \frac{1}{\sum_{i=1}^{n}\sum_{j=1}^{n} c_{ij}} \sum_{i=1}^{n} \left[\frac{(y_i - \overline{y})}{\sqrt{\sum_{i=1}^{n}(y_i - \overline{y})^2 / n}} \right] \left[\sum_{i=1}^{n} c_{ij} \frac{(y_j - \overline{y})}{\sqrt{\sum_{i=1}^{n}(y_i - \overline{y})^2 / n}} \right], \tag{2.6}
$$

which refers to the ordered pairs $(z_i, \sum_{j=1}^{n} c_{ij} z_j)$. In other words:

Step 1. Convert each y_i to a z-score.
Step 2. Plot each z-score (horizontal axis) against its corresponding sum of surrounding z-scores (vertical axis).

The trend line for this scatterplot is the unstandardized MC (i.e., the slope of the line needs to be divided by $\sum_{i=1}^{n}\sum_{j=1}^{n} c_{ij}$).

The quadrants of the Moran scatterplot allow interpretation of the portrayed trend. Concentration of values in the first (top right) and third (bottom left) quadrants indicates positive spatial autocorrelation, with the degree increasing as the cloud of points forms a straight line sloping downward from right to left and having a 45° angle with the horizontal axis. This type of scatter indicates that high values are nearby high values, intermediate values are nearby intermediate values, and low values are nearby low values (Figure 2.4a); data values are saying "I am like my neighbors." In contrast, concentration of values in the second (top left) and fourth (bottom right) quadrants indicates negative spatial autocorrelation, with the degree increasing as the cloud of points forms a straight line sloping downward from left to right and having a 45° angle with

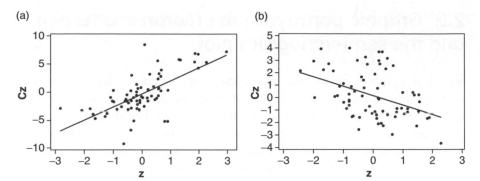

Figure 2.4   Example Moran scatterplots (*z* denotes z-score Cz denotes sum of surrounding *z*-scores) (a) Positive spatial autocorrelation. (b) Negative spatial autocorrelation.

the horizontal axis. This type of scatter indicates that high values are nearby low values, intermediate values are nearby intermediate values, and low values are nearby high values (Figure 2.4b); data values are saying "I differ from my neighbors." In either case, points falling into the other two quadrants indicate heterogeneity that can be detected with local Moran statistics.

The semi–variogram scatterplot is a two–dimensional diagram using Cartesian coordinates of the first quadrant (i.e., all values are non–negative) to display pairs of values in a manner that summarizes the relationship between the variation for a univariate georeferenced variable and distance separating the georeferenced observations. As Figure 2.5 illustrates, its construction relates to equation (2.5).

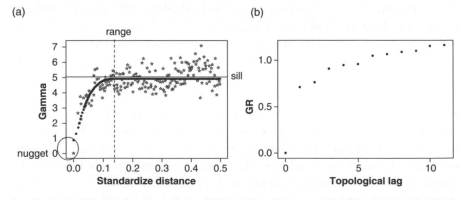

Figure 2.5   (a) An example semi-variogram plot with a trend line superimposed on it. (b) The corresponding GR correlogram plot.

Features of the semi-variogram plot include the concepts of sill, range, and nugget. The sill is the limit of the trend line implied by the scatter of points as distance goes to infinity. The range is the distance at which spatial autocorrelation becomes zero. Many semi-variogram trend line models asymptotically converge on 0 in the limit, and for them an effective range (i.e., where spatial autocorrelation is nearly 0) can be calculated. This is the distance at which the difference between the implied trend line and the sill is negligible. The nugget is a discontinuity at the origin, such that the trend line does not go to 0 when distance is 0. A nugget arises because of, for example, measurement error in data, or specification error in a trend line model specification.

2.3. Impacts of spatial autocorrelation

The single most conspicuous impact of positive spatial autocorrelation is variance inflation. One effect of this for a bell-shaped curve is that its tails, which extend to $\pm \infty$, become heavier (Figure 2.6a). As data values concentrate around the mean, variance decreases. As the central bell part of the distribution is pushed toward the horizontal axis, data values spread along that axis, and the tails inflate.

Because a Poisson distribution has a minimum of 0, variance inflation for it involves increasingly larger outliers and a concentration of 0 values (Figure 2.6b). As the columns of counts concentrating around the mean are pushed toward the horizontal axis, these counts spread along that axis, bunching up at 0 and moving far to the right of the mean. Preservation of the mean constrains this dispersion.

Because a binomial distribution has both a minimum of 0 and a maximum at N_{tr} (the number of trials involved), variance inflation for it involves increasingly moving toward an all-or-nothing dichotomous distribution (Figure 2.6c). As the columns of counts concentrating around the mean are pushed toward the horizontal axis, these counts spread along that axis, bunching up at 0 and at N_{tr}. In the extreme case, the frequencies of all of the intervening counts (i.e., $1, 2, \ldots, N_{tr} - 1$) go to zero.

2.4. Testing for spatial autocorrelation in regression residuals

Cliff and Ord (1981, p. 202) furnish distributional theory for testing linear regression residuals for the presence of spatial autocorrelation using the MC. Expression (2.4) can replace their complicated standard error formulae for values

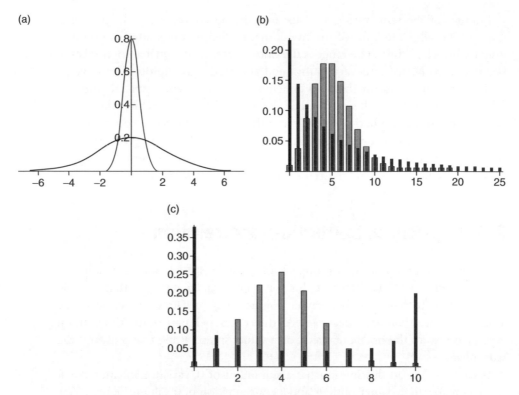

Figure 2.6 Gray denotes the original theoretical distribution; red denotes
the positively spatially autocorrelated theoretical distribution.
(a) Bell-shaped (i.e., normal) distribution. (b) Poisson distribution ($\mu = 5$).
(c) Binomial distribution ($N_{tr} = 10$, $p = 0.4$).

of $n - k$ (where k is the number of covariates plus 1 for the intercept term) of
at least 25. Using matrix notation, the expected value of the MC is given by

$$-n\,\mathrm{tr}[(\mathbf{X}^T\mathbf{X})^{-1}\mathbf{X}^T\mathbf{CX}]/[(n-k)\mathbf{1}^T\mathbf{C1}], \tag{2.7}$$

where tr denotes the matrix trace operator, $\mathbf{X}$ is the $n \times k$ matrix of covariates,
in which the first column is all 1s, and $\mathbf{1}$ is an $n \times 1$ vector of 1s. The term
$\mathbf{1}^T\mathbf{C1}$ counts all of the 1s in matrix $\mathbf{C}$. The diagonal of the term $\mathbf{X}^T\mathbf{CX}$
contains the numerators of the individual MCs for each covariate X in matrix
$\mathbf{X}$, plus the expected value for response variable Y. For a bivariate regression,
Cliff and Ord show that expression (2.7) reduces to

$$-(1 + \mathrm{MC}_X)/(n - 2).$$

If the X covariates are orthogonal, then this expected value reduces to

$$-(1 + \sum_{j=1}^{k-1} \mathrm{MC}_{X_j}) / (n - k)$$

Regardless, equation (2.4) furnishes a good approximation for the standard error of the residual autocorrelation across a wide range of random variable types.

2.5. R code for concept implementations

A spatial weights matrix can be defined from a neighborhood structure. In the *spdep* package, *nb* is a class to store and manage spatial neighbors, and *listw* is a class for spatial weights that supports defining different types of spatial weights, such as binary or row standardized ones (Chapter 4 discusses this in detail). After creating an *nb* object, the neighbor structure may be visualized and utilized for spatial analysis purposes in R. Computer Code 2.1 illustrates how to read and visualize a spatial neighbor structure from a GAL file that can be created with GeoDa software (Anselin et al., 2006). It also shows how to create a choropleth map in R using the *classInt* package for common classification methods, such as equal interval and quantile; Figure 2.7a illustrates this. Then, with a *listw* object created from an *nb* object, the MC and GR for a variable can be calculated, and a Moran scatterplot can be created; Figure 2.7b illustrates this. Finally, Computer Code 2.2 illustrates how an empirical variogram model (i.e., trend line) may be estimated with an experimental variogram, and visualized; Figure 2.7c illustrates this. Computer Code 2.2 presents how to conduct a simple linear regression, and to evaluate the nature and degree of any spatial autocorrelation in the resulting regression residuals. The visualization of the residuals through choropleth mapping can further provide information about spatial autocorrelation; Figure 2.7d illustrates this.

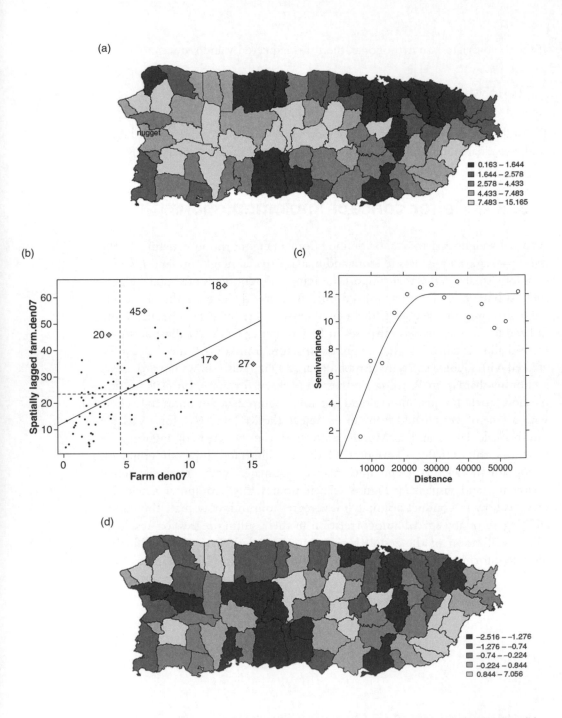

Figure 2.7   Density of number of farms in 2007 (Farm den07). (a) Geographic distribution. (b) Moran scatterplot. (c) Semi-variogram and trend line. (d) Residuals from bivariate regression on 2002 density of number of farms.

Computer Code 2.1. Creation of the topological network, calculation of the MC and the GR, and construction of the Moran scatterplot and the semi-variogram plot.

```# Loading libraries and data```	
```library(spdep)```	Load *spdep* package.
```library(classInt)```	Load *classInt* package.
```pr <- readShapePoly("PuertoRico_SPCS.shp")```	Read PuertoRico.shp (municipalities) file and its spatial neighbor file.
```pr.nb <- read.gal("PuertoRico.GAL")```	Create a *listw* object for binary type
```pr.listw <- nb2listw(pr.nb, style="B")```	spatial weights.
```# Plotting spatial connectivity```	Extract the centroids of the
```cent <- coordinates(pr)```	municipalities.
```plot(pr,lwd=1.5)```	Plot the boundaries of the municipalities.
```plot(pr.nb, cent, add=T, col="gray")```	Plot the neighborhood connectivity over the boundaries in gray color.
```# Farm density in 2007```	
```farm.den07 <- pr$nofarms_07/pr$area```	Calculating farm density in 2007.
```# Plotting the density of farms in 2007```	
```pal.gray <- gray.colors(5)```	Create a palette with 5 gray colors.
```q5.den <- classIntervals(farm.den07,5, style="quantile")```	Define 5 classes for farm.den07 with the quantile option.
```cols.den <- findColours(q5.den,pal.gray)```	Match colors for each farm.den07 value.
```plot(pr, col=cols.den)```	Plot the municipalities with the matched colors.
```brks.den <- round(q5.den$brks,3)```	Get the break values for a legend.
```leg.txt <- paste(brks.den[-5], brks.den[-1], sep=" - ")```	Create formatted legend texts with the break texts.
```legend("bottomright",fill=attr(cols.den, "palette"),legend=leg.txt, bty="n")```	Add a legend to the map.
```# Spatial autocorrelation tests```	Conduct spatial autocorrelation test for
```moran.test(farm.den07, pr.listw)```	the density of farms with Moran coefficient
```geary.test(farm.den07, pr.listw)```	and Geary's ratio.
```# Moran scatterplot```	Plot Moran scatterplot for the density of
```moran.plot(farm.den07, pr.listw, pch=20)```	farms.
```# Variogram```	
```library(gstat)```	Load *gstat* package.
```pr.v <- variogram(farm.den07 ~ 1, pr)```	Calculate an empirical variogram.
```pr.v.fit <- fit.variogram(pr.v, vgm(11,"Sph", "30000", 1))```	Fit the empirical variogram with a theoretical variogram (spherical model).
```plot(pr.v, pr.v.fit)```	Plot the empirical and fitted variograms.

Computer Code 2.2. Calculation of the residual autocorrelation, and testing it for significance.

```# Farm density in 2002``` ```farm.den02 <- pr$nofarms_02/pr$area```	Calculate the density of farms in 2002.
```lm.farm <- lm(farm.den07 ~ farm.den02)```	Run a linear regression of the farm density in 2007 on the farm density in 2002.
```summary(lm.farm)```	Report the regression results.
```lm.morantest(lm.farm,pr.listw)```	Test spatial autocorrelation among the regression residuals.
```#Plotting the regression residuals``` ```res <- resid(lm.farm)```	Get the regression residuals.
```q5.res <- classIntervals(res,5,``` ```style="quantile")```	Define 5 classes for the residuals with quantile option.
```cols.res <- findColours(q5.res,pal.gray)```	Match colors for each residual.
```plot(pr, col=cols.res)```	Plot the municipalities with the matched colors.
```brks.res <- round(q5.res$brks,3)```	Get the break values for a legend.
```leg.txt <- paste(brks.res[-5],``` ```brks.res[-1], sep=" - ")```	Create formatted legend texts.

```legend("bottomright",```
```fill=attr(cols.res, "palette"),```
```legend=leg.txt ,bty="n")```
	Add a legend to the map.

3

Spatial Sampling

LEARNING OBJECTIVES:

- To review the basic effective sampling designs for collecting spatial data
- To describe how to implement the resampling bootstrap technique
- To describe how to implement the resampling jackknife technique
- To outline the concept of effective geographic sample size

Empirical quantitative research often involves probability sampling – frequently referred to as scientific sampling – for data collection. In other words, a researcher identifies the population of objects to which s/he wants to generalize, and selects a subset from this population according to assigned probabilities. Equal probabilities are the most common ones assigned: every object has the same chance of being selected for a sample. Accordingly, a research utilizes some type of random sampling (i.e., selection is equally likely across all objects in a population). If a population is discrete, its members need to be tagged one-to-one with the consecutive positive integers, followed by drawing a random sample of those integers (with a pseudo-random number generator). If a population is continuous, then drawing a sample involves pseudo-random numbers from a continuous uniform distribution. Lotteries employ this type of sampling, either with or without replacement (i.e., a member of the population can or cannot be selected more than once to be in a sample).

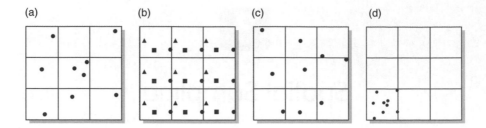

Figure 3.1   Sampling over a unit square. (a) A random sample. (b) Three
systematic random samples (denoted by star, triangle, solid circle).
(c) A geographically stratified (by quadrat) random sample.
(d) A geographical cluster sample.

3.1. Selected spatial sampling designs

One drawback of simple random sampling is the possibility of drawing a very
unrepresentative (geographic) sample. For example, it tends to yield patchy
results over a population, with parts of the population being oversampled, and
parts being undersampled. Consider the sampling of points on a surface; this is
a continuous, infinite population. Construct a 1×1 square region (the horizontal axis is for one of the uniform random variables, and the vertical axis is for the
other). Drawing a sample whose coordinates each come from a uniform distribution produces a Poisson distribution on the surface: parts of the region are
oversampled, and parts are undersampled (Figure 3.1a). Geographically stratify-
ing the sample by quadrat (Figure 3.1b) forces sample points to disperse: quadrats
with multiple simple random sample points end up with only one, as do empty
quadrats. Consequently, the sample retains a random component and becomes
more representative (e.g., all sample points can never fall in a single quadrat). This
is the type of sampling design devised for the US Environmental Protection
Agency EMAP project, which employs hexagons rather than squares because
hexagons furnish the optimal coverage of a planar surface;[1] Figure 3.2a portrays
part of the US coverage. Figure 3.2b shows the coverage of a hexagon that is
spread across a geographic landscape by a hexagonal stratification; in other
words, if all sample points are contained in a single hexagon, its area becomes
completely covered by a sample of size infinity. Stehman and Overton (1996)
furnish additional discussion of spatial sampling.

---

[1] See www.epa.gov/emap/html/pubs/docs/resdocs/mglossary.html.

(a)   (b)

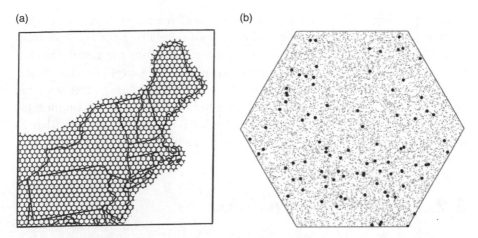

Figure 3.2   (a) Part of the US Environmental Protection Agency national hexagonal
tessellation overlaying the northeastern United States. (b) One hundred
replications of samples of size 90, with dots denoting the sample
appearing in Figure 3.4c.

In addition to seeking a more representative sample, researchers desire data
collection convenience. One way to achieve this goal is with systematic random sampling, which involves randomly selecting a starting point, and then
systematically selecting subsequent sample points by employing a predefined
interval between points. Figure 3.1c illustrates three different implementations
of this design in two dimensions: a point is randomly selected in a quadrat, and
then the remaining eight sample points are those defined by adding a fixed
east–west and a fixed north–south increment to its respective geocode coordinates. This is the type of sampling historically used by the US Bureau of the
Census to collect census survey data with what was called its long form: a
random address was selected at the beginning of a street, and then, beginning
with the selected house, every tth house was given a questionnaire. Surveyors
in malls and stores often use this type of sampling, too, randomly selecting an
initial person entering the facility and then selecting every tth person entering
thereafter.

Cluster sampling offers another approach to incorporating convenience
into a sampling design. But it rests on a very strong assumption that a given
population comprises heterogeneous subgroups that are microcosms of the
parent population. A sample involves randomly selecting one of these subgroups. If the groups are sufficiently large, a second stage of sampling involves
selecting a simple random sample of the members constituting the selected

subgroup. In Figure 3.1d, if each quadrat is considered a heterogeneous microcosm of the unit square parent population, then numbering the quadrats from 1 to 9 allows a random selection of a single quadrat. Once the sample quadrat is selected, then either all points within it constitute the sample, or, as in Figure 3.1d, when the number of points is too large (here, it is infinite), then a simple random sample of points is selected. Companies use this type of sampling for test marketing purposes: find a community that is socio-economically/demographically similar to the target market, and use it to gauge the viability of a product or service in the target market.

3.2. Puerto Rico DEM data

Roughly 9,181 one-kilometer-square pixels, each containing an elevation measure (ranging from 0 to 1,144 meters), constitute the digital elevation model (DEM) covering Puerto Rico (Figures 3.3a and 3.3b). These georeferenced data constitute a geographic population for illustrative sampling purposes. This population is skewed (Figure 3.3c), containing 347 zeros, with an average of 223.63 and a variance of 219.85^2; these are population parameters that random sampling seeks to recover. Figure 3.3d is a scatterplot portraying the relationship between the DEM raster values and elevation in meters recorded for each station; deviations from the perfect fit trend line reflect the difference between square kilometer averages and GPS positions.

Currently a network of 90 weather stations (Figure 3.4d) monitors such events as rainfall across the island. These locations constitute a convenience/purposeful sample: most locations are in settlements or other privileged locations. Figure 3.4a portrays a specific random sample of points across the island. Figure 3.4b portrays a specific systematic sample of points across the island. The random selection occurs in the southwest corner of the island, with fixed increments added to the longitude and to the latitude of a single selected sample point. Figure 3.4c portrays a specific hexagonal tessellation random sample of points across the island. Figure 3.2b contextualizes this sample within a single hexagon. The random selection is from a single hexagon, and then each selected point has one and only one of the tessellation centroids added to it. Puerto Rico is covered by 65 complete hexagons (in its interior), and 58 hexagon fragments along its boundary. The hexagonal tessellation stratified random sample is difficult to implement because of edge effects. In the Puerto Rico case, 58 hexagon fragments need to be aggregated into 25 pseudo-hexagons (i.e., not necessarily adjacent pieces of hexagons whose combined area equals that of a complete hexagon) with an area of

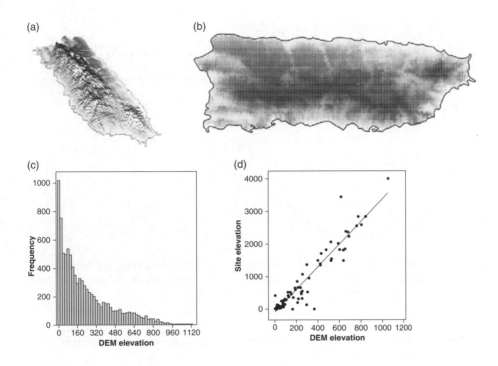

(a)

(b)

(c)

(d)

Figure 3.3 The Puerto Rico DEM; the gray scale increases in darkness with
increasing elevation. (a) Three-dimensional view. (b) Geographic
distribution. (c) Histogram. (d) Scatterplot of DEM pixel values in meters
versus weather station site elevation in feet.

0.00825887 (see footnote 2) (i.e., the total island area[3] in decimal degrees
divided by 90), which is that of each complete hexagon – this aggregation
retains the property of equally likely selection, and ensures geographic coverage of the boundary area in the sampling design. Because the fragments are
discrete pieces, achieving exactly the same area for each is unlikely. Figure 3.5
presents an aggregation for the 58 Puerto Rico hexagon fragments.

Sampling results for elevation mean and variance appear in Table 3.1. The
95% confidence interval (CI) for the arithmetic mean,[4] based on the central

[2] The radius of the sampling hexagon is given by $\sqrt{\text{area}\left(2/\left(3\sqrt{3}\right)\right)}$.

[3] The total island area computed by ArcMap is 0.7432983, which is equivalent to 9,104 square
kilometers (note that the DEM contains 9,181 one-kilometer squares that cover the island).

[4] The margin of error is $\pm1.96 \times 219.85/\sqrt{90}$.

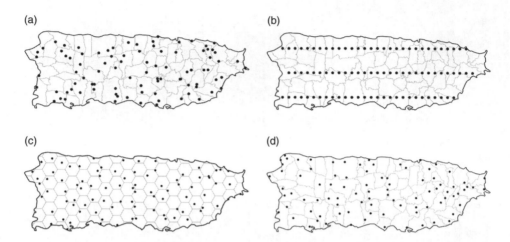

Figure 3.4 Sampling 90 points across the main island of Puerto Rico. (a) Simple random sample. (b) Systematic random samples. (c) Tessellation stratified random sample. (d) Actual weather station points.

Table 3.1 Sample statistics for the sampling design realizations appearing in Figure 3.4

Sample	Arithmetic mean	Variance	Median	Mean deviation
Population	223.63	219.85^2	152.00	167.00
Random	228.74	230.21^2	174.50	179.23
Systematic	217.79	223.44^2	136.00	157.88
Hexagon stratified	258.37	228.75^2	203.50	242.86
Purposeful (actual)	233.43	249.76^2	122.00	185.48

limit theorem[5] and a sufficiently large sample size of 90 to ensure a good normal distribution approximation, is (178.21, 269.05). This CI contains all of the sample means yielded by the various sampling designs. The 95% CI for the variance[6] is $(187.58^2, 252.06^2)$, and the 95% CI for the median[7] is (95.09,

[5] As the sample size n goes to infinity, the distribution of the sample mean has a mean equaling the population mean, a variance equaling σ^2/n, and a frequency distribution that conforms to a normal distribution.

[6] The lower bound is $219.85^2 \times 64.7934/89$ the upper bound is $219.85^2 \times 116.9891/89$

[7] The margin of error is $\pm 1.96 \times 1.253 \times 219.85/\sqrt{90}$

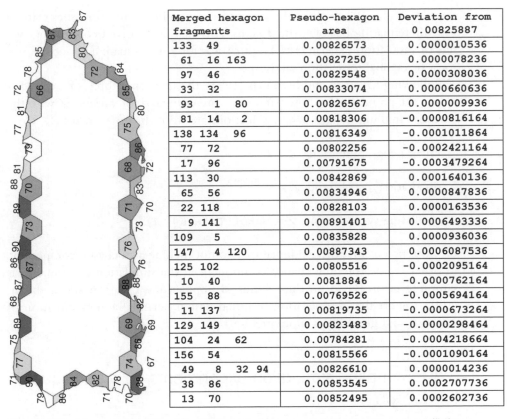

Merged hexagon fragments			Pseudo-hexagon area	Deviation from 0.00825887
133	49		0.00826573	0.0000010536
61	16	163	0.00827250	0.0000078236
97	46		0.00829548	0.0000308036
33	32		0.00833074	0.0000660636
93	1	80	0.00826567	0.0000009936
81	14	2	0.00818306	-0.0000816164
138	134	96	0.00816349	-0.0001011864
77	72		0.00802256	-0.0002421164
17	96		0.00791675	-0.0003479264
113	30		0.00842869	0.0001640136
65	56		0.00834946	0.0000847836
22	118		0.00828103	0.0000163536
9	141		0.00891401	0.0006493336
109	5		0.00835828	0.0000936036
147	4	120	0.00887343	0.0006087536
125	102		0.00805516	-0.0002095164
10	40		0.00818846	-0.0000762164
155	88		0.00769526	-0.0005694164
11	137		0.00819735	-0.0000673264
129	149		0.00823483	-0.0000298464
104	24	62	0.00784281	-0.0004218664
156	54		0.00815566	-0.0001090164
49	8	32 94	0.00826610	0.0000014236
38	86		0.00853545	0.0002707736
13	70		0.00852495	0.0002602736

Figure 3.5   The aggregation of the fragmented hexagons in the hexagon tessellation superimposed on Puerto Rico.

208.91), both of which also contain all of their respective sample statistics reported in Table 3.1.

3.3. Properties of the selected sampling designs: simulation experiment results

Results reported in Table 3.1 fail to differentiate between the three sampling designs. All CIs contain the sample statistics. Such a differentiation requires the drawing of multiple samples. A set of simulation experiments utilizing pseudo-random number generators and involving 10,000 replications (i.e., repeated samples of size 90) exploits the law of large numbers,[8] and furnishes criteria for differentiating between the designs. This analysis involved conducting two sets of simulation experiments. The first was for a unit square. The second was for a hexagonal tessellation landscape.

Following Overton and Stehman (1993), the following three surfaces constitute the populations whose parameters are estimated for variable Z with the various sampling designs, where selections are from the coordinates (U, V):

linear geographic trend, $Z = U + V$;

quadratic type of trend, $Z = e^{-[(U-0.5)^2+(V-0.5)^2]/2}$;

oscillating type of trend, $Z = \sin(5U\pi) + \sin(4V\pi)$.

Of note here is that these populations do not include a stochastic component; in other words, the only chance component in the simulation experiments is sampling error. Based on these kinds of populations, Overton and Stehman (1993) report that a tessellation stratified design permits better estimation of variance, and generally is more precise.

3.3.1. Sampling simulation experiments on a unit square landscape

Figure 3.6 portrays the populations for the simulation experiments, both as two-dimensional contour maps and three-dimension maps. Because all three of these variables are deterministic trends, standard calculus calculations render the parameter values of Z.

Table 3.2 summarizes sample sampling distribution results for these geographic landscapes. Simulation results reported in this table for simple random sampling confirm two parts of the central limit theorem: the mean of the sampling distribution equals the population mean, and the standard error of the sample mean is $\sigma/\sqrt{100}$. Figures 3.7a–c indicate that all three conform closely to a normal frequency distribution with a sample size of only 100. All three sampling designs render good average means and variances. Systematic

---

[8] As the sample size, n, goes to infinity, the empirical probability of each event approaches its theoretical probability (given by its probability mass function or probability density function): the frequency distribution of a random sample tends to resemble the distribution for its parent population more closely as n increases.

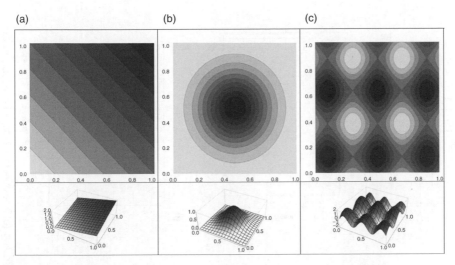

Figure 3.6 Simulation experiment populations for a unit square. (a) Linear geographic gradient. (b) Quadratic type of trend. (c) Oscillating type of trend.

Table 3.2 Summary results for random samples of size $n = 100$ drawn from a unit square

Parameter	Population	Random	Systematic	Stratified
Linear				
Mean	1	0.99956	1.00009	0.99995
Standard error		0.04080	0.04088	0.00412
Variance	0.40825^2	0.40814^2	0.40825^2	0.41027^2
Standard error		0.01985	0	0.00333
Quadratic type				
Mean	0.23101	0.23145	0.23101	0.23110
Standard error		0.02526	0.00024	0.00499
Variance	0.25373^2	0.25412^2	0.25501^2	0.25509^2
Standard error		0.01066	0.00010	0.00309
Oscillating type				
Mean	0.12732	0.12756	0.12938	0.12802
Standard error		0.09936	0.01248	0.03966
Variance	0.99186^2	0.99147^2	0.99678^2	0.99581^2
Standard error		0.11220	0.00312	0.06852

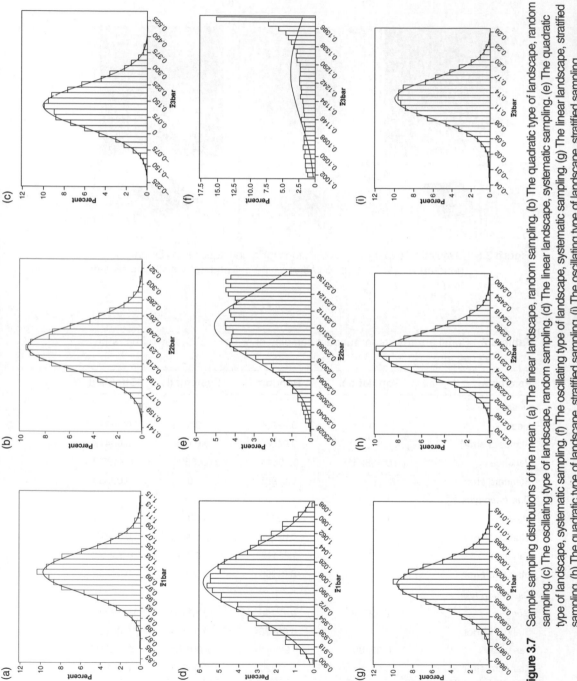

Figure 3.7 Sample sampling distributions of the mean. (a) The linear landscape, random sampling. (b) The quadratic type of landscape, random sampling. (c) The oscillating type of landscape, random sampling. (d) The linear landscape, systematic sampling. (e) The quadratic type of landscape, systematic sampling. (f) The oscillating type of landscape, systematic sampling. (g) The linear landscape, stratified sampling. (h) The quadratic type of landscape, stratified sampling. (i) The oscillating type of landscape, stratified sampling.

sampling yields the lowest standard errors, but at the severe cost of non-standard frequency distributions (Figures 3.7d–f). Tessellation stratified random sampling offers the best results, with standard errors that are substantially lower than their random sampling counterparts, and histograms that conform to a normal frequency distribution even with $n = 100$ (Figures 3.7g–i). These results corroborate those reported by Overton and Stehman (1993).

3.3.2. Sampling simulation experiments on a hexagonal landscape structure

Figure 3.8 portrays the populations for the simulation experiments, both as two-dimensional contour maps and three-dimension maps. Because all three of these variables are deterministic trends over a surface with a circuitous boundary, the surfaces were superimposed on a set of 650,606 points in order to calculate the parameter values of Z.

Table 3.3 summarizes sample sampling distribution results for these geographic landscapes. Associated histograms mirror those appearing in Figure 3.7, although those for the systematic design are distorted in a slightly different fashion (Figure 3.9). These results corroborate the preceding ones reported for the unit square. Specifically, tessellation stratified random sampling offers the

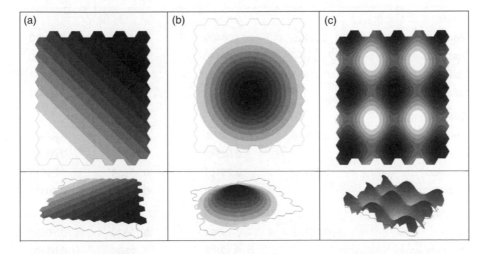

Figure 3.8 Simulation experiment populations for a hexagonal structured landscape. (a) Linear geographic gradient. (b) Quadratic type of trend. (c) Oscillation type of trend.

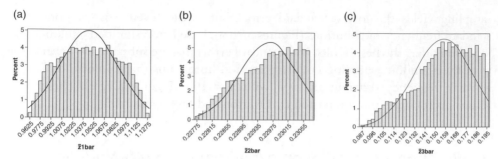

Figure 3.9 Sample sampling distributions of the mean. (a) Linear landscape, systemic sampling. (b) Quadratic type of landscape, systemic sampling. (c) Oscillating type of landscape, systematic sampling.

best results, with standard errors that are substantially lower than their random sampling counterparts, and histograms that conform to a normal frequency distribution even with $n = 100$. Consequently, the preferred results reported in Table 3.1 are for the hexagon stratified random sampling design.

Table 3.3 Summary results for random samples of size $n = 100$ drawn from a unit area 10 × 10 hexagonal region

Parameter	Population	Random	Systematic	Stratified
Linear				
Mean	1.04495	1.04409	1.04515	1.04490
Standard error		0.04180	0.04007	0.00400
Variance	0.41453^2	0.41431^2	0.41430^2	0.41621^2
Standard error		0.02064	0	0.00331
Quadratic type				
Mean	0.22928	0.22933	0.22962	0.22968
Standard error		0.02542	0.00074	0.00500
Variance	0.25479^2	0.25467^2	0.25614^2	0.25613^2
Standard error		0.01065	0.00030	0.00313
Oscillating type				
Mean	0.15752	0.15784	0.15689	0.15582
Standard error		0.10146	0.02506	0.03803
Variance	1.00561^2	1.00607^2	1.01062^2	1.01023^2
Standard error		0.11679	0.02398	0.06421

3.4. Resampling techniques: reusing sampled data

A major purpose of sampling is to avoid assessing an entire population. Consequently, constructing a sampling distribution by repeatedly drawing samples of a given size n defeats this primary purpose and advantage of sampling. However, once a sample is selected, resampling techniques allow the conducting of simulation experiments with this single sample that parallel the preceding simulation experiments. Two popular resampling techniques are the bootstrap (Diaconis and Efron, 1983; Shalizi, 2010) and the jackknife (Matloff, 1980; Hinkley, 2006; Abdi and Williams, 2010). Their goal is to estimate the precision of the estimates (i.e., the standard errors) by determining variability between subsamples of a single selected sample. Because the bootstrap draws a very large number of samples of size n, it yields results that vary when repeating an analysis with a given selected sample. In contrast, because the jackknife does all possible samples of a given size, it yields fixed, recurring results when repeating an analysis with a given selected sample. Variance estimation with the jackknife is superior to that with the bootstrap. Distribution estimation with the bootstrap is superior to that with the jackknife.

3.4.1. The bootstrap

The bootstrap involves constructing a sample sampling distribution with replicate samples by random sampling with replacement from a single selected sample, using a sample of size n. It differs from the preceding simulation experiments because they draw replicate samples from a parent population. It offers, for example, a robust alternative to inference based on the central limit theorem when this theorem's underlying assumptions are in doubt. Results reported in Tables 3.2 and 3.3 indicate that the standard error formula for the central limit theorem fails to hold for tessellation stratified random sampling.

The samples portrayed in Figure 3.4, whose results appear in Table 3.1, may be subjected to bootstrapping. In keeping with the simulation experiments, the bootstrapping exercise involves 10,000 replications. Results summarized in Table 3.4 indicate that the purposeful sample yields the poorest results, with a systematic design producing considerably more variability in the variance than either the random or the stratified designs. Although the tessellation stratified design has a much better coverage of the island (Figure 3.4), the random sample outperforms it. In all cases, the sample sampling distribution closely aligns with a normal frequency distribution (Figure 3.10).

Table 3.4 Summary results for bootstrapping the selected Puerto Rico DEM samples

Parameter	Random	Systematic	Stratified	Actual
Mean	228.280	218.216	258.256	233.374
Standard error	18.412	17.900	18.523	20.093
Variance	230.305²	223.632²	228.678²	249.783²
Standard error	6843.579	7259.737	6880.709	8035.089

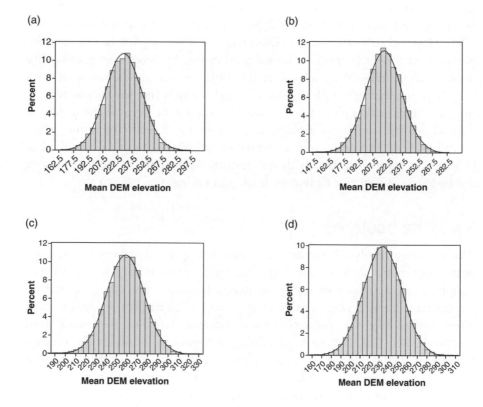

Figure 3.10 The bootstrap sample sampling distribution of the sample mean. (a) Random sample design. (b) Systematic design. (c) Tessellation stratified design. (d) Actual weather station locations.

3.4.2. The jackknife

The jackknife involves constructing a sample sampling distribution by systematically leaving out k observations at a time from a selected sample, and recomputing a given statistic with the remaining sample size of $n - k$. The total number of

Table 3.5 Summary results for jackknifing the selected Puerto Rico DEM samples

Parameter	Random	Systematic	Stratified	Actual
Leaving 1 out (90 replicates; n = 89)				
Mean	228.744	217.878	258.367	233.433
Standard error	24.267	23.553	24.113	26.327
Variance	230.212^2	223.441^2	228.753^2	249.761^2
Standard error	8968.353	9526.657	8991.772	10548.430
Leaving 2 out (4,005 replicates; n = 88)				
Mean	228.744	217.878	258.367	233.433
Standard error	24.268	23.554	24.114	26.329
Variance	230.212^2	223.441^2	228.753^2	249.761^2
Standard error	8969.359	9527.622	8992.767	10549.615
Leaving 3 out (117,480 replicates; n = 87)				
Mean	228.744	217.878	258.367	233.433
Standard error	24.267	23.553	24.113	26.327
Variance	230.212^2	223.441^2	228.753^2	249.761^2
Standard error	8969.288	9527.440	8992.681	10549.532

samples for $k = 1$ is n, for $k = 2$ is $n(n - 1)/2$, and for $k = 3$ is $n(n - 1)(n - 2)/6$. It allows estimation of the bias and standard error of a statistic based on a single selected sample. Because both the mean and the variance (its denominator is $n - 1$) estimators are unbiased, their jackknife calculations appearing in Table 3.5 are exactly the same for 1, 2, and 3 deletions (i.e., their bias is 0). Standard errors reported in this table vary only by rounding error. Cressie (1981) indicates that the variance, because it is a nonlinear statistic, should be transformed (using its cubed root) for this analysis.

Jackknife results also indicate that the tessellation stratified sampling design is the best. It yields the smallest standard error for the sample mean, and yields a standard error for the variance that is competitive with that produced by random sampling. In addition, its sampling distribution is far better behaved than those of the other designs; this distribution appears to be converging on a normal distribution faster than those of the other designs (Figure 3.11). Unfortunately, confirming this situation requires at least 10 deletions (i.e., more than 5.72×10^{12} subset samples).

Common jackknife results are for only a single deletion. Jackknife results tend not to be as useful for unbiased estimators, such as the mean and the variance computed with $n - 1$ in its denominator; but these two statistics allow confirmation of results for multiple deletion cases. Here the jackknife standard

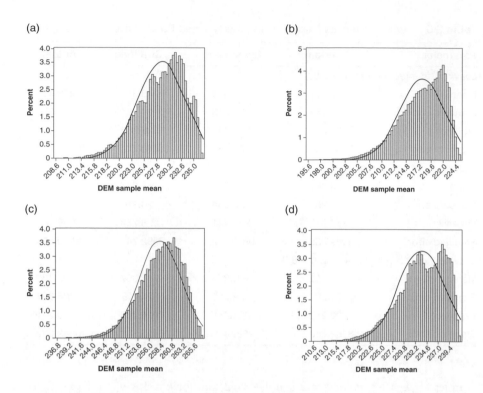

Figure 3.11   The jackknife sampling distribution of the sample mean with three left out. (a) Random sample design. (b) Systematic design. (c) Tessellation stratified design. (d) Actual weather station locations.

errors are larger than their bootstrap counterparts (see Table 3.4). Finally, the jackknife closely relates to cross-validation techniques.

A jackknife analysis of the correlation between weather station elevations and DEM pixel measures (Figure 3.3d) indicates an absence of bias, and a standard error of 0.01839 for deletions of 1, 2, and 3 observations. The corresponding histograms appear in Figure 3.12. Cressie (1981) and Hinkley (2006) both indicate that the correlation coefficient, because it is a nonlinear statistic, should be transformed for this analysis (using the standard Fisher logarithmic transformation, which is equivalent to the hyperbolic arctangent transformation).

3.5. Spatial autocorrelation and effective sample size

The presence of positive spatial autocorrelation indicates the presence of redundant information in data values, with this redundancy being attributable to the

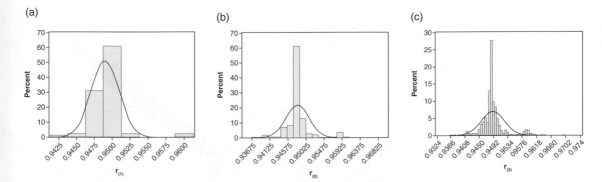

Figure 3.12   Jackknife distribution of a correlation coefficient. (a) One deletion. (b) Two deletions. (c) Three deletions.

relative locations of the values. Effective sample size is the equivalent number of independent values (the classical statistics situation). As spatial autocorrelation increases from 0 to 1, the effective sample size decreases from n to 1 (Figure 3.13b). The DEM data contain substantial positive spatial autocorrelation (Figure 3.13a),[9] with an MC value of 0.97066 (standard error 0.00743).

The spatial autocorrelation regression parameter is 0.9967. Substituting this value into the equation reported in Griffith (2003, p. 83) yields

$$9181 \times \left[1 - \frac{1}{1 - e^{-1.92349}} \frac{9181 - 1}{9181} \left(1 - e^{-2.12373 \times 0.9967 + 0.20024 \sqrt{0.9967}} \right) \right] \approx 12.$$

In other words, on average, 12 judiciously spaced pixels across the island of Puerto Rico contain all of the DEM information furnished by the 9,181 values. Figure 3.14 portrays this result. Twelve points were selected in a systematic dispersed pattern from across the island (i.e., a 3 × 4 square lattice was superimposed on the island, and a single point was judiciously selected from within each square in order to minimize the spatial autocorrelation in the resulting geographic distribution of elevation values). The Moran Coefficient (MC) for these values is 0.01642 (standard error 0.24). These values capture the coastal–lowlands and interior–highlands trends across the island (Figure 3.3a,b), and contain virtually

---

[9] The left truncation occurs because the minimum recorded elevation is 0 (i.e., sea level). Of the 9,181 pixels, about 212 distortions occur along the coast because of the clipping of the DEM in ArcMap. The maximum number of neighbors is 8. North–south distances between pixel centroids are about 5% greater than east–west distances.

(a)   (b)

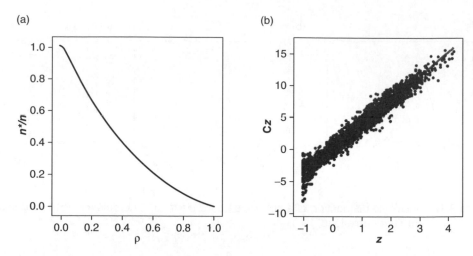

Figure 3.13   (a) Effective sample size for $n = 9{,}181$ across the range of positive spatial autocorrelation values. (b) Moran scatterplot for the Puerto Rico DEM, with a trend line (gray).

no spatial autocorrelation. Furthermore, the effective sample size (the spatial autocorrelation regression parameter is 0.00403) for this geographic distribution is 12 (the same as n).

3.6. R code for concept implementations

Tessellation stratified random sampling is the preferred sampling design. Computer Code 3.1 presents an implementation of this design with R. R allows a map to be overlayed with a hexagonal tessellation, and supports the automatic drawing of a single sample point from each hexagon. Computer Code 3.2 presents code for drawing random samples from a single hexagon that then can have each hexagonal tessellation centroid added to one and only one of the sample points. These are equivalent sampling implementations, with Computer Code 3.2 allowing inspection of aggregate coverage of the hexagon (Figure 3.2b), as well as furnishing an overview for implementation in other software packages that do not support automatic sampling from each hexagon in a hexagonal tessellation. One advantage of the R sampling function is that the complete and fragmented hexagons can be sampled at the same time (the fragmented hexagons still need to be merged into their synthetic hexagons before sampling, so that the sampling function draws a point based upon all of the pieces of a synthetic hexagon).

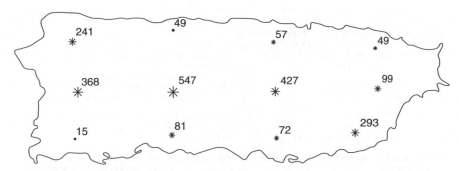

Figure 3.14 Judiciously selected effective sample size pixels (an asterisk is proportional to the DEM value) labeled by DEM elevation values.

Computer Code 3.3 implements the bootstrap and the jackknife using the bootstrap and jackknife functions in the bootstrap package in R. It allows replication of results in Sections 3.4.1 and 3.4.2.

Computer Code 3.1. Simultaneous and automatic random sampling from the hexagons forming a hexagonal tessellation.

```# Purpose: Sampling with spdep package``` ```library(spdep)```	Load *spdep* package.

```# Read Puerto Rico shapefile```
```pr <- readShapePoly("PuertoRico.shp")```
```n <- 90```
	Read PuertoRico.shp file.
	Set *n* with a number of samples.

```# Draw samples randomly```
```samp.rand <- spsample(pr, n,```
```type="random")```
```plot(pr)```
```points(samp.rand, pch=20)```
	Draw spatially random samples.
	
	Plot the boundaries of Puerto Rico.
	Plot the spatially random samples.

```# Regular samples```
```samp.reg <- spsample(pr, n,```
```type="regular")```
```plot(pr, border="gray")```
```points(samp.reg, pch=20)```
	Draw spatially regular samples.
	
	Plot the boundaries of Puerto Rico.
	Plot the spatially regular samples.

```# Stratified with hexagons```
```pr.hex <- readShapePoly("pr-```
```hexagons.shp")```
```n <- length(pr.hex)```
	Read a hexagon shapefile.
	
	Set *n* with a number of hexagons.

```samp.xy <-```
```sapply(slot(pr.hex,"polygons"),```
```   function(x) t(coordinates(spsample(x,```
```   1, type="random"))))```
```samp.str <-```
```cbind(samp.xy[1,],samp.xy[2,])```
	Draw one spatially random sample
	inside of each hexagon.
	
	Save *x,y* coordinates in columns.

```plot(pr, border="gray", lty=2)```
```plot(pr.hex, add=T)```
```points(samp.str, pch=20)```
	Plot the boundaries of Puerto Rico.
	Plot the hexagons.
	Plot the stratified samples.

Computer Code 3.2. Random sampling from a single hexagon, with each sample point then added to one and only one hexagonal tessellation centroid.

```
sample.hex <- function(n, Area,              Define a function, which has 3
                link="vertical") {           arguments.
                                              n: the number of hexagons
  # Draw samples in quadrat I                 Area: area of a hexagon
  # of a hexagon                              link: type of hexagon arrangements

  loc <- matrix(0,n,2)                        Create an object for samples.
  i <- 1                                      Set an index variable.
  rad <- sqrt(Area*2/(3*sqrt(3)))            Set a radius.

  # Draw n samples depending on hexagon       Two options: (1) East/West adjacency
  # arrangements.                                          (2) North/South adjacency
  if (link == "vertical") {                   If East/West adjacency,
    while (i <= n) {
      uv <- runif(2)                          Draw x, y coordinates in a unit hexagon.
      if (uv[1] < 1 - 0.5*uv[2]) {            Accept a sample in quadrat I of a unit
        loc[i,] <- uv                         hexagon.
        i <- i + 1                            Increase a value of the index variable.
      }
    }
    # Scaling to a hexagon from a unit
one
    loc[,1] <- rad * loc[,1]                  Scale x coordinates of samples.
    loc[,2] <- sqrt(3)/2 * rad * loc[,2]      Scale y coordinates of samples.
  }
  else if (link == "horizontal") {            Same sampling for North/South
    while (i <= n) {                          adjacency.
      uv <- runif(2)
      if (uv[2] < 1 - 0.5*uv[1]) {            Draw x, y coordinates in a unit hexagon.
        loc[i,] <- uv                         Accept a sample in quadrat I of a unit
        i <- i + 1                            hexagon.
      }                                       Increase a value of the index variable.
    }
    loc[,1] <- sqrt(3)/2 * rad * loc[,1]      Scale x coordinates of samples.
    loc[,2] <- rad * loc[,2]                  Scale y coordinates of samples.
  }
  else
    stop("The link is not correctly set")

  # Assign a quadrat
  qd <- sample(1:4,n,replace=T)               Draw quadrats randomly.
  loc[,1] <- ifelse((qd==2)|(qd==3),          Change the sign of x coordinate for
            loc[,1]* -1, loc[,1])             quadrat 2 and 3.
  loc[,2] <- ifelse((qd==3)|(qd==4),          Change the sign of y coordinate for
            loc[,2]* -1, loc[,2])             quadrat 3 and 4.
  return (loc)                                Return the samples.
}

library(spdep)                               Load spdep library.

# Read a hexagon shapefile
comp.hex <- readShapePoly("complete-         Read a hexagon shapefile.
hexagons.shp")
n <- length(comp.hex)                         Set n with the number of hexagons.

# Get the area of a hexagon
hex1 <- slot(comp.hex,"polygons")[[1]]        Get the first hexagon.
Area <- slot(hex1,"area")                     Get the area of the hexagon.

# Draw random samples in a hexagon
loc <- sample.hex(n, Area,                    Draw samples (the hexagons are arranged
link="vertical")                              with North/South adjacency).
```

```
# Plot samples in a hexagon
cent <- coordinates(comp.hex)              Get the centroids of the hexagons.
plot(comp.hex[1,])                         Plot the first hexagon.
points(loc[,1] + cent[1,1],                Plot the samples in the first hexagon.
       loc[,2] + cent[1,2], pch=20)

# Distribute one sample to each hexagon    Add the centroids to x, y of the
samples.xy <- loc + cent                   samples.
plot(comp.hex)                             Plot the hexagons.
points(samples.xy, pch=20)                 Plot the samples.
```

Computer Code 3.3. A bootstrap and a jackknife implementation.

```
library(bootstrap)                          Load bootstrap package.

pr.rd <- read.csv("pr_sample_random.csv",   Read sample values from a file.
header=T)
pr.samp <- pr.rd[,"DEM_rs"]                  Get sample values.

# Bootstrap (1000 times)
n.s <- 1000                                 Set 1000 for a number of resamples.
f.mean <- function(x){mean(x)}              Define a function for bootstrap.
bs.mean <- bootstrap(pr.samp, n.s,          Bootstrapping for mean.
f.mean)
mean(bs.mean$thetastar)                      Mean of the means.
sd(bs.mean$thetastar)                        Standard deviation of the means.

f.var <- function(x){var(x)}                Define a function for bootstrap.
bs.var <- bootstrap(pr.samp, n.s, f.var)    Bootstrapping for variance.
mean(bs.var$thetastar)                       Mean of the variances.
sd(bs.var$thetastar)                         Standard deviations of the variances.

#Jackknifing
jk.mean <- jackknife(pr.samp, f.mean)       Jackknifing for mean.
mean(jk.mean$jack.values)                    Mean of the means.
jk.mean$jack.se                              Standard error of the means.

jk.var <- jackknife(pr.samp, f.var)         Jackknifing for variance.
mean(jk.var$jack.values)                     Mean of the variances.
jk.var$jack.se                               Standard error of the variances.
```

4

Spatial Composition and Configuration

LEARNING OBJECTIVES:

- To differentiate between homogeneity and heterogeneity in spatial data
- To describe common ways to quantify geographic contiguity
- To differentiate between static geographic distributions and spatial interaction cases

---

Statistical heterogeneity frequently refers to a lack of uniform variability across a data dimension. In classical statistics, the dimension commonly is value size. In spatial statistics, it is also geographic landscape. The statistical assumption of independent and identically distributed (iid) is equivalent to assuming homogeneous data. In other words, the mean and the variance of a random variable are constant across observations, as are all other moments (e.g., those used to calculate skewness and kurtosis). Therefore, in an empirical context, the question to address is whether or not the mean and the variance of some phenomenon vary across regions into which a geographic landscape is divided. Because areal units tend to vary in size, the phenomenon under study needs to be standardized to, for example, a percentage of a total or a density. Otherwise, size effects tend to dominate spatial analyses.

4.1. Spatial heterogeneity: mean and variance

A mean can vary systematically across a geographic landscape. This variability may be captured with covariates in a regression model. Simple 0–1 indicator variable covariates can account for regional differences. Often power transformations can stabilize variability in variance across a geographic landscape. For some variable Y (e.g., density of cuerdas[1] in farmland in a municipality), this transformation takes on one of the following forms (Box and Tidwell, 1962; Manly, 1976):

$$Y\star = (Y + \delta)^{\lambda}, \quad \lambda \neq 0,$$
$$Y\star = \ln(Y + \delta), \quad \lambda = 0,$$
$$Y\star = e^{-\lambda Y}.$$

Because the underlying probability distribution is given by the normal probability model, coefficients δ and λ are selected to maximize correspondence between Y and its corresponding normal quantile value (nonlinear least squares may be used to calibrate them). These are the two types of spatial heterogeneity addressed in this section.

Often analysts employing a variable transformation want to discuss results in terms of the original measurement scale. To do so requires a back-transformation. Normal curve theory reveals that such a back-transformation is a function of the mean and the variance of the transformed variable. The estimated mean is the predicted value, whereas the estimated variance is the mean squared error. An excellent approximation equation for calculating back-transformation values is given by the following conjecture: If $(Y + \delta)^{\lambda} \sim N(\mu, \sigma)$ and $\lambda > 0$, the fractal moments about the origin are well approximated by the equations

$$E\{[(Y + \delta)^{\lambda}]^{1/\lambda}\} = \begin{cases} \mu^{1/\lambda} + \sum_{j=1}^{[0.5/\lambda]} C_j \mu^{1/\lambda - 2j} \sigma^{2j}, & \text{if } \frac{1}{\lambda} \geq 2, \\ \mu^{1/\lambda}, & \text{if } 0 < \frac{1}{\lambda} < 2, \end{cases} \tag{4.1}$$

where C_j are combinatorial coefficients, and $[0.5/\lambda]$ denotes the integer value of $0.5/\lambda$.

For both integer and non-integer values of $1/\lambda$, the combinatorial coefficients are given by

$$C_j = \prod_{h=1}^{j} \frac{0.5}{h} \left[-\frac{1}{4} + \left(\frac{1}{\lambda} - 2h + \frac{3}{2} \right)^2 \right], \quad \frac{1}{\lambda} \geq 1. \tag{4.2}$$

---

[1] 1 cuerda = 0.00393040km^2 = 0.00151753 mile^2

Simulation experiments were used to establish this for $\lambda > 0$. The standard back-transformation result for $E[\ln(Y + \delta)]$, $\lambda = 0$ is $e^{\mu + \sigma^2/2}$ but that for $E(e^{-\lambda Y})$ remains to be established. In all three cases, the desired result is $E(Y)$, which means δ needs to be subtracted from each side of the final equation.

4.1.1. ANOVA

Analysis of variance (ANOVA) is a classical technique that accounts for difference of means across groups when the variance is homogeneous. An accompanying assumption is that data conform to a bell-shaped curve within each group. ANOVA (Griffith and Amrhein, 1997) furnishes the tool needed for a quantitative evaluation of pairwise and simultaneous differences between regional means. The inferential basis for ANOVA in this context is from a model-based perspective: an infinite superpopulation (given by the ANOVA model describing the data-generating process) that includes a random component generates the observed data at a given point in time; and inference is conditional on the observed data, which are considered to be an accurate representation of the parent population. Inference here is to the infinite superpopulation.

4.1.2. Testing for heterogeneity over a plane: regional supra-partitionings

Consider the density of farmland across Puerto Rico in 2002. Many decades ago, the Commonwealth's Department of Agriculture divided the island into five agricultural administrative regions (Figure 4.1a). Does this farmland density (cuerdas per square mile) vary across these regions (Figure 4.1b)? The corresponding statistics appear in Table 4.1. The statistical question asks whether or not these natures and degrees of differences persist across repeated samples from the parent superpopulation.

The first diagnostic evaluation addresses the assumption of a bell-shaped curve. The probability of conforming to a normal frequency distribution (based upon the Shapiro–Wilk diagnostic statistic) indicates a rejection of the null hypothesis for the San Juan region, suggesting the presence of specification error in the model-based inferential basis. Adjusting for simultaneous testing (e.g., using a Bonferroni adjustment, which for the most liberal overall 10% level becomes 2% for each individual region) of five null hypotheses reverses this statistical decision.

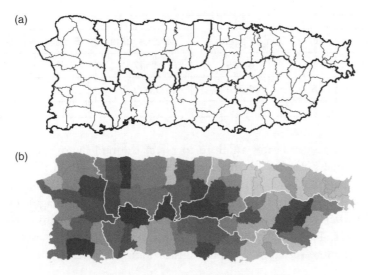

Figure 4.1 Agricultural production across Puerto Rico. (a) Agricultural administrative regions. (b) Geographic distribution of 2002 density of farmland (density directly proportional to gray scale darkness).

Table 4.1 Selected sample statistics for the agricultural administration regions of Puerto Rico

Region	San Juan	Arecibo	Mayaguez	Ponce	Caguas
Mean	128.3778	250.0856	222.7726	219.5620	191.5862
Variance	109.5681^2	124.7694^2	72.0148^2	101.4183^2	88.9903^2
Normal distribution probability	0.0259	0.1211	0.1296	0.4796	0.2043

The next diagnostic evaluation concerns homogeneity of variance across the regions. Its null hypothesis may be stated (see Griffith and Amrhein, 1991, pp. 292–3) as

$$\sigma_1^2 = \sigma_2^2 = \sigma_3^2 = \sigma_4^2 = \sigma_5^2.$$

Levene's test[2] is used here to evaluate this null hypothesis, yielding:

---

[2] Analyses here employ the robust version, based on the mean deviation (i.e., the absolute values of deviations from sample medians).

Source	df	Sum of squares	Mean square	F-ratio	Pr > F
Regions	4	10,069	2,517.4	0.65	0.6320
Error	68	265,222	3,900.3		

This diagnostic test indicates a failure to reject the null hypothesis, implying that the regional variances are the same in the superpopulation.

One conventional approach to adjust for deviation from the assumption of normality is to treat the heterogeneity as a function of the magnitude of Y values. A power transformation differentially inflates and shrinks values in order to better align the corresponding transformed variable Y^* with a bell-shaped curve. Here the most suitable transformation is given by

$$Y^* = (Y + 445)^{-0.15}.$$

The corresponding sample statistics appear in Table 4.2. The probability of conforming to a normal frequency distribution indicates a failure to reject the null hypothesis for all five regions, even without adjusting for simultaneous testing. The cost of the improved diagnostic test is the requirement of a back-transformation at the end of the data analysis.

Now Levene's test yields:

Source	df	Sum of squares	Mean square	F-ratio	Pr > F
Regions	4	0.000129	0.000032	1.22	0.3103
Error	68	0.001790	0.000026		

Table 4.2 Selected transformed variable sample statistics

Agricultural administrative region	San Juan	Arecibo	Mayaguez	Ponce	Caguas
Mean	0.3867	0.3756	0.3773	0.3779	0.3803
Variance	0.0104^2	0.0095^2	0.0058^2	0.0085^2	0.0079^2
Normal distribution probability	0.1306	0.5093	0.4329	0.6526	0.2163

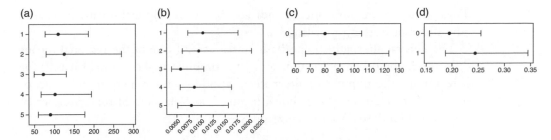

Figure 4.2 Bonferroni 95% confidence intervals for variance estimates. (a) Untransformed 2002 density of farmland. (b) Transformed 2002 density of farmland. (c) Untransformed 2007 density of farmland. (d) Transformed 2007 density of farmland.

Because this homogeneity of variance test lacks strong statistical power, Figure 4.2 allows its graphical assessment: the confidence intervals (CIs) overlap about the same before and after the variable transformation. Therefore, the gain here is in terms of the underlying probability model.

The null hypothesis of interest may be stated as

$$\mu_1 = \mu_2 = \mu_3 = \mu_4 = \mu_5.$$

Ignoring the potential assumption violation (i.e., normality) yields the following ANOVA table:

Source	df	Sum of squares	Mean square	F-ratio	Pr > F
Regions	4	138,552.7049	34,638.1762	3.47	0.0122
Error	68	678,304.3598	9,975.0641		
Corrected total	72	816,857.0647			

The statistical decision is to reject the null hypothesis. Additional uncertainty about this decision arises from impacts of possible specification error. Adjusting for possible non-normality changes the ANOVA table as follows:

Source	df	Sum of squares	Mean square	F-ratio	Pr > F
Regions	4	0.0013	0.0003	4.22	0.0041
Error	68	0.0051	0.0001		
Corrected total	72	0.0063			

These results more emphatically indicate that some regional means are markedly different in the population.

The general alternative hypothesis is that at least one of the regional means differs from the other regional means. The combinatorial counting formula for determining the number of alternative hypotheses for K regions, in terms of the number of groups (G) of equal means, is as follows (a Stirling number of the second kind; see Abramowitz and Stegun, 1972):

$$\frac{1}{G!} \sum_{h=0}^{G} (-1)^{G-h} \binom{G}{h} h^{K}, \text{ for } G = 2, 3, \ldots, K.$$

$G = 1$ is the null hypothesis (i.e., all means are equal). Here the number of possible alternative hypotheses is 51. A multiple comparison technique, such as the Scheffé test, allows this set to be reduced. Here only the following two possibilities remain in the set:

$$\mu_1 \neq \mu_2 = \mu_3 = \mu_4 = \mu_5 \text{ and } \mu_1 = \mu_3 = \mu_4 = \mu_5 \neq \mu_2.$$

This first alternative states that the San Juan metropolitan region differs from the remaining parts of the island. This second alternative states that Arecibo metropolitan region differs from the remaining parts of the island.

4.1.2.1. Establishing a relationship to the superpopulation

A simulation experiment allows these findings to be related to the parent superpopulation. Sample sampling distributions appearing in Figure 4.3 were generated using the means and variances reported in Table 4.2 for pseudorandom number generation, and are based on 10,000 replications. These results suggest that the model-based inferential basis does a good job of mostly rejecting the null hypothesis. The extreme probabilities' portions of the sampling distribution are: 61.1% for $p < 0.0041$, 71.7% for $p < 0.01$, 87.4% for $p < 0.05$, and 92.6% for $p < 0.10$.

4.1.2.2. A null hypothesis rejection case with heterogeneity

The preceding example illustrates a case where a variable transformation better aligns collected data with model assumptions. But a researcher has no guarantee that such a variable transformation exists. Consider the density of farmland across Puerto Rico in 2007 (i.e., $Y = $ [2007 cuerdas in farmland]/area), within the context of a coastal lowlands/interior highlands regionalization scheme, illustrated in Figure 4.4a. Elevation (Figure 3.3) furnishes a

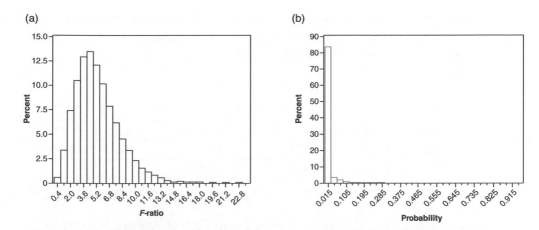

Figure 4.3   Simulated sampling distributions for the agricultural administrative region classification model-based inference. (a) F-ratio. (b) Null hypothesis probability.

rationale for such a two–group classification scheme. The following transformation, whose geographic distribution appears in Figure 4.4b, improves the normality diagnostic statistics (Table 4.3):

$$Y^\star = \ln(Y + 211).$$

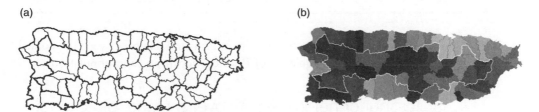

Figure 4.4   Agricultural production across Puerto Rico. (a) Elevation-based regions. (b) Geographic distribution of transformed 2007 density of farmland (density directly proportional to gray scale darkness).

Table 4.3   Selected sample statistics for the elevation-based regions of Puerto Rico

Region	Coastal lowlands ($n = 42$)		Interior highlands ($n = 31$)	
Type of data	Raw	Transformed	Raw	Transformed
Mean	140.7869	5.8292	196.3858	5.9930
Variance	97.5435^2	0.2583^2	73.8305^2	0.1892^2
Normal distribution probability	0.0033	0.4386	0.1591	0.0693

This transformation overcompensates for non–normality in the coastal low-lands region at the expense of normality in the interior highlands region, which now is significant at the 10% level.

Levene's test yields:

Source	df	Sum of squares	Mean square	F-ratio	Pr > F
Regions	1	0.0267	0.0267	1.38	0.2445
Error	71	1.3756	0.0194		

Its accompanying CI plots appear in Figures 4.2c,d. A significant difference between regional variances is present at the 10% level. This assumption violation brings into question the standard ANOVA F-ratio probability of 0.0039. Welch's (1951) variance–weighted adjustment, which involves effective degrees of freedom, may be used to account for this heterogeneity:

Source	df	F-ratio	Pr > F
Regions	1	9.78	0.0026
Error	70.9993		

The implication is that the average density of farmland differs between the coastal lowlands and the interior highlands of Puerto Rico, in its superpopulation.

4.1.3. Testing for heterogeneity over a plane: directional supra-partitionings

Besides regional heterogeneity, directional heterogeneity is of concern to spatial scientists. One assessment of this situation evaluates variability across the four plane quadrants of a landscape (northeast, NE; northwest, NW; southeast, SE; southwest, SW). Figure 4.5a portrays one such regionalization scheme. These four groups result in 15 possible alternative hypotheses.

Consider the 2002 density of farms across the island of Puerto Rico, whose appropriate power transformation is $\ln(Y + 0.35)$. Figure 4.5b depicts its geographic distribution. This transformation improves conformity to a bell-shape curve, in terms of the normal distribution probability:

Quadrant	Northeast	Northwest	Southwest	Southeast
Untransformed	0.0001	0.0549	0.0018	0.0002
Transformed	0.2482	0.6663	0.8398	0.4331

(a)   (b)

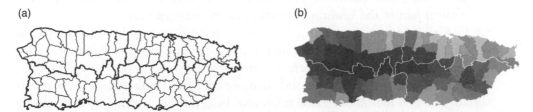

Figure 4.5   Agricultural production across Puerto Rico. (a) Quadrants of the plane regions. (b) Geographic distribution of transformed 2002 density of farms (density directly proportional to gray scale darkness).

Figure 4.6 reports Levene's test results together with its corroborating graphical portrayal. The ANOVA results are as follows:

Source	df	Sum of squares	Mean square	F-ratio	Pr > F
Regions	3	11.5660	3.8553	6.66	0.0005
Error	69	39.9393	0.5788		
Corrected total	72	51.5053			

(a)   (b)

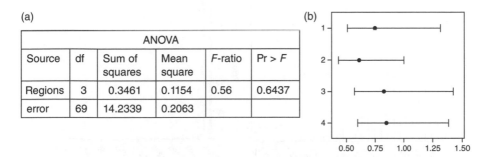

ANOVA

Source	df	Sum of squares	Mean square	F-ratio	Pr > F
Regions	3	0.3461	0.1154	0.56	0.6437
error	69	14.2339	0.2063		

Figure 4.6   (a) Levene's test results. (b) Bonferroni 95% confidence intervals for the transformed variable variance estimates.

The implication is that the null hypothesis is rejected. The Scheffé tests suggest that one of the two following alternative hypotheses is most likely:

$$\mu_{NE} \neq \mu_{NW} = \mu_{SE} = \mu_{SW} \quad \text{and} \quad \mu_{NE} = \mu_{SE} \neq \mu_{NW} = \mu_{SW}.$$

This first alternative hypothesis states that the San Juan quadrant differs from the other three quadrants. This second alternative hypothesis states that the eastern part of the landscape differs from the western part.

A simulation experiment allows these findings to be related to the parent superpopulation. Sample sampling distributions appearing in Figure 4.7 were generated using the transformed variable means and variances for pseudo-random number generation, and are based on 10,000 replications. These results suggest that the model–based inferential basis does an excellent job of mostly rejecting the null hypothesis. The extreme probabilities' portions of the sampling distribution are: 56.8% for $p < 0.0005$, 85.8% for $p < 0.01$, 95.2% for $p < 0.05$, and 97.7% for $p < 0.10$.

4.1.4. Covariates across a geographic landscape

The preceding sections address variance and normality heterogeneity for geo-referenced data. In those contexts, the desired assessment concerns regional means across a geographic landscape, where n areal units are grouped into a relatively small number of regions. Shrinking these regions to n individual

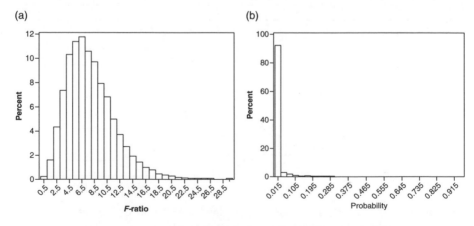

Figure 4.7   Simulated sampling distributions for the directional model-based inference. (a) F-ratio. (b) Null hypothesis probability.

(a)   (b)

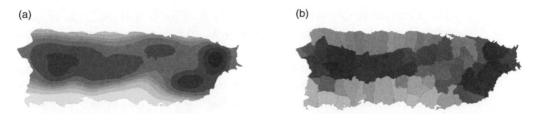

Figure 4.8 The gray scale increases in darkness with increasing rainfall. (a) Contour map of rainfall. (b) Average (of raster values for contour map) rainfall by municipality.

areal units focuses attention on mean responses, moving an analysis from ANOVA to linear regression. By necessity, analyzing the variability in n mean responses links a study to covariates. Assumptions remain important: in the simplest of analyses, the bell-shaped curve should describe the error distribution; variance needs to be constant across the magnitude of the Y values; and Y needs to have a linear relationship with each covariate. Transformations and weightings still furnish tools for satisfying these assumptions.

Because crops require water, rainfall is a potential covariate of farming variables. Consider the 2007 distribution of the density of the number of farms engaging in irrigation (IRRF) practices across the island of Puerto Rico. Because these are counts, not surprisingly the appropriate Box–Cox power transformation is ln(IRRF/area + 0.04) (Figure 4.8a); the normality diagnostic statistic probability is 0.611 (failing to reject the null hypothesis). The expectation is a negative relationship between the number of these farms and the average rainfall in a municipality: as the annual average rainfall in a location increases, the number of farms needed to irrigate tends to decrease. Figure 4.8b confirms this expectation for Puerto Rico.

(a)   (b)

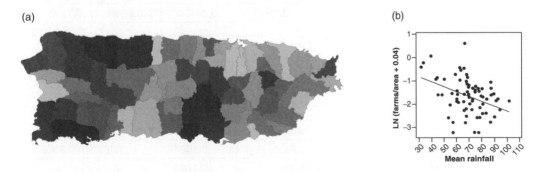

Figure 4.9 (a) Geographic distribution of IRRF (the gray scale darkness is directly proportional to the number of farms). (b) Scatterplot for transformed IRRF density versus mean rainfall.

The bivariate regression analysis for the transformed IRRF, whose geographic distribution appears in Figure 4.9a, and average rainfall indicates a significant covariation between them: average rainfall accounts for roughly 13% of the geographic variation in the transformed IRRF. The trend line and scatterplot in Figure 4.9b illustrate this relationship. The probability for the accompanying homogeneity of variance diagnostic test (i.e., White test) statistic is 0.095. The PRESS statistic – a summary cross-validation statistic – is 39.9394, which is very close to the corresponding regression error sum of squares value of 38.0104 (it is roughly 5% greater). Finally, the probability of the normality diagnostic statistic for the regression residuals is 0.210. Moreover, the model–based inferential assumptions appear to be satisfied.

One interesting feature of the preceding analysis is that an ANOVA based upon the five agricultural administration regions suggests that the average IRRF differs across these regions:

Source	df	Sum of squares	Mean square	F-ratio	Pr > F
Regions	4	8.0092	2.0023	3.77	0.0079
Error	68	36.1008	0.5309		
Corrected total	72	44.1100			

The normality diagnostic statistic probabilities are:

Region	San Juan	Arecibo	Mayaguez	Ponce	Caguas
Probability	0.6838	0.1637	0.4497	0.9966	0.7696

Meanwhile, Levene's test yields:

Source	df	Sum of squares	Mean square	F-ratio	Pr > F
Regions	4	0.7935	0.1984	1.05	0.3906
Error	68	12.9081	0.1898		

But, adjusting for the covariation with average rainfall reverses this statistical inference, with the following *t*-statistic probabilities for difference of means:

Region	San Juan	Arecibo	Mayaguez	Ponce	Caguas
Probability	0.5686	0.3199	0.5052	0.3452	0.7888

The homogeneity of variance test statistic probability accompanying these results is 0.2403. And the residual normality test statistic probabilities are:

Region	San Juan	Arecibo	Mayaguez	Ponce	Caguas
Probability	0.5688	0.2476	0.0152	0.5387	0.2916

The Bonferroni adjustment for doing five simultaneous tests here means that a 10% overall level translates into a 0.02 individual threshold probability, and a 5% overall level translates into a 0.01 individual threshold probability.

In conclusion, average annual rainfall accounts for what appears to be regional differences in average IRRF in the superpopulation.

4.2. Spatial weight matrices

The introduction to Chapter 2 presents an initial discussion of the spatial weight matrix. In that description, it is topologically based and constructed as an $n \times n$ table of binary 0–1 indicator variables, one for each location on a map. The table cell entries are 1 when the table row and column locations are designated as neighbors, and 0 otherwise. One very common definition of "neighbor" is when two areal units in a surface partitioning share a common non–zero–length border. This is called the rook's case, making an analogy with chess. Sometimes neighbors are defined with both zero- and non–zero–length borders; this is called the queen's case (it is the default definition in, for example, GeoBUGS). We denote this table by the $n \times n$ matrix **C**. Figures 2.1 and 2.3 illustrate it.

Tiefelsdorf et al. (1999) outline a family of spatial weight matrices. Patuelli et al. (2011) present specific empirical comparisons of selected members of this family.

4.2.1. Weight matrices for geographic distributions

The previously defined matrix $\mathbf{C}$ is the spatial weight matrix version frequently used when calculating indices of spatial autocorrelation. It is the one used in Sections 2.1.1 and 2.1.2 for computing MCs and GRs. This matrix can be constructed for a geographic distribution of points, by constructing Thiessen polygons and using their boundaries to determine neighbors.

Converting the matrix $\mathbf{C}$ into one in which each row sums to 1 (i.e., row standardization) produces another popular version of the spatial weight matrix. This version, denoted by $\mathbf{W}$, is obtained as follows:

$$w_{ij} = \frac{c_{ij}}{\sum\limits_{j=1}^{n} c_{ij}}, \text{ or in matrix notation } \mathbf{W} = \begin{pmatrix} \mathbf{1}^\mathrm{T}\mathbf{c}_1 & \cdots & 0 \\ \vdots & \ddots & \vdots \\ 0 & \cdots & \mathbf{1}^\mathrm{T}\mathbf{c}_n \end{pmatrix}^{-1} \mathbf{C},$$

where $\mathbf{1}$ is an $n \times 1$ vector of ones, superscript T denotes the matrix transpose operation, and $\mathbf{c}_j$ is the jth row vector of matrix $\mathbf{C}$. Matrix $\mathbf{W}$ is the spatial weight matrix repeatedly found in spatial statistics and spatial econometrics.

A third common version of the spatial weight matrix derives directly from the numerator of the MC formula, denoted here as $\mathbf{MCM}$, and is constructed as follows:

$$(\mathbf{I} - \mathbf{11}^\mathrm{T}/n)\ \mathbf{C}\ (\mathbf{I} - \mathbf{11}^\mathrm{T}/n).$$

The pre- and post-multiplying matrix $(\mathbf{I} - \mathbf{11}^\mathrm{T}/n)$ is one version of a projection matrix found throughout linear statistical theory (see Schott, 2005, pp. 55–61). Here it causes the first eigenfunction of $\mathbf{C}$ to be replaced with a constant vector (i.e., proportional to vector $\mathbf{1}$) and accompanying eigenvalue of 0, while asymptotically preserving the remaining $n - 1$ eigenfunctions. The eigenvectors represent all of the distinct (i.e., orthogonal and uncorrelated) spatial autocorrelation map patterns, from maximum positive to maximum negative spatial autocorrelation.[3] The matrix $\mathbf{MCM}$ is the spatial weight matrix furnishing the basis of eigenvector spatial filtering (Griffith, 2003, 2010b).

Rather than being based upon topological geographic relationships on a surface, spatial weights also can be based upon distance, as in geostatistical

---

[3] Eigenvectors are unique to a multiplicative factor of –1. Consequently, when used as covariates in analyses, eigenvectors calculated with different algorithms can result in a change in sign for their coefficients.

analysis (see Section 2.2). One formulation uses only nearest neighbors (e.g., LeSage and Pace, 2009, p. 272): if two locations are nearest neighbors, then $c_{ij} = 1$; otherwise $c_{ij} = 0$. A second formulation establishes a threshold: $c_{ij} = 1$ for all distances less than the designated threshold; otherwise, $c_{ij} = 0$. Either of these spatial weight matrices also can be converted to their row standardized versions. A third possibility is to use some power of inverse distance between all distinct locations (diagonal entries are defined to be 0), and then convert the resulting $n \times n$ tabulation to a row standardized $\mathbf{W}$ matrix. These matrices can be constructed for a polygonal surface partitioning by using the centroids of the polygons as points representing their locations.

4.2.2. Weight matrices for geographic flows

Construction of spatial weight matrices for $n \times n$ spatial interaction between locations involves Kronecker products, and produces $n^2 \times n^2$ matrices (LeSage and Pace, 2009, pp. 212–16). Conceptualizations include the following four cases (see Chun and Griffith, 2011):

$$\mathbf{C}^N = \mathbf{C} \otimes \mathbf{I}, \tag{4.3}$$

$$\mathbf{C}^N = \mathbf{I} \otimes \mathbf{C}, \tag{4.4}$$

$$\mathbf{C}^N = \mathbf{C} \oplus \mathbf{C} = \mathbf{C} \otimes \mathbf{I} + \mathbf{I} \otimes \mathbf{C}, \tag{4.5}$$

$$\mathbf{C}^N = \mathbf{C} \otimes \mathbf{C}, \tag{4.6}$$

where $\otimes$ and $\oplus$ denote Kronecker product and Kronecker sum, respectively, and superscript N denotes the $n^2 \times n^2$ connectivity matrix. Figure 4.10 illustrates each of these cases.

4.3. Spatial heterogeneity: spatial autocorrelation

One of the first treatments of spatially heterogeneous spatial autocorrelation is by Cliff and Ord (1975). But they analyze the special case of non-coterminous regions, which simplifies the problem by allowing two distinct spatial autocorrelation parameters (i.e., the two geographic weight matrices are block diagonal

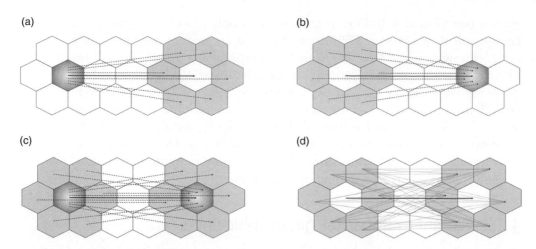

Figure 4.10   (a) Destination correlated flows from a given origin. (b) Origin correlated flows to a given destination. (c) Combination of (a) and (b). (d) Correlated origin to correlated destination flows.

components of a composite geographic weight matrix). Another popular treatment is for directional differences, either in lattice structures (e.g., Besag, 1974) or in semi-variogram model specifications (e.g., Cressie, 1991).

4.3.1. Regional differences

Consider the following pairings of non-coterminous agricultural administrative regions of Puerto Rico (Figure 4.1a): San Juan and Mayaguez, Caguas and Mayaguez, and Caguas and Arecibo. Of the 348 connections in the binary geographic weight matrix, 98 are regional border connections that disappear from any spatial autocorrelation analysis. Moran coefficient results are as follows:

Region	San Juan	Arecibo	Mayaguez	Caguas
Moran coefficient	0.6602	0.0712	−0.0252	0.1767
s_{MC}	0.175	0.223	0.169	0.201
Geary ratio	0.4696	0.8379	0.9432	0.7101

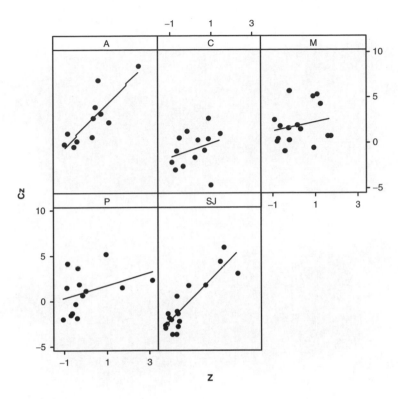

Figure 4.11 Regional Moran scatterplots for Puerto Rico.

The t-statistic for the San Juan–Mayaguez comparison is 2.82 (33 df), which is significant ($p < 0.0001$). The t-statistics for the Caguas–Mayaguez and Caguas–Arecibo comparisons are 0.77 and 0.35, respectively, neither of which is significant. Even with a Bonferroni adjustment, evidence exists that the spatial dependency relationship for the 2007 density of farms varies across the regions of Puerto Rico. The disaggregated Moran scatterplot (Figure 4.11), which includes the 98 regional border connections, implies this same conclusion.

4.3.2. Directional differences: anisotropy

Consider the 66 × 179 complete rectangular grid subset of Puerto Rican digital elevation model (DEM) values ($n = 9,114$ out of 11,814; Figure

(a)

(b)

Figure 4.12   (a) Geographic distribution of elevation for the Puerto Rico DEM pixels. (b) Kriged values of the power-transformed DEM elevation values.

4.12a). The difference between this figure and Figure 3.3b is that 123 pixel fragments (created by clipping the DEM to the outline of the island) are converted into 56 complete pixels here. These elevation measures do not conform to a normal frequency distribution (Figure 4.13a); the DEM Box–Cox power transformation, $DEM^{0.35}$, better aligns these values with a normal distribution (Figure 4.13b), but with noticeable deviations in both tails. Especially problematic is the large number of zero values. Meanwhile, the Moran scatterplots reveal directional spatial dependency: there is spatial dependence along the east–west axis, but not along the north–south axis (Figures 4.13d,e).

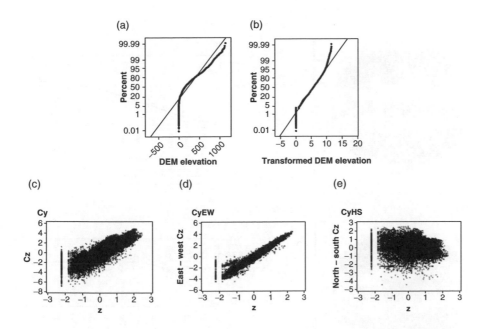

Figure 4.13   (a) DEM elevation normal quantile plot. (b) Power-transformed DEM
elevation normal quantile plot. (c) Moran scatterplot. (d) East–west
Moran scatterplot. (e) North–south Moran scatterplot.

The Moran Coefficient (MC) value for these data is 0.4138 (s_{MC} =
0.0078). This global value can be disaggregated into both a north–south and
an east–west MC: MC_{NS} = −0.0671 (s_{MCNS} = 0.0093) and MC_{EW} = 0.8901
(s_{MCEW} = 0.0092). The difference between these two disaggregate values is
substantial. Consequently, evidence exists implying a spatial dependency difference between the two directions.

A geostatistical analysis utilizing ordinary kriging also indicates heterogeneity −
anisotropy (i.e., closer elevations tend to be more similar in an approximately
east–west direction than in a north–south direction) − with an ellipse rather
than a circle characterizing the geographic variance (Figures 4.14a,c) in the
geographic distribution of power-transformed DEM elevation values (Figure
4.12a). The empirically determined orientation involves a slight clockwise
rotation of 9° from the east–west (i.e., horizontal) axis. This result, which
includes a major axis range parameter of 0.47 (Figure 4.14b) versus a minor
axis ranges parameter of 0.18 (Figure 4.14d), mostly appears to reflect the

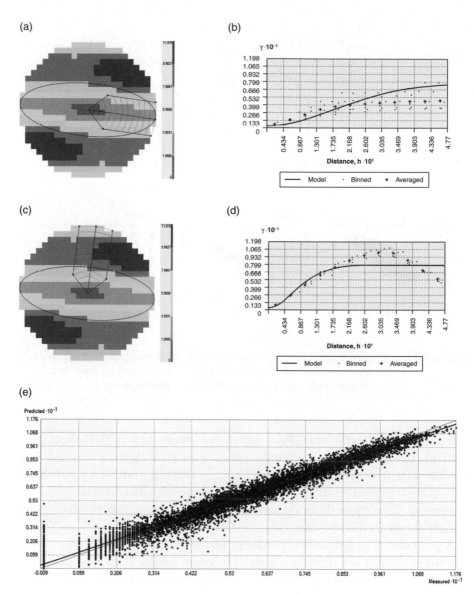

Figure 4.14 Geostatistical analysis results for power-transformed elevation values (from ArcMap). (a) Anisotropic semi-variogram cloud with major axis directional. (b) Semi-variogram with major axis K-Bessel function trend line. (c) An isotropic semi-variogram cloud with minor directional ellipse. (d) Semi-variogram with minor axis K-Bessel function trend line. (e) Cross-validation results.

east–west mountain chain traversing the 66 × 179 lattice landscape. Kriging predictions for the power-transformed values are extremely good (Figure 4.14e).

4.4. R code for concept implementations

Computer Code 4.1 presents how to duplicate the Section 4.1 results in R. It contains basic functions that calculate a mean and standard deviation, and functions that furnish diagnostic statistics, such as the Shapiro–Wilk normality test statistic, or implement statistical techniques, such as ANOVA and linear regression. Here, the *leveneTest* function in the *car* package is used to conduct Levene's homogeneity of variance test. Also the *tapply* function is extensively utilized to calculate statistics for each group defined with a factor variable (e.g., means for the five agricultural administrative regions). Note that because R very efficiently executes vector or matrix operations, the use of vector operations such as the *tapply* function (which avoids employing a loop) can considerably reduce computation time, especially for a large dataset.

Computer Code 4.1. Implementing ANOVA, together with model diagnostics.

`library (car)`	Load *car* package.
`pr.farm <- read.csv(file="PR-farm-data.csv")`	Read a data file for Puerto Rico farm information.

`# 4.1.2`
`adm <- factor(pr.farm$ADM, levels=1:5,`
`      labels=c("San Juan", "Arecibo",`
`      "Mayaguez", "Ponce", "Caguas"))`
	Create a factor variable, *adm*, for 5 agricultural administrative regions.

`land.den02 <-`
`pr.farm$cuerdas_02/pr.farm$area`
`mean(land.den02[adm=="San Juan"])`
`sd(land.den02[adm=="San Juan"])`
`shapiro.test(land.den02[adm=="San Juan"])`
	Calculate the farmland densities in 2002.
	Calculate the mean and std dev. of the farmland density for San Juan region.
	Conduct Shapiro-Wilk (S-W) test for San Juan region.

`tapply(land.den02,adm,mean)`
`tapply(land.den02,adm,sd)`
`sw.p <- function(x){`
`    shapiro.test(x)$p.value`
`}`
`tapply(land.den02,adm,sw.p)`
	Calculate means for the 5 regions.
	Calculate std devs for the 5 regions.
	Create a function to get only *p*-values for S-W test.
	
	Calculate probabilities of S-W test for the 5 regions.

`leveneTest(land.den02, adm, center=mean)`	Conduct Levene's test.

`lden02.tr <- (land.den02+445)^-0.15`
`tapply(lden02.tr, adm,mean)`
`tapply(lden02.tr, adm,sd)`
`tapply(lden02.tr, adm,sw.p)`
	Transform the farmland density.
	Calculate means, std devs, and S-W test probabilities for the transformed farmland densities in 2002.

`leveneTest(lden02.tr, adm, center=mean)`	Conduct Levene's test for the transformed variable.

`lm.102.org <- lm(land.den02 ~ adm)`
`anova(lm.102.org)`
`lm.102.tr <- lm(lden02.tr ~ adm)`
`anova(lm.102.tr)`
	Run ANOVA for the untransformed farmland densities in 2002.
	Run ANOVA for the transformed farmland densities in 2002.

`land.den07 <-`
`pr.farm$cuerdas_07/pr.farm$area`
`cl_ih <- factor(pr.farm$cl_ih,levels=0:1,`
`        labels=c("CL","IH"))`
`lden07.tr <- log(land.den07 + 211)`
	Calculate the farmland densities in 2007.
	Create a factor variable, *cl_ih*, for the elevation-based regions.
	Transform the variable.

`tapply(land.den07,cl_ih,mean)`
`tapply(land.den07,cl_ih,sd)`
`tapply(land.den07,cl_ih,sw.p)`
	Calculate means, std devs, and S-W test probabilities for the farmland densities in 2007.

`tapply(lden07.tr,cl_ih,mean)`
`tapply(lden07.tr,cl_ih,sd)`
`tapply(lden07.tr,cl_ih,sw.p)`
	Calculate means, std devs, and S-W test probabilities for the transformed farmland densities in 2007.

`leveneTest(lden07.tr, cl_ih, center=mean)`	Conduct Levene's test for the transformed variable.

`lm.107.org <- lm(land.den07 ~ cl_ih)`
`anova(lm.107.org)`
`lm.107.tr <- lm(lden07.tr ~ cl_ih)`
`anova(lm.107.tr) library (car)`
	Run ANOVA for the untransformed farmland densities in 2007.
	Run ANOVA for the transformed farmland densities in 2007.

`# 4.1.3`
`farm.den02 <-`
`pr.farm$nofarms_02/pr.farm$area`
`quad <- factor(pr.farm$quad,levels =`
`c(4,3,1,2),labels=c("NE","NW","SW","SE"))`
	Calculate the farm densities in 2002.
	Create a factor variable, *quad*, for the 4 quadrants.

`fden02.tr <- log(farm.den02 + 0.35)`	Transform the variable.
`tapply(farm.den02,quad,sw.p)` `tapply(fden02.tr,quad,sw.p)`	Calculate p-values of S-W test for untransformed and transformed variables.
`leveneTest(fden02.tr, quad, center=mean)`	Conduct Levene's test for the transformed variable.
`lm.f02.tr <- lm(fden02.tr ~ quad)` `anova(lm.f02.tr)`	Run ANOVA for the transformed farm densities in 2002.

`#4.1.4`
`rain <- pr.farm$rain_mean`
`ifarm.den07 <-`
`pr.farm$irr.farms_07/pr.farm$area`
	Get average rainfall data.
	Calculate the IRRF farms densities in 2007.

`ifden07.tr <- log(ifarm.den07 + 0.04)` `shapiro.test(ifden07.tr)`	Transform the variable. Conduct S-W test.
`plot(rain,ifden07.tr, pch=20)` `abline(lm(ifden07.tr ~ rain))`	Plot a scatterplot with average rainfall and IRRF farm densities with a fitted line.
`lm.ifden07.tr <- lm(ifden07.tr ~ adm)` `anova(lm.ifden07.tr)`	Run ANOVA for the transformed IRRF farm densities in 2007.
`tapply(ifden07.tr,adm,sw.p)`	Calculate S-W probabilities for the 5 agricultural administrative regions.
`leveneTest(ifden07.tr, adm, center=mean)`	Conduct Levene's test for the transformed variable.

`lm.ifden07.tr.rain <- lm(ifden07.tr ~ adm`
`+ rain - 1)`
`summary(lm.ifden07.tr.rain)`
	Fit a linear regression model without intercept.
	Report the summary of the regression result.

`resids <- resid(lm.ifden07.tr.rain)`
`leveneTest(resids, adm, center=mean)`
`tapply(resids, adm, sw.p)`
	Get the residuals.
	Run Levene's test for the residuals.
	Calculate S-W probabilities for the residuals.

5

Spatially Adjusted Regression and Related Spatial Econometrics

LEARNING OBJECTIVES:

- To reformulate linear regression models to account for spatial autocorrelation

- To reformulate binomial/logistic regression models to account for spatial autocorrelation

- To reformulate Poisson regression models to account for spatial autocorrelation

- To differentiate between static geographic distributions and spatial interaction cases

Regression analysis seeks to establish an equation for predicting some response variable, Y, from a set of P covariates, X_1, X_2, ..., X_P. One statistical problem is to estimate the coefficients for these covariates in order to construct this prediction equation. Classical statistics attaches a probability distribution to the residuals (i.e., differences between observed and predicted values of Y) of this prediction equation. Spatial statistics modifies this situation by specifying a prediction function that has Y on both sides of the equation. In other words, a value at location i is at least partially a function of the values of Y at nearby locations. This conceptualization captures the essence of spatial autocorrelation.

5.1. Linear regression

Cliff and Ord (1973) furnish much of the seminal work for a linear regression model. Griffith (1993b) details the translation of a range of linear regression model specifications, from ANOVA, through product moment correlation coefficients, to two-group discriminant function analysis. This section features the autoregressive model most commonly employed in spatial statistics, namely the simultaneous autoregressive (SAR) specification,

$$\mathbf{Y} = \rho \mathbf{W} \mathbf{Y} + (\mathbf{I} - \rho \mathbf{W})\mathbf{X}\boldsymbol{\beta} + \boldsymbol{\varepsilon}, \tag{5.1}$$

which is the spatial statistical counterpart to the standard linear regression model specification of

$$\mathbf{Y} = \mathbf{X}\boldsymbol{\beta} + \boldsymbol{\varepsilon}, \tag{5.2}$$

where $\mathbf{W}$ is the row standardized geographic connectivity matrix (see Section 4.2), $\mathbf{I}$ is an $n \times n$ identity matrix, ρ is the spatial autocorrelation parameter, $\boldsymbol{\beta}$ is a $(P + 1) \times 1$ vector of regression coefficients (including the intercept term), and $\boldsymbol{\varepsilon}$ is an $n \times 1$ vector of iid $N(0, \sigma^2)$ random variables, which may be written in matrix form as the multivariate normal distribution $MVN(\mathbf{0}, \mathbf{I}\sigma^2)$. Positing a row standardized geographic connectivity matrix $\mathbf{W}$ restricts positive spatial autocorrelation values of ρ to be in the interval [0, 1). The presence of non–zero spatial autocorrelation means equation (5.2) has the modified specification

$$\mathbf{Y} = \mathbf{X}\boldsymbol{\beta} + (\mathbf{I} - \rho \mathbf{W})^{-1}\boldsymbol{\varepsilon}, \tag{5.3}$$

where the spatial linear operator $(\mathbf{I} - \rho \mathbf{W})^{-1}$ embeds spatial autocorrelation into the error term, and hence the calculated residual. In other words, equation (5.2) becomes

$$\mathbf{Y}, = \mathbf{X}\boldsymbol{\beta} + [\rho \mathbf{W}(\mathbf{Y} - \mathbf{X}\boldsymbol{\beta}) + \boldsymbol{\varepsilon}] = \mathbf{X}\boldsymbol{\beta} + \boldsymbol{\xi},$$

with $\boldsymbol{\xi}$ no longer being distributed as $MVN(\mathbf{0}, \mathbf{I}\sigma^2)$. The conventional (i.e., ordinary least squares, or OLS) estimates $\mathbf{b}$ of $\boldsymbol{\beta}$ remain unbiased. But spatial autocorrelation alters their sampling distribution variances (i.e., their standard errors) as well as the regression model R^2 value (see Dutilleul et al., 2008).

Although equation (5.1) is properly specified, its estimation requires employment of a weighting function that achieves two goals: first, it ensures that the probabilities in both the autocorrelated and its corresponding unauto-correlated mathematical space integrate to 1; and second, it restricts the value of ρ to the interval $[0, 1)$. This estimation version of equation (5.1) is (Griffith, 1988)

$$\frac{\mathbf{Y}}{\exp\left(\sum_{i=1}^{n}(1-\rho\lambda_i)\right)} = \frac{\rho\mathbf{WY}}{\exp\left(\sum_{i=1}^{n}(1-\rho\lambda_i)\right)} - \frac{\rho\mathbf{WX\beta}}{\exp\left(\sum_{i=1}^{n}(1-\rho\lambda_i)\right)} + \frac{\mathbf{X\beta}}{\exp\left(\sum_{i=1}^{n}(1-\rho\lambda_i)\right)} + \frac{\varepsilon}{\exp\left(\sum_{i=1}^{n}(1-\rho\lambda_i)\right)},$$

where the λ_i are the n eigenvalues of matrix $\mathbf{W}$. Estimation requires nonlinear techniques because ρ appears in both the numerator and the denominator of the first two terms on the right-hand side of this equation. Furthermore, the derivatives are not straightforward, and their calculation is cumbersome. These technical complications become hidden in software implementations of spatial autoregression estimation procedures.

Consider the 2007 geographic distribution of number of farms utilizing irrigation. The Box–Cox power transformation better aligning it with a bell-shaped curve is $\ln(Y/\text{area} + 0.04)$; normal diagnostic probability increases from < 0.001 to 0.611 (see Section 4.1.4). Results for regressing this response variable on average annual rainfall include the following:

Estimation	$\hat{\rho}$	$\hat{\beta}_0$	$\hat{\beta}_1$	(pseudo-)R^2	Normality probability
OLS	0	−0.2067	−0.0207	0.138	0.210
		(0.4360)	(0.0061)		
SAR	0.5760	−0.4327	−0.0174	0.379	0.213
		(0.5129)[1]	(0.0071)		

These results imply the presence of moderately strong positive spatial auto-correlation, and illustrate the effects on standard errors and the increase in variance accounted for (e.g., R^2).

---

[1] Standard error results may differ slightly because of differences in the nonlinear optimization algorithm used and/or the type of standard error computed (e.g., asymptotic).

Spatial autocorrelation can affect a pairwise correlation coefficient calculated for two georeferenced variables (see Clifford et al., 1989), again largely in terms of its standard error. The Pearson product moment correlation coefficient for the power-transformed 2007 geographic distribution of number of farms utilizing irrigation and the average annual rainfall is −0.3719. The SAR spatial autocorrelation parameter estimates for these two variables respectively are 0.6469 and 0.8239. In order to adjust for these levels of spatial autocorrelation, the correlation coefficient to calculate is between the variables

$$(\mathbf{I} - 0.6469\ \mathbf{W})\langle\ln(Y/\text{area} + 0.04)\rangle \text{ and } (\mathbf{I} - 0.8239\ \mathbf{W})\ \mathbf{X},$$

where the wide angle brackets denote a vector. Adjusting for the latent spatial autocorrelation in this way reduces the correlation coefficient to −0.2426. In other words, spatial autocorrelation makes the relationship between these two variables look stronger than it actually is in the superpopulation.

In Section 4.1.4, the initial statistical decision is that a difference exists in regional means of the power-transformed 2007 geographic distribution of number of farms utilizing irrigation. Accounting for average annual rainfall reverses this decision. But after adjusting for spatial autocorrelation of 0.6469 in this transformed variable, the ANOVA results change as follows:

Source	df	Sum of squares	Mean square	F-ratio	Pr > F
Regions	4	2.2023	0.5506	1.35	0.2603
Error	68	27.7215	0.4077		
Corrected total	72	29.9239			

The normality diagnostic statistic probabilities are:

Region	San Juan	Arecibo	Mayaguez	Ponce	Caguas
Probability	0.5666	0.1938	0.2120	0.9804	0.8066

Meanwhile, Levene's test yields:

Source	df	Sum of squares	Mean square	F-ratio	Pr > F
Regions	4	0.2654	0.0713	0.47	0.7541
Error	68	10.2194	0.1503		

These model diagnostics support the underlying assumptions for model-based inference. Consequently, the initial differences detected in regional means disappear after accounting for spatial autocorrelation. This finding explains why adjusting for average annual rainfall, with its high level of positive spatial autocorrelation, also reverses the statistical decision.

The two-group discriminant function analysis (DFA) model is the final classical linear model treated here (see Tatsuoka, 1988). It also can be formulated as a linear regression specification, for which the response variable is binary (i.e., takes the value 0 or 1). The bivariate regression results are as follows (with standard errors in parentheses):

Estimation	$\hat{\rho}$	$\hat{\beta}_0$	$\hat{\beta}_1$	(pseudo-)R^2
OLS	0	−0.4440	0.0125	0.124
		(0.2795)	(0.0039)	
SAR	0.7426	−1.5004	0.0272	0.494
		(0.3276)	(0.0044)	

The normality assumption no longer is valid with this analysis; the response variable is binary, not continuous. In addition, the linear model specification does not guarantee that the 0–1 response values are contained in the interval [0, 1]. Nevertheless, the coefficients are proportional to discriminant function analysis coefficients in multivariate statistical theory.

5.2. Nonlinear regression

In the preceding section, implementation of spatial autoregressive models requires nonlinear regression techniques. But the error term assumption is still the normal probability model. Nonlinear regression also involves non–normal probability models, such as those for binomial and Poisson random variables. The generalized linear model (GLM) is the implementation of the latter models.

Eigenvector spatial filtering furnishes a sound methodology for estimating non–normal probability models with georeferenced data containing non–zero spatial autocorrelation. This methodology accounts for spatial autocorrelation in random variables by incorporating heterogeneity into parameters in order to model non–homogeneous populations. It renders a mixture of distributions that can be used to model observed georeferenced data whose various characteristics differ from those that are consistent with a single, simple, underlying distribution with constant parameters across all observations. The aim of this technique is to capture spatial autocorrelation effects with a linear combination of spatial proxy variables – namely, eigenvectors – rather than to identify a global spatial auto-correlation parameter governing average direct pairwise correlations between selected observed values. As such, it utilizes the misspecification interpretation of spatial autocorrelation, which assumes that spatial autocorrelation is induced by missing exogenous variables, which themselves are spatially autocorrelated, and hence relates to heterogeneity.

Eigenvector spatial filtering conceptualizes spatial dependency as a common factor that is a linear combination of synthetic variates summarizing distinct fea-tures of the neighbors' geographic configuration structure for a given georefer-enced dataset. The synthetic variates may be the eigenvectors of the matrix $(\mathbf{I} - \mathbf{1}\mathbf{1}^T/n)\mathbf{C}(\mathbf{I} - \mathbf{1}\mathbf{1}^T/n)$ discussed in Section 4.2.1, a term appearing in the Moran Coefficient (MC) index of spatial autocorrelation.[2] De Jong et al. (1984) show that the extreme eigenfunctions of this matrix define the most extreme levels possible of spatial autocorrelation for a given surface partitioning, a result in combination with Tiefelsdorf and Boots (1995) and Griffith (1996) that attaches conceptual meaning to the extracted synthetic variates. These variates summarize distinct map pattern features because they are both orthogonal and uncorrelated.

The eigenfunction problem solution is similar to that obtained with principal components analysis in which the covariance matrix is given by $[\mathbf{I} + k(\mathbf{I} - \mathbf{1}\mathbf{1}^T/n) \times \mathbf{C}(\mathbf{I} - \mathbf{1}\mathbf{1}^T/n)]$, for some suitable value of k; sequential, rather than simultaneous, variance extraction is desired in order to preserve interpretation of the extremes. This solution relates to the following decomposition theorem (after Tatsuoka, 1988, p.141):

> the first eigenvector, say $\mathbf{E}_1$, is the set of numerical values that has the largest MC achievable by any set of real numbers for the spatial arrangement defined by matrix $\mathbf{C}$; the second eigenvector is the set of real numbers that has the largest achievable MC by

---

[2] The Geary ratio counterpart to this matrix also could be used.

any set that is uncorrelated with $\mathbf{E}_1$; the third eigenvector is the third such set of values; and so on through $\mathbf{E}_n$, the set of values that has the largest negative MC achievable by any set that is uncorrelated with the preceding $(n - 1)$ eigenvectors.

The corresponding eigenvalues index these levels of spatial autocorrelation: $MC = n\mathbf{E}^T\mathbf{CE}/\mathbf{1}^T\mathbf{C1}$. But, in contrast to principal components analysis, rather than using the resulting eigenvectors to construct linear combinations of attribute variables (which would be the n 0–1 binary indicator variables forming matrix $\mathbf{C}$), the eigenvectors themselves (instead of principal components scores) are the desired synthetic variates, each containing n elements, one for each areal unit (i.e., location). Figure 5.1 illustrates global, regional, and local geographic patterns of spatial autocorrelation portrayed by selected eigenvectors.

5.2.1. Binomial/logistic regression

The preceding discriminant function analysis can be recast as a logistic regression problem, which ensures that the predicted values corresponding to the observed 0–1 values are contained in the interval [0, 1]. The Bernoulli (i.e., binomial with number of trials (N_{tr}) equal to 1) probability model underlies

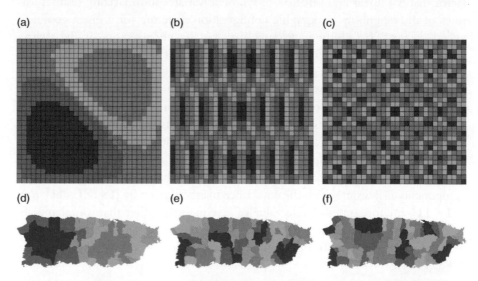

Figure 5.1　Spatial filter map patterns for (a–c) a regular square tessellation (top) and (d–f) the Puerto Rico municipality surface partitioning; quintile eigenvector value classes (which are relative to a factor of –1) range from dark green to dark red. (a,d) Global map pattern. (b,e) Regional map pattern. (c,f) Local map pattern.

this model specification. The spatial filter (SF) conceptualization enables this model to be implemented with a GLM while still accounting for positive spatial autocorrelation.

Figure 5.2a portrays the coastal lowlands/interior highlands classification scheme. This distribution contains weak positive spatial autocorrelation: MC = 0.2374 (standard error 0.075), Geary Ratio (GR) = 0.8120. Average rainfall accounts for roughly 12% of the variation in the binary classification. A stepwise selection procedure adjusting for non-constant variance includes nine eigenvectors in the model to account for spatial autocorrelation. This spatial autocorrelation component accounts for an additional approximately 64% of the variation in the classification scheme. The residuals for the binary predicted values contain only trace amounts of spatial autocorrelation: MC = −0.1244, GR = 1.1879. Figure 5.2b is the geographic distribution of the estimated probability of a municipality being a member of the interior highlands group. Rounding all values between 0 and 0.5 to 0, and all values between 0.5 and 1 to 1, Figure 5.2c portrays the predicted classification scheme. Figures 5.2a and 5.2c are very similar.

The preceding example illustrates a dichotomous classification case. But many georeferenced variables are percentages. For these variables, a binomial model specification is appropriate. Such a specification involves both a lower limit (i.e., 0) as well as an upper limit (i.e., N_{tr}) on counts. The percentage of farms in a municipality utilizing irrigation furnishes one example of this type of variable (Figure 5.3a). This geographic distribution contains weak positive spatial autocorrelation: MC = 0.1533, GR = 0.6665. Because the variable is linked to a binomial probability model, the relationship between its mean and its variance is given as follows: variance = $(1 - p)$ mean. Overdispersion occurs when deviations from this relationship are such that variance > $(1 - p)$ mean. The deviance statistic that indexes this overdispersion has an ideal value of 1. For the Puerto Rico farm irrigation example, average rainfall accounts for roughly 29% of the geographic variance in percentage of farms utilizing irrigation, with an accompanying deviance statistic of 9.67 (i.e., excessive overdispersion). Spatial

(a)   (b)   (c)

Figure 5.2 The coastal lowlands/interior highlands classification scheme.
(a) Geographic distribution of the observed classification. (b) Predicted probabilities for the observed classification. (c) Predicted classification.

(a)   (b)   (c)

Figure 5.3   Gray scale darkness is directly proportional to values. (a) Geographic
distribution of percentage of farms utilizing irrigation. (b) Predicted
geographic distribution of percentage of farms utilizing irrigation.
(c) Constructed spatial filter.

autocorrelation (Figure 5.3c) accounts for an additional roughly 32% of geographic variance, reducing the deviance statistic to 4.42 (i.e., a substantial reduction, but still indicating excessive overdispersion). The SF (Figure 5.3c) represents
strong positive spatial autocorrelation: MC = 0.8097, GR = 0.2598. Meanwhile,
the model residuals contain little spatial autocorrelation: MC = –0.1415, GR =
0.9572. Of note is that the GR values[3] here suggest the presence of some data
complications (e.g., messiness, dirtiness, noisiness).

5.2.2. Poisson/negative binomial regression

One difference between Poisson and binomial variables is that the only bound
the former have is a lower one of 0. Counts for a Poisson variable are not
constrained by an upper bound (i.e., N_{tr}), and can go to infinity. Another difference is that the presence of overdispersion can be conceptualized as a non-
constant mean, which when characterized by a gamma probability model
converts a Poisson into a negative binomial variable.

5.2.2.1. Geographic distributions

The Box–Cox power transformation for 2007 farm count density (Y) can be
recast as a Poisson variable for farm counts coupled with an area offset variable
(i.e., a variable whose regression coefficient is set to 1 rather than being estimated). Because the area variable is introduced into an exponential function, it
must be done in its natural logarithm form (i.e., $e^{\ln(x)} = x$). A model specification
of this type avoids specification error arising from employing a bell-shaped curve
with a power-transformed variable, as well as avoiding the need to calculate a
back-transformation after completing an analysis (see equation [4.1]).

---

[3] A heuristic test for well-behaved data is that MC + GR should be very close to 1.

The Box–Cox power transformation renders the variable $(Y - 0.12)^{0.38}$ as approximately normally distributed; the Shapiro–Wilk probability, P(S-W), increases from less than 0.0001 to 0.5688. Regressing the transformed variable on mean annual rainfall yields a set of predicted values together with a mean squared error of 0.2550 (i.e., $\hat{\sigma}^2$). Mean annual rainfall accounts for roughly 13% of the variance in the transformed variable. The back-transformation involves the exponent $1/0.38 = 2.6315789$. Equation (4.2) yields

$$C_1 = \prod_{h=1}^{1} \frac{0.5}{h}\left[-\frac{1}{4} + \left(\frac{1}{0.38} - 2h + \frac{3}{2} \right)^2 \right] = 2.14681$$

and equation (4.1) yields, for the n values of $E(Y)$,

$$\hat{\mu}_i^{1/0.38} + \sum_{j=1}^{1} (2.14681)\hat{\mu}_i^{2-2j} \left(\sqrt{0.25496} \right)^{2j} + 0.12 , \qquad i = 1, 2, \ldots, n,$$

which accounts for roughly 16% of the variance in Y (Figure 5.4a). The range of these back-transformed predicted values is roughly 2 to 7, whereas that for the observed values is 0 to 15. The bivariate regression of Y on these back-transformed predicted values renders an intercept of -0.8048 and a slope of 1.2244.

Employing the Poisson model specification yields a deviance statistic of nearly 94, indicating that the variance and the mean are not equal. Respecifying this Poisson model as a negative binomial model (i.e., a Poisson random variable with a gamma-distributed mean) reduces this deviance statistic value to 1.11 (which mostly affects the calculation of standard errors); accordingly, $\hat{\sigma}^2 = \hat{\mu} + 0.5067\hat{\mu}^2$. Densities computed with the predicted counts account for about 15% of the variance in Y (Figure 5.4b). The range of these predicted values is roughly 2 to 9, an improvement upon the normal approximation results. The bivariate regression of Y on these predicted values renders an intercept of 0.5078 and a slope of 0.8858, both of which are closer to their respective ideal values of 0 and 1 than the normal approximation results. The difference between these GLM and the bell-shaped curve results is attributable to specification error: the paired results are reasonably similar (i.e., the approximation is very good), but have conspicuous differences.

Positive spatial autocorrelation can be detected not only in variable Y (MC = 0.3343, GR = 0.7732), but also in the residuals from both model specifications (normal approximation MC = 0.3847, GR = 0.7104; negative binomial MC = 0.4040, GR = 0.6788). Constructing an SF to account for this

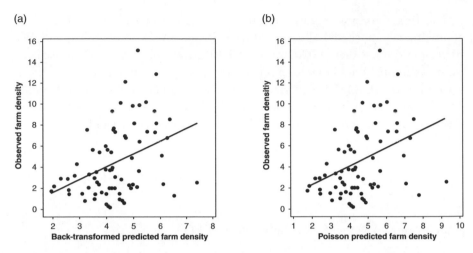

Figure 5.4   Observed versus predicted scatterplots. (a) Normal probability model
results. (b) Poisson probability model results.

spatial autocorrelation results in eight vectors being selected for the normal
approximation specification, and five of these same eight vectors being selected
for the negative binomial specification (using $\alpha = 0.01$ in this second case).
Now roughly 73% of the variation is accounted for in the transformed variable, and roughly 72% of the variation in Y (Figure 5.5a) after calculating the
back-transformation. The range of these back-transformed predicted values
improves to roughly 1 to 14. The bivariate regression of Y on these back-
transformed predicted values renders an intercept of 0.1867 and a slope of
0.9635. In contrast, the negative binomial specification yields predicted values
that account for roughly 68% of the variation in Y, and produces a 1 to 14
range of predicted values. Its bivariate regression results include an intercept of
0.4136 and a slope of 0.8993. In other words, the normal approximation outperforms the GLM.

Equation (2.7) furnishes the expected value for normally distributed residuals from a linear regression analysis. Here the value is -0.1059 for the normal
approximation regression analysis, and -0.0777 for the negative binomial
regression analysis. Spatial autocorrelation index values for the back-transformed residuals are MC $= -0.1751$ and GR $= 1.2692$. In contrast, spatial
autocorrelation index values for the negative binomial residuals are MC $=
-0.1276$ and GR $= 1.2484$. The GR values suggest possible overcorrection by
the SFs for detected spatial autocorrelation.

These results can be extended to ANOVA problems by introducing
the appropriate indicator variables into the regression model specifications,

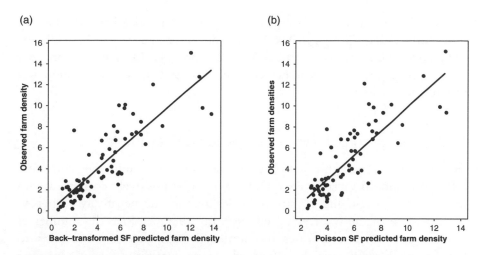

(a)   (b)

Figure 5.5   Observed versus predicted scatterplots. (a) Spatial filter normal probability model results. (b) Spatial filter Poisson probability model results.

allowing the assumed ANOVA probability model to be non-normal. The
transformed variable results for a one-way ANOVA, in which the classification is based upon urban and non-urban municipalities, yields the following
results:

unadjusted

   for variable Y: $P(S-W) = 0.5376$ and 0.7834

   for variable Y: P(Levene statistic) $= 0.2976$

   ANOVA $F = (-6.18)^2 = 38.19$, $P(F) < 0.0001$

adjusted for spatial autocorrelation[4]

   for regression residuals: $P(S-W) = 0.5054$ and 0.7594

   for regression residuals: P(Levene statistic) $= 0.3216$

   ANOVA $F = (-2.94)^2 = 8.64$, $P(F) = 0.0046$

In other words, a difference in farm densities between the urban and non-urban
groups is expected to exist in the superpopulation. Meanwhile, the negative binomial

---

[4] The spatial filter construction with stepwise regression includes one additional
eigenvector when the model specification includes the classification variable.

yields a significant regression coefficient for the difference between the two indicator variables ($P(b_{class})$ = 0.0005). The deviance statistic is 1.22, while the individual group deviance statistics are 1.29 and 1.49. Overall, both analyses furnish the same statistical inference, and indicate that this implication is a sound model-based inference.

5.2.2.2. Geographic flows: a journey-to-work example

Because the n^2 geographic flows between locations are counts, they constitute a Poisson random variable. Each flow tends to be positively correlated with the size of its origin and the size of its destination, and negatively correlated with the size of the intervening distance. In other words, as the number of workers at a location increases, the number leaving that origin location to travel to work tends to increase. Similarly, as the number of jobs at a location increases, the number of workers arriving at that destination to work tends to increase. And, as the distance separating an origin and a destination location increases, the number of workers tending to travel from that origin to that destination tends to decrease. The following simple equation furnishes a very good description of this situation (see Section 4.2.2; Griffith, 2011):

$$F_{ij} \approx \kappa A_i O_i B_j D_j e^{-\gamma d_{ij}} e^{SF_{O_i \times D_j}} , \tag{5.4}$$

where

F_{ij} denotes the flow (e.g., number of workers) between locations i and j;

κ is a constant of proportionality;

A_i denotes an origin balancing factor;

O_i denotes the total amount of flow leaving from origin i (e.g., number of workers residing at an origin);

B_j denotes a destination balancing factor;

D_j denotes the total amount of flow arriving at destination j (e.g., the number of jobs available at a destination);

d_{ij} denotes the distance separating origin i and destination j;

γ denotes the global distance decay rate.

SF_{O_i} denotes the origin i spatial filter accounting for spatial autocorrelation in flows, calculated by holding D_j constant in $SF_{O_i \times D_j}$

SF_{D_j} denotes the destination j spatial filter accounting for spatial autocorrelation in flows, calculated by holding O_i constant in $SF_{O_i \times D_j}$

Selected results from the estimation of equation (5.4) for the Puerto Rico 2000 journey-to-work data (874,832 inter-municipality trips for $73^2 = 5,329$ dyads) include the following:

Set values	$\hat{\kappa}$	$\hat{\gamma}$	Overdispersion	pseudo-R^2
$SF_{O_i} = 0$, $SF_{D_j} = 0$, $A_i = 1$, $B_j = 1$	9.4×10^{-6}	0.1625	14.5227^2	0.8039
$SF_{O_i} = 0$, $SF_{D_j} = 0$	5.6×10^{-6}	0.2286	7.9801^2	0.9825
None	5.1×10^{-6}	0.2084	6.4750^2	0.9892

The spatial filter comprises 85 of 121 candidate eigenvectors (those with an MC of at least 0.25), from a total of 5,329 possible eigenvectors. These results illustrate the failure to estimate an accurate global distance decay parameter value when ignoring spatial autocorrelation in flows. Spatial autocorrelation in flows contributes to excess Poisson variation, too. Adjusting for spatial autocorrelation in flows yields a better alignment of the largest predicted and observed values, which slightly improves the pseudo-R^2 value (Figure 5.6). The following bivariate regression results quantify this improved alignment, which signifies a reduction in model misspecification:

Set values	Intercept	Slope	PRESS/ESS[5]	Predicted R^2
$SF_{O_i} = 0$, $SF_{D_j} = 0$, $A_i = 1$, $B_j = 1$	95.36	0.42	3.53	0.3086
$SF_{O_i} = 0$, $SF_{D_j} = 0$	7.09	0.96	1.41	0.9753
None	4.08	0.98	1.21	0.9876

The ideal values here are 0 for the intercept, 1 for the slope, 1 for the PRESS/ESS ratio, and 1 for the predicted R^2.

Figure 5.7 portrays the balancing factors and spatial filters for the Puerto Rico journey-to-work example. The A_i and B_j values display conspicuous geographic patterns (Figures 5.7a,b). The origin balancing factors display an east–west trend from values between 0 and 1 (deflating departure flows), to values greater than 1 (inflating departure flows). The destination balancing factors display the opposite trend. Spatial autocorrelation accounts for roughly 90% of the variation in each of these geographic distributions. Meanwhile, the origin spatial filter (Figure 5.7c) contrasts the San Juan metropolitan region

---

[5] ESS is error sum of squares, PRESS is predicted error sum of squares.

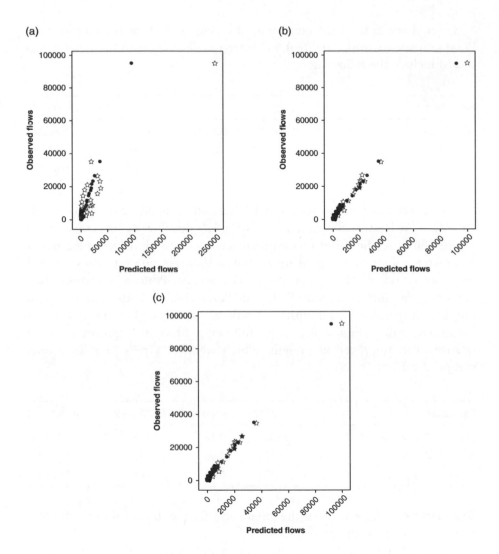

Figure 5.6 Scatterplots of the journey-to-work trips predicted by equation (5.4) and observed. (a) $SF_{O_i} = 0$, $SF_{D_j} = 0$, $A_i = 1$, $B_j = 1$. (b) $SF_{O_i} = 0$, $SF_{D_j} = 0$. (c) All parameters estimated. Solid circle denotes observed flow values; star denotes predicted flow values.

with the remainder of the island. This contrast is consistent with the origin balancing factors map pattern. The destination spatial filter highlights the four urban catchment areas (San Juan–Caguas, Arecibo, Mayaguez, and Ponce; see Figure 4.1).

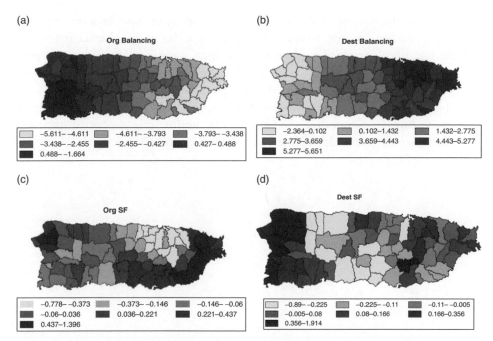

Figure 5.7   Geographic distributions of equation (5.4) terms. (a) Origin balancing factor, A_i. (b) Destination balancing factor, B_j. (c) Origin spatial filter. (d) Destination spatial filter. Darkness of gray scale is directly proportional to value.

5.3. R code for concept implementations

Computer Code 5.1 demonstrates implementations of the spatially adjusted regression models presented in this chapter. These implementations include eigenvector spatial filter specifications for the normal, binomial, Poisson, and negative binomial models. Standard stepwise regression methods in R, such as the *step* and *stepAIC* functions, make selections based upon such measures as the Akaike information criterion (AIC). The stepwise procedure with AIC tends to select more eigenvectors than are chosen by the traditional stepwise procedure based upon statistical significance. All data analyses in this chapter were performed with SAS, including the eigenvector selections. The R code implementations in this section utilize the *stepwise.forward* function (which is defined in the all_functions.R file) for the normal cases, and the *stepAIC* function for the non-normal distribution cases. Hence, when compared with the eigenvectors selected for the normal cases, slightly more eigenvectors tend to be selected with *stepAIC* for the non-normal cases. Nevertheless, many eigenvectors are common to these two sets. In order to replicate the data analyses in this chapter, the results from traditional stepwise regression based upon statistical significance are presented as well as R code using the *stepAIC* function. Results obtained with R code need to be manually adjusted to match those obtained with SAS.

The *mapping.seq* function is utilized in order to avoid redundant and lengthy R code lines in Computer Code 5.1 when performing repetitive mapping tasks. This function is also defined in the all_functions.R file.

Computer Code 5.1. Implementing spatially adjusted regression and spatial interaction models

```# load libraries and data``` ```library(car)``` ```library(spdep)``` ```library(RColorBrewer)``` ```library(classInt)```	Load *car*, *spdep*, *RColorBrewer*, and *classInt* packages.
```pr.f <- read.csv(file="PR-farm-data.csv")```	Read Puerto Rico farm data.
```# 5.1``` ```ifarm.den07 <- pr.f$irr_farms_07/pr.f$area``` ```y <- log(ifarm.den07 + 0.04)``` ```rain <- pr.f$rain_mean```	Calculate irrigated farm density in 2007. Transform the density. Get mean rainfall.
```if.lm <- lm(y ~ rain)``` ```summary(if.lm)``` ```shapiro.test(resid(if.lm))```	Run linear regression and summarize the results. Conduct a normality test.
```pr.nb <- read.gal("PuertoRico.GAL")``` ```pr.listw <- nb2listw(pr.nb, style="W")``` ```pr.listb <- nb2listw(pr.nb, style="B")``` ```if.sar <- errorsarlm(y ~ rain, listw =``` ```pr.listw)``` ```summary(if.sar)``` ```if.res <- residuals(if.sar)``` ```shapiro.test(if.res)```	Read spatial neighbor information. Generate *listw* objects with W and B styles. Run a spatial autoregressive model and summarize the results. Get residuals and conduct Shapiro-Wilk normality test.
```cor(y, rain)``` ```y.sar <- errorsarlm(y ~ 1, listw=pr.listw)``` ```y.sar$lambda``` ```x.sar <- errorsarlm(rain ~ 1, listw=``` ```pr.listw)``` ```x.sar$lambda```	Calculate correlation between the two variables. Estimate SAR spatial autocorrelation parameters for the two variables.
```y.sa <- y - y.sar$lambda *``` ```lag.listw(pr.listw,y)``` ```rain.sa <- rain - x.sar$lambda *``` ```lag.listw(pr.listw,rain)``` ```cor(y.sa, rain.sa)```	Adjust for the latent spatial autocorrelation in the variables. Calculate correlation between the adjusted variables.
```adm <- factor(pr.f$ADM, levels=1:5, labels=``` ```c("San Juan", "Arecibo", "Mayaguez",``` ```"Ponce", "Caguas"))``` ```lm.if.sa <- lm(y.sa ~ adm)``` ```anova(lm.if.sa)```	Create a factor variable. Conduct ANOVA for the spatial autocorrelation adjusted farm densities.
```sw.p <- function(x){``` ``` shapiro.test(x)$p.value}``` ```tapply(resid(lm.if.sa),adm,sw.p)``` ```leveneTest(resid(lm.if.sa), adm,``` ```center=mean)```	Create a function and conduct Shapiro-Wilk test for each administrative region. Conduct Levene's test.
```ci <- pr.f$cl_ih``` ```ci.lm <- lm(ci ~ rain, data=pr.f)``` ```summary(ci.lm)``` ```ci.sar <- errorsarlm(ci ~ rain,``` ```listw=pr.listw)``` ```summary(ci.sar)```	Get a binary variable. Run a linear regression and summarize the result. Run an SAR model and summarize the result.

| ```
#5.2.1
moran.test(ci, pr.listb)
geary.test(ci, pr.listb)
``` | Conduct spatial autocorrelation tests. |
| ```
n <- length(pr.nb)
M <- diag(n) - matrix(1,n,n)/n
B <- listw2mat(pr.listb)
MBM <- M %*% B %*% M
eig <- eigen(MBM,symmetric=T)
``` | Generate eigenvalues and eigenvectors. from a transformed spatial weight matrix (MBM in the R codes). |
| ```
EV <- as.data.frame( eig$vectors[ ,
eig$values/eig$values[1] > 0.25])
colnames(EV) <- paste("EV", 1:NCOL(EV),
sep="")
``` | Construct a candidate set of eigenvectors. Add column names for the eigenvectors. |
| ```
ci.full <- glm(ci ~ rain + ., data=EV,
family=binomial)
ci.sf <- stepAIC(glm(ci ~ rain, data=EV,
family=binomial), scope=list(upper=
ci.full), direction="forward")
``` | Conduct spatial filtering with *stepAIC* function.This selects more eigenvectors than a selection procedure based solely on significance. |
| ```
ci.sf <- glm(ci ~ rain + EV4 + EV2 + EV7 +
EV9 + EV6 + EV14 + EV13 + EV18 + EV12,
                data=EV, family=binomial)
summary(ci.sf)
``` | Get a spatial filter model in the text which is constructed based on significance. Summarize the result. |
| ```
ci.sf.res <- round(residuals(ci.sf,
type="response"))
moran.test(ci.sf.res , pr.listb)
geary.test(ci.sf.res , pr.listb)
``` | Get the residuals of the spatial filter model. Conduct spatial autocorrelation tests. |
| ```
pr <- readShapePoly("PuertoRico.shp")
pal.wr <- c("white","red")
cols.wr <- pal.wr[ci+1]
plot(pr, col=cols.wr)
leg <- c("coastal", "interior")
legend("bottomright", fill=pal.wr,
legend=leg, bty="n")
``` | Read Puerto Rico shapefile. Set a color list with white and red. Find colors for each polygon. Plot the polygons with the colors. Set legend texts. Locate a legend. |
| ```
pal.red <- brewer.pal(5,"Reds")
q5 <- classIntervals(ci.sf$fitted, 5,
style="quantile")
cols.red <-findColours(q5, pal.red)
plot(pr, col=cols.red)
brks <- round(q5$brks,3)
leg <- paste(brks[-6], brks[-1], sep=" - ")
legend("bottomright", fill=pal.red,
legend=leg, bty="n")
``` | Create a color palette with 5 colors. Classify the fitted values into 5 classes with quantile option. Find colors for the polygons. Plot the polygons with the colors. Get break information. Create legend texts. Locate a legend. |
| ```
cols.wr <- pal.wr[round(ci.sf$fitted)+1]
plot(pr, col=cols.wr)
leg <- c("coastal", "interior")
legend("bottomright", fill=pal.wr,
legend=leg,bty="n")
``` | Convert the fitted values into a binary variable, then map them similarly. |
| ```
# The percent of farms utilizing irrigation
fp <- pr.f$irr_farms_02/pr.f$nofarms_02
fp.col <- cbind(pr.f$irr_farms_02,
pr.f$nofarms_02-pr.f$irr_farms_02)
``` | Get irrigated farm densities in 2002. Create a dependent variable for binomial regression: (# of success, # of fail). |
| ```
fp.base <- glm(fp.col ~ rain, family=
quasibinomial)
disp <- summary(fp.base)$dispersion
fp.full <- glm(fp.col ~ rain + ., data=EV,
family=binomial)
``` | Run a binomial regression. Get Pearson-type overdispersion value. Conduct stepwise regression with *stepAIC*. |
```

```fp.sf <- stepAIC(glm(fp.col~rain, data=EV, family=binomial), scale=disp, scope= list(upper=fp.full), direction="forward")```	
```fp.sf <- glm(fp.col ~ rain + EV1 + EV13 + EV4 + EV12 + EV2 + EV15, data=EV, family=quasibinomial)```	Get a spatial filter model in the text estimated based on significance.
```summary(fp.sf)```	Summarize the result.
```moran.test(fp, pr.listb) geary.test(fp, pr.listb)```	Conduct spatial autocorrelation tests.
```summary(fp.base)$deviance/fp.base$df.residual summary(fp.sf)$deviance/fp.sf$df.residual```	Calculate deviance statistics for the base and spatial filter models.
```summary(fp.sf)$dispersion```	Get Pearson-type overdispersion value.
```# Mapping the percentages source("all_functions.R") mapping.seq(pr, fp, 5)```	Load functions in all_functions.R file. Map the farm percentage with 5 classes.
```# Mapping the predicted mapping.seq(pr, fp.sf$fitted, 5)```	Map the predicted values.
```# Mapping the spatial filter sfilter <- as.matrix(EV[,c(1,13,4,12,2,15)]) %*% as.matrix(fp.sf$coefficients[c(-1,-2)])```	Construct the spatial filter.
```moran.test(sfilter, pr.listb) geary.test(sfilter, pr.listb)```	Conduct spatial autocorrelation test for the spatial filter.
```sf.res <- residuals(fp.sf, type="response") moran.test(sf.res, pr.listb) geary.test(sf.res, pr.listb)```	Get residuals of the spatial filter model, and conduct spatial autocorrelation tests.
```mapping.seq(pr, sfilter, 5, main="SF")```	Map the constructed spatial filter.
```#5.2.2.1```	
```farm.den07 <- pr.f$nofarms_07/pr.f$area y.fd <- (farm.den07 - 0.12)^0.38```	Calculate farm densities in 2007 and transform it.
```shapiro.test(y.fd)```	Conduct Shapiro-Wilk test.
```lm.fd <- lm(y.fd ~ rain)```	Run a linear regression.
```lm.fd.s <- summary(lm.fd)```	Store the summaries of the regression.
```s2 <- round(lm.fd.s$sigma^2,5) c1 <- round(0.5 * (-0.25+(1/0.38-2+1.5)^2),5)```	Calculate components for back-transformation.
```pred <- lm.fd$fitted y.fd.e <- pred^(1/0.38) + c1*s2 + 0.12```	Calculate back-transformed predicted values.
```lm.bt <- lm(farm.den07 ~ y.fd.e) summary(lm.bt)```	Run linear regression between observed and predicted values, and summarize the result.
```pois.fd <- glm(nofarms_07 ~ rain_mean, offset=log(area), family=poisson, data=pr.f)```	Run a Poisson regression with offset values.
```pois.fd$deviance/pois.fd$df.residual```	Calculate deviance statistic.
```nb.fd <- glm.nb(nofarms_07 ~ rain_mean + offset(log(area)), data=pr.f)```	Run a negative binomial model.
```nb.fd$deviance/nb.fd$df.residual```	Calculate deviance statistic.
```1/nb.fd$theta```	Get dispersion parameter estimate.
```nb.fit <- nb.fd$fitted/pr.f$area```	Calculate predicted densities.
```nb.back <- lm(farm.den07 ~ nb.fit) summary(nb.back)```	Run linear regression and summarize it.

``` par(mfrow=c(1,2)) plot(y.fd.e, farm.den07, pch=20) abline(0,1, col=2) nb.den <- fitted(nb.fd)/pr.f$area plot(nb.den, farm.den07, pch=20) abline(0,1, col=2) par(mfrow=c(1,1)) ```	Plot observed versus predicted plots from the normal model and negative binomial model.
``` moran.test(farm.den07, pr.listb) geary.test(farm.den07, pr.listb) moran.test(farm.den07-y.fd.e, pr.listb) geary.test(farm.den07-y.fd.e, pr.listb) moran.test(farm.den07- nb.fd$fitted/pr.f$area, pr.listb) geary.test(farm.den07- nb.fd$fitted/pr.f$area, pr.listb) ```	Conduct spatial autocorrelation tests for the three sets of values: the farm densities in 2007, residuals from the normal model, and residuals from the negative binomial model.
``` lm.full <- lm(y.fd ~ rain + ., data=EV) lm.sf <- stepwise.forward(lm.full, lm(y.fd ~ rain, data=EV), 0.1, verbose=F) summary(lm.sf)$r.squared pred.sf <- lm.sf$fitted ```	Conduct stepwise regression with *stepwise.forward*. Summarize the result. Get predicted values.
``` s2.sf <- round(summary(lm.sf)$sigma^2,5) y.e.sf <- pred.sf^(1/0.38) + c1*s2.sf + 0.12 lm.sf.bt <- lm(farm.den07 ~ y.e.sf) summary(lm.sf.bt) ```	Conduct back-transformation. Examine its model fit.
``` plot(y.e.sf, farm.den07, pch=20) abline(lm.sf.bt) ```	Plot a scatterplot with observed and predicted values.
``` lm.sf.res <- farm.den07 - y.e.sf moran(lm.sf.res, pr.listb, n, Szero(pr.listb)) geary(lm.sf.res, pr.listb, n, n-1, Szero(pr.listb)) ```	Get residuals of the normal model. Calculate Moran's I. Calculate Geary's C.
``` X <- as.matrix(cbind(rep(1,n), lm.sf$model[,-1])) num <- -n*sum(diag(solve(crossprod(X), crossprod(X,B)%*%X))) den <- lm.sf$df.residual * sum(B) num/den ```	Get independent variables to calculate the expected value of Moran's I: numerator denominator the expected value of Moran's I.
``` nb.full <- glm.nb(pr.f$nofarms_07 ~ rain + offset(log(pr.f$area)) + ., data=EV) nb.sf <- stepAIC(glm.nb(pr.f$nofarms_07 ~ rain + offset(log(pr.f$area)), data=EV), scope=list(upper=nb.full), direction="forward") ```	Run stepwise negative binomial regression with *stepAIC*.
``` nb.sf <- glm.nb(pr.f$nofarms_07 ~ rain + EV12 + EV4 + EV1 + EV2 + EV18 + offset(log(pr.f$area)), data=EV) summary(nb.sf) ```	Get a spatial filter model in the text estimated based on significance. Summarize the result.
``` glm.sf.bt <- lm(farm.den07 ~ I(nb.sf$fitted/pr.f$area)) summary(glm.sf.bt) ```	Examine the model fit of the negative binomial model.
``` plot(nb.sf$fitted/pr.f$area, farm.den07, pch=20) abline(glm.sf.bt) ```	Create a scatterplot of observed versus predicted values.

Code	Comment

`glm.sf.res <- farm.den07 - nb.sf$fitted/pr.f$area`
`moran(glm.sf.res, pr.listb, n, Szero(pr.listb))`
`geary(glm.sf.res, pr.listb, n, n-1, Szero(pr.listb))`
	Get the residuals of the negative binomial model.
	Calculate Moran's *I*.
	
	Calculate Geary's *C*.

`X <- as.matrix(cbind(rep(1,n), nb.sf$model[,c(-1,-8)]))`
`num <- -n*sum(diag(solve(crossprod(X), crossprod(X,B)%*%X)))`
`den <- nb.sf$df.residual * sum(B)`
`num/den`
	Get independent variables to calculate the expected value of Moran's *I*.
	numerator
	
	denominator
	the expected value of Moran's *I*.

`ur <- factor(pr.f$u_r, levels=0:1, labels=c("urban", "rural"))`
`tapply(y.fd, ur, sw.p)`
`leveneTest(y.fd, ur, center=mean)`
`anova(lm(y.fd ~ ur))`
	Create a factor variable for urban & rural.
	Conduct normality tests.
	Conduct Levene's test.
	Conduct ANOVA.

`ur.d <- ifelse(pr.f$u_r==0,-1,1)`
`lm.full <- lm(y.fd ~ rain+ur.d+., data=EV)`
`lm.ur <- stepwise.forward(lm.full, lm(y.fd ~ rain + ur.d, data=EV), 0.1, verbose=F)`
`lm.ur.res <- residuals(lm.ur)`
`tapply(lm.ur.res, ur, sw.p)`
`leveneTest(lm.ur.res, ur, center=mean)`
`summary(lm.ur)$coefficients[3,]`
	Create a dummy variable with -1 & 1.
	Run stepwise regression for a spatial filter model.
	
	Get residuals of the spatial filter model, and then conduct normality and Levene's tests.
	Get statistics for ur.d variable (mean difference test).

`nb.ur <- update(nb.sf, . ~ . + EV10 + EV15 + ur.d)`
`summary(nb.ur)$coefficients[10,]`
`nb.ur$deviance/nb.ur$df.residual`
	Get a spatial filter model in the text estimated based on significance.
	Get statistics of ur.d variable.
	Get deviance statistic.

`#5.2.2.2`	
`pr.j2w <- read.csv("PR_journey-to-work_2000.csv")` `n <- sqrt(NROW(pr.j2w))`	Load journey-to-work data. The number of regions (i.e., municipalities).

`# model1`
`f.os <- function(x,flow.df,n){`
`sum(flow.df[flow.df[,"ResID"]==x,"Count"])}`
`Oi.sum <- sapply(1:n, f.os, flow.df=pr.j2w, n=n)`
`Oi.sum <- rep(Oi.sum, each=n)`
 	
`f.ds <- function(x,flow.df,n){`
`sum(flow.df[flow.df[,"WorkID"]==x,"Count"])`
`}`
`Dj.sum <- sapply(1:n, f.ds, flow.df=pr.j2w, n=n)`
`Dj.sum <- rep(Dj.sum, n)`
`lnOiDj <- log(Oi.sum) + log(Dj.sum)`
	Define a function to calculate sums of flows from each origin.
	Get sums of flows from each origin.
	
	Match the sums to the origin/destination (OD) list.
	Define a function to calculate sums of flows from each origin.
	
	Get sums of flows from each destination.
	Match the sums to the OD list.
	Prepare an offset variable.

`si.nc <- glm(Count ~ dist, offset=lnOiDj, data=pr.j2w, family=poisson)`
`exp(si.nc$coefficients[1])`
`si.nc$coefficients[2]`
`si.nc$deviance/si.nc$df.res`
`lm.nc <- lm(pr.j2w$Count~si.nc$fitted)`
	Run Poisson regression with only distance variable.
	Constant estimate.
	Distance-decay estimate.
	Deviance type overdispersion estimate.
	Examine the model fit.

```
summary(lm.nc)

# model2
b.id <- 63                                Set a base level for dummy variables.
fid.f <- as.factor(pr.j2w$ResID)          Get a factor variable for origins.
contr.f <- contr.treatment(levels(fid.f), Create dummy variables for origins with
base=b.id)                                b.id region as base.
xo <- contr.f[fid.f,]                     Match the dummy variable to the OD list.
colnames(xo) <- paste("R", levels(fid.f)[- Set column names for the dummy
b.id], sep="")                            variables.
rownames(xo) <- 1:(n^2)                   Set row names.

tid.f <- as.factor(pr.j2w$WorkID)         Similarly create dummy variables for
contr.t <- contr.treatment(levels(tid.f), destinations.
base=b.id)
xd <- contr.t[tid.f,]
colnames(xd) <- paste("W", levels(tid.f)[-
b.id], sep="")
rownames(xd) <- 1:(n^2)

si.dc <- glm(Count ~ dist + xo + xd,      Run a Poisson regression with the dummy
offset=lnOiDj, data=pr.j2w, family=poisson) variables and distance.
exp(si.dc$coefficients[1])                Constant estimate.
si.dc$coefficients[2]                      Distance-decay estimate.
si.dc$deviance/si.dc$df.res                Deviance type overdispersion estimate.
lm.dc <- lm(pr.j2w$Count~si.dc$fitted)    Examine the model fit.
summary(lm.dc)                            Summarize the result.


# model3
attach(pr.j2w)                            Add pr.j2w to a search space.
# eigenvector treatment for flows
evec <- read.table("pr_evecs.txt",        Read eigenvectors from the transformed
header=T)                                 spatial weight matrix.
evec <- evec[,c(-1,-2)]                   Drop two ID columns.
EV <- evec[,1:11]                         Select the first 11 eigenvectors.
EVo <- apply(EV,2, function(x,n)          Match the 11 eigenvectors to the
{rep(x,each=n)}, n=n)                     origins in the OD list.
EVd <- apply(EV,2, function(x,n)          Match the 11 eigenvectors to the
{rep(x,n)}, n=n)                          destinations in the OD list.
EVod <- kronecker(EVo, matrix(1,1,11)) *  Generate 121 eigenvectors by
kronecker(matrix(1,1,11),EVd) * 100       multiplying the matched eigenvectors
                                          for origins and destinations.
colnames(EVod) <- paste("EV",1:121,sep="") Set column names.
EVod.df <- as.data.frame(EVod)            Convert a matrix to a data frame.

#disp <- si.dc$deviance/si.dc$df.res      Conduct stepwise regression to
#si.full <- glm(Count ~ dist + xo + xd + ., construct a spatial filter model. Note
data=EVod, family=poisson)                that this stepAIC function will take a
#si.sf <- stepAIC(glm(Count ~ dist + xo + while. Also note that the selected
xd, data=EVod, family=poisson), scale=disp, eigenvectors with significance in the
scope=list(upper=si.full),                text are stored in pr_flow_sel_evec.txt
direction="forward", trace=0)             file.

evs <- scan("pr_flow_sel_evecs.txt")      Read selected eigenvector information.
EVod.sel <- EVod[,evs]                     Get only the selected eigenvectors.

si.sf <- glm(Count ~ dist + xo + xd +      Run a Poisson with distance, dummy
EVod.sel, offset=lnOiDj, family=poisson)   variables, and the selected
                                           eigenvectors.
exp(si.sf$coefficients[1])                 Constant estimate.
si.sf$coefficients[2]                      Distance-decay estimate.
si.sf$deviance/si.sf$df.res                Deviance type overdispersion estimate.
```

`lm.sf <- lm(Count~si.sf$fitted)` `summary(lm.sf)`	Examine the model fit. Summarize the result.

`plot(si.nc$fitted, Count, pch=4)`
`points(Count, Count)`
`plot(si.dc$fitted, Count, pch=4)`
`points(Count, Count)`
`plot(si.sf$fitted, Count, pch=4)`
`points(Count, Count)`
	Scatterplots of observed versus
	predicted values for the three models.

`detach(pr.j2w)`	Remove pr.j2w from the search space.
`ai.v <-substr(names(si.sf$coef),1,3)=="xoR"` `ai <- si.sf$coef[ai.v]`	Find origin dummy variables. Get estimated coefficients of origin dummy variables.
`bj.v <-substr(names(si.sf$coef),1,3)=="xdW"` `bj <- si.sf$coef[bj.v]`	Find destination dummy variables. Get estimated coefficients for destination dummy variables.

`insert <- function(v,e,pos){`
`  return(c(v[1:(pos-1)], e,`
`  v[(pos):length(v)]))}`
`ai <- insert(ai, 0, b.id)`
`bj <- insert(bj, 0, b.id)`
	Create a function to insert zero for
	base regions of the dummy variables.
	
	Put zero for the origin base region.
	Put zero for the destination base
	region.

`ev.v <- substr(names(si.sf$ coef),1,8) ==`
`"EVod.sel"`
`ev.beta <- si.sf$coef[ev.v]`
`sf.if <- EVod.sel %*% ev.beta`
`sf.df <- pr.j2w[,c("ResID", "WorkID")]`
`sf.df$sfij <- sf.if`
	Get estimated coefficients for
	eigenvectors.
	
	Calculate a spatial filter.
	Combine the filter values with origin
	and destination IDs.

`f.oi <- function(x,flow.df) { median(`
`flow.df[flow.df[,"ResID"]==x,"sfij"])}`
`sf.oi <- sapply(1:n, f.oi, flow.df=sf.df)`
	Define a function to get medians of the
	spatial filter vales for each origin.
	Get medians for origins.

`f.dj <- function(x,flow.df) {median(`
`flow.df[flow.df[,"WorkID"]==x,"sfij"])}`
`sf.dj <- sapply(1:n, f.dj, flow.df=sf.df)`
	Similarly, get medians for
	destinations.

`mapping.seq(pr,ai,7,main="Org Balancing")`
`mapping.seq(pr,bj,7,main="Dest Balancing")`
`mapping.seq(pr,sf.oi,7,main="Org SF")`
	Map the balancing factors and spatial
	filters.

6

Local Statistics: Hot and Cold Spots

LEARNING OBJECTIVES:

- To quantify small-scale spatial clustering
- To relate local to global measures of spatial autocorrelation
- To specify bivariate relationships that vary across space

A global spatial relationship is an average of n local spatial relationships, specific locations on a map that have clusters of similar or dissimilar neighboring values for a given attribute (see Lloyd, 2007). For example, the Moran coefficient (MC) spatial autocorrelation statistic is the average of n local MC terms, one for each location, each involving $\sum_{j=1}^{n} c_{ij}$ values to determine a local spatial relationship. Inspection of these n values, which permit the construction of a geographic distribution map, allows an assessment of variability in spatial dependency across a geographic landscape: the focus of an analysis is on identifying and understanding differences rather than similarities across space (Fotheringham, 1997). One general concern is for homogeneity in the terms used to calculate a global statistic. Another general concern is the presence of spatial clusters, or local regions of strong spatial autocorrelation (usually positive in nature). This assessment also can reveal a mixture of positive and negative spatial autocorrelation, resulting in a global statistic implying no spatial autocorrelation. And a third concern is the simultaneous testing of n statistics, the multiple testing problem, which seeks to minimize false discoveries of statistically significant results.

6.1. Multiple testing with positively correlated data

Treating n local statistics simultaneously introduces the complication of multiple testing. The simplest way to address this complication is to employ a Bonferroni (or similar) adjustment. In other words, the decided–upon overall alpha level ($\alpha\star$) statistical significance is divided by n (e.g., $\alpha\star = 0.05$ becomes $\alpha = 0.05/n$). This adjustment becomes increasingly poor as the level of positive spatial autocorrelation increases. It is most suitable for the unlikely case of zero spatial autocorrelation. Figure 6.1a illustrates this type of situation over the full range of positive correlation, but for selected non–spatial cases of 2 and 10 items to be compared, equal correlation among all items, and a 5% level of significance. These trajectories may be approximated, for $P > 1$ items to be compared and a constant correlation among them of ρ_e (i.e., equicorrelation), by the equation[1] $\alpha = 1 - (1 - \alpha\star)^{1/P^a}$, where

$$a = 1 - \cfrac{\cfrac{\ln[1 + \ln(2\varphi_0 + 2\varphi_1 e^{-\varphi_2 n})]}{\ln[1 - \ln(2\varphi_0 + 2\varphi_1 e^{-\varphi_2 n})]} - (1 + \rho_e)^{\varphi_0 + \varphi_1 e^{-\varphi_2 n}} \cfrac{\ln[1 + \ln(2\varphi_0 + 2\varphi_1 e^{-\varphi_2 n} + \rho_e^{\varphi_0 + \varphi_1 e^{-\varphi_2 n}})]}{\ln[1 - \ln(2\varphi_0 + 2\varphi_1 e^{-\varphi_2 n} + \rho_e^{\varphi_0 + \varphi_1 e^{-\varphi_2 n}})]}}{\cfrac{\ln[1 + \ln(2\varphi_0 + 2\varphi_1 e^{-\varphi_2 n})]}{\ln[1 - \ln(2\varphi_0 + 2\varphi_1 e^{-\varphi_2 n})]} - 2^{\varphi_0 + \varphi_1 e^{-\varphi_2 n}} \cfrac{\ln[1 + \ln(2\varphi_0 + 2\varphi_1 e^{-\varphi_2 n} + 1)]}{\ln[1 - \ln(2\varphi_0 + 2\varphi_1 e^{-\varphi_2 n} + 1)]}},$$

with the following coefficient estimates:[2]

Landscape wide	$\alpha\star$	$\hat{\varphi}_0$	$\hat{\varphi}_1$	$\hat{\varphi}_2$
	0.050	0.8578	0.0016	−0.1679
	0.025	0.8583	0.0010	−0.0946

This equation yields the exact independent result (which the Bonferroni adjustment approximates) for $\rho_e = 0$, and $\alpha\star = 0.025$ or 0.05 for the perfectly correlated result for which $\rho_e = 1$. Figure 6.1a displays 0.05 minus the value rendered by this equation, for the cases of $P = 2$ and $P = 10$.

---

[1] See http://bit.ly/KczvAl for the database.

[2] These coefficient estimates were obtained with nonlinear least squares. The respective relative error sums of squares are 1.4×10^{-4} and 6.0×10^{-4}.

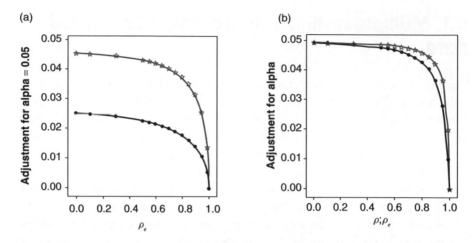

Figure 6.1   The amount of correction to $\alpha = 0.05$. (a) for $P = 10$ (gray plot) and $P = 2$ (black plot), equicorrelation aspatial data. (b) for $P = 73$ for spatial (black plot) and aspatial (gray plot) data.

For spatial data, de Castro and Singer (2006) allude to an approach that exploits the effective sample size (see Section 3.5). For the Puerto Rico data, this sample size is given by the expression

$$P = 73 \times \left[1 - \frac{1}{1 - e^{-1.92349}} \frac{73 - 1}{73} \left(1 - e^{-2.12373 \times \rho + 0.20024 \sqrt{\rho}} \right) \right].$$

Figure 6.1b shows 0.05 minus the value rendered by this equation, for the case of $P = 73$, comparing the aspatial and spatial equations. One reason why these two plots differ, although these differences are not too marked, is that the spatial case is not an equicorrelation one (i.e., correlation between two locations decreases with increasing distance separating them).

6.2. Local indices of spatial association

Local indices of spatial association (LISA) relate to the Moran scatterplot (Anselin, 1995). The MC defined by equation (2.6) can be more explicitly re-written as:

$$MC = \frac{n}{\sum\limits_{i=1}^{n}\sum\limits_{j=1}^{n}c_{ij}} \frac{\sum\limits_{i=1}^{n}\sum\limits_{i=1}^{n}c_{ij}(y_i - \overline{y})(y_j - \overline{y})}{\sum\limits_{i=1}^{n}(y_i - \overline{y})^2} = \frac{1}{\sum\limits_{i=1}^{n}\sum\limits_{j=1}^{n}c_{ij}} \frac{\sum\limits_{i=1}^{n}(y_i - \overline{y})\sum\limits_{j=1}^{n}c_{ij}(y_j - \overline{y})}{\sqrt{\sum\limits_{i=1}^{n}(y_i - \overline{y})^2 / n}\sqrt{\sum\limits_{i=1}^{n}(y_i - \overline{y})^2 / n}}$$

$$= \frac{1}{\sum\limits_{i=1}^{n}\sum\limits_{j=1}^{n}c_{ij}}\sum\limits_{i=1}^{n}z_i\sum\limits_{j=1}^{n}c_{ij}\,z_j\;.$$

This is the version employed in Section 2.2 to construct Moran scatterplots, using the biased sample variance estimate (i.e., division by n rather than $n-1$).

Each MC_i LISA is a component of this preceding version of the MC:

$$MC_i = z_i \sum\limits_{j=1}^{n} c_{ij}z_j. \tag{6.1}$$

Moreover, it is the product of the corresponding horizontal and vertical axis values in a Moran scatterplot. These calculations allow identification of the following type of clusters: a high value surrounded by high values (HH, the first quadrant of a Moran scatterplot); a low value surrounded by low values (LL, the third quadrant of a Moran scatterplot); a low value surrounded by high values (LH, the second quadrant of a Moran scatterplot); and a high value surrounded by low values (HL, the fourth quadrant of a Moran scatterplot). One weakness of this statistic is that it identifies geographic cluster outliers without indicating whether they comprise high values or low values. MC is the average of the MC_i, which is calculated as follows:

$$\frac{\sum\limits_{i=1}^{n}MC_i}{\sum\limits_{i=1}^{n}\sum\limits_{j=1}^{n}c_{ij}}$$

For a binary 0–1 geographic weighting scheme, the denominator is the number of non-zero entries in the sum appearing in the numerator. This average is the standardized (i.e., divided by $\sum_{i=1}^{n}\sum_{j=1}^{n}c_{ij}$) slope of the linear regression trend line for a Moran scatterplot.

The expected value of MC_i is $-\left(\sum_{j=1}^{n}c_{ij}\right)/(n-1)$, paralleling the expected value of MC of $-1/(n-1)$. The average of the expected values of the separate n MC_i values contained in an MC value equals the expected value of MC. Meanwhile, because the number of neighbors for a given location i is almost always relatively small, the corresponding adjusted version of equation (2.4) does not furnish a good approximation for the variance of MC_i. Rather, because of the small sample size involved, randomization (i.e., a permutation test) frequently is used to calculate it. Accordingly, for a binary 0–1 geographic weighting scheme,

$$\text{Var}(\text{MC}_i) = \frac{n - \sum_{i=1}^{n} z_i^4 \big/ \left(\sum_{i=1}^{n} z_i^2\right)^2}{n-1} \sum_{j=1}^{n} c_{ij} + \frac{2\left[2\sum_{i=1}^{n} z_i^4 \big/ \left(\sum_{i=1}^{n} z_i^2\right)^2 - n\right]}{(n-1)(n-2)}$$

$$\left(\sum_{j=1}^{n} c_{ij}\right)\left(\sum_{j=1}^{n} c_{ij} - 1\right) - \left[\frac{\sum_{j=1}^{n} c_{ij}}{n-1}\right]^2. \tag{6.2}$$

For a normally distributed attribute variable, the quantity $\sum_{i=1}^{n} z_i^4 \big/ \left(\sum_{i=1}^{n} z_i^2\right)^2$ is close to 3. The calculation $[\text{MC}_i - \text{E}(\text{MC}_i)]/\sqrt{\text{Var}(\text{MC}_i)}$ furnishes a test statistic here that can be referenced to a t-distribution (because of small sample size) for statistical inference purposes.

Figure 6.2a furnishes an example of a LISA map for the 2002 density of farmland across Puerto Rico, based upon contiguity, using a threshold normal z-score value of 1.96 for a two-tailed 5%, and 1.65 for a two-tailed 10%, level of significance. This map was generated in the ESRI™ ArcMap software, using the single-item critical values to identify statistically significant densities (it erroneously classifies two municipalities as outliers). Using the SAR model specification (see

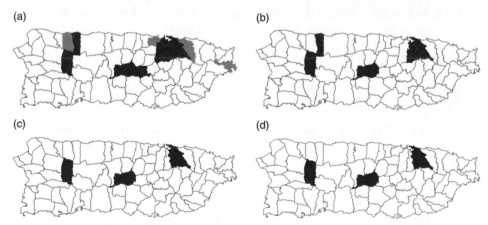

Figure 6.2 Extreme LISA values for the 2002 density of farmland across Puerto Rico. Gray together with black denotes two-tailed 10% level, and black denotes two-tailed 5% level of significance results. (a) Results ignoring multiple testing. (b) Results accounting for correlated multiple testing using z-scores. (c) Results accounting for correlated multiple testing using t-statistics. (d) Results based upon a Bonferroni adjustment.

Section 5.1), the spatial autocorrelation parameter estimate for this geographic distribution is $\hat{\rho} = 0.5055$. This level of spatial autocorrelation implies an effective sample size of 21.9, and hence a two–tail probability of roughly 0.0023 for a 10% island-wide, and 0.0012 for a 5% island-wide, overall level of significance. Accordingly, the respective adjusted threshold normal z-score values are 2.8284 and 3.0471; the corresponding threshold t-statistics (with 19.9 degrees of freedom) are 3.1845 and 3.4920. Figure 6.2b portrays the correct set of municipalities identified in Figure 6.2a using the adjusted z-scores; Figure 6.2c uses the adjusted t-statistics. In this example, three of the outlier clusterings remain the same, but two of their geographic extents shrink with the simultaneous testing adjustments. A Bonferroni adjustment produces z-scores of 3.2009 (island-wide 10% level of significance) and 3.3955 (island-wide 5% level of significance), which incorrectly eliminate two outliers based on the z-score criterion (Figure 6.2d).

6.3. Getis–Ord statistics

The Getis–Ord G_i and $G_i^\star$ statistics (Getis and Ord, 1992; Ord and Getis, 1995) relate more to a semi-variogram than to a Moran scatterplot. The difference between these two statistics is that G_i excludes observation i in its calculation, whereas $G_i^\star$ does not. For a selected distance range d (a threshold within which all locations are neighbors, and beyond which all locations are not neighbors),

$$
G_i^\star = \frac{\sum\limits_{j=1}^{n} w_{ij}(d)x_j - \overline{x}\sum\limits_{j=1}^{n} w_{ij}(d)}{s_x \sqrt{\dfrac{(n-1)\sum\limits_{j=1}^{n} w_{ij}^2(d) - \left[\sum\limits_{j=1}^{n} w_{ij}(d)\right]^2}{n-2}}},
$$

where s_x denotes the standard deviation of variable X, and w_{ij} is the geographic weight (see Chapter 1) linking locations i and j. Positive values of $G_i^\star$ indicate the presence of a spatial cluster of high values; negative values of $G_i^\star$ indicate the presence of a spatial cluster of low values. One weakness of this statistic is that variable X must be non–negative.

Figure 6.3 furnishes an example of a Getis–Ord-based LISA map for the 2002 density of farmland across Puerto Rico generated with ESRI ArcMap. Multiple comparison adjustments need to be employed in order to determine whether or not the identified clusters are statistically significant. Based upon z-scores (± 2.8284 and ± 3.0471), part of suburban San Juan constitutes a geographic cluster of low values (island-wide 10% level of significance),

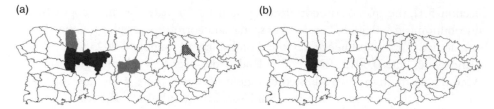

Figure 6.3   Extreme Getis–Ord statistic values for the 2002 density of farmland
across Puerto Rico. Gray denotes 5% upper-tail outliers, black denotes
2.5% upper-tail outliers, and cross-hatch denotes 5% lower-tail outliers.
(a) Values based upon z-score. (b) Values based upon t-statistics.

which is sensible. This cluster disappears with the use of t-statistics ($\pm$
2.9618 and $\pm$ 3.2815). This local indicator of spatial autocorrelation statistic fails
to identify the same clusters uncovered with LISA (Figure 6.2) (although similarities exist), and identifies two other outliers not appearing in Figure 6.2.

6.4. Spatially varying coefficients

Local statistics seek to address one feature of the more general theme of
geographically varying relationships. A geographically varying mean is the focus
in specifications such as the standard spatial autoregressive and spatial filtering models. This type of specification can be extended to regression coefficients, too. One technique producing such geographically varying coefficients
requires the construction of interaction variables with a set of candidate spatial
filter eigenvectors and geographic variables (Griffith, 2008). Then geographically varying coefficients may be determined by employing a stepwise regression selection technique, followed by factoring each X variable from the set of
interaction terms containing it. The sum of the resulting set of eigenvectors
for each X furnishes geographically varying coefficients.

   Consider the relationship between 2002 density of farmland and whether
or not a municipality is predominantly urban (an indicator variable, where
1 denotes urban and -1 denotes non-urban; this is a contrast definition). A
spatial filter specification captures spatial autocorrelation and geographically
varying coefficients, yielding the following two vectors for this case study
(after converting the densities to z-scores):

   intercept: $0.00521 + 3.0909\mathbf{E}_1 - 1.4900\mathbf{E}_3 - 1.2975\mathbf{E}_9 + 3.0649\mathbf{E}_{10} +$
   $1.4365\mathbf{E}_{12}$, and

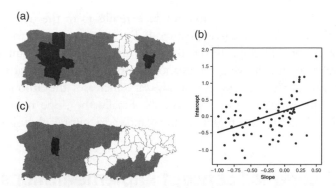

Figure 6.4   Spatial varying coefficients. (a) Spatial filter intercept. (b) Scatterplot for the two spatially varying coefficients. (c) Spatial filter slope.

slope: $-0.25791 + 2.3006\mathbf{E}_1 + 2.4197\mathbf{E}_8$.

The intercept ranges from -1.24 to 1.82 (Figure 6.4a), indicating that some municipalities have less than, while others have more than, average density of farmland. The slope ranges from -0.98 to 0.49 (Figure 6.4b), indicating a relationship between urban predominance and density of farmland that is negative in some places, non-existent in other places, and positive in yet other places. These two spatially varying coefficients share a common eigenvector, $\mathbf{E}_1$, which results in a correlation of 0.427 (Figure 6.4b) between them. Interestingly, the primary contrast is between the San Juan urban area and the rural interior highlands.

The bivariate regression equation for this example may be written as

$$z_y = a + bU,$$

where z_y denotes the z-score version of 2002 density of farmland, a denotes the spatially varying intercept term, b denotes the spatially varying slope term, and U denotes the $-1/1$ urban–rural indicator variable. Construction of these spatially varying coefficients involved a linear regression analysis employing covariates $E_1, E_3, E_9, E_{10}, E_{12}, U, E_1 \times U$, and $E_8 \times U$. A stepwise linear regression procedure selected these spatial filter components from the full set of 18 eigenvectors together with 18 eigenvector–U interaction terms. Summary statistics from the final regression analysis include:

Covariate	R^2	$P(S–W)$
None	0	0.1628
U	0.1930	0.0005
U, a	0.4051	0.0022
a, b (which includes U)	0.5350	0.0022

The production of non–normal residuals results from the use of an indicator variable; this is an ANOVA (see Chapter 4). Because no eigenvectors are common to the intercept and slope terms, they are uncorrelated. Accounting for spatial autocorrelation and allowing the relationship between the indicator variable and the response variable to geographically vary increases the amount of variance accounted for roughly from 19% to 54%. Finally, the slope map also produces geographic clustering that highlights the island's agricultural administrative regions.

6.5. R code for concept implementations

Computer Code 6.1 demonstrates how to conduct a data analysis in R with local spatial statistics. First, this computer code shows how to calculate the MC_i and G_i^* statistics. The corresponding statistical inferences for the LISAs are determined with different threshold values, adjusting for multiple testing. Second, a geographically varying coefficient model with an eigenvector spatial filter specification is presented. An extended set of candidate eigenvectors is prepared by combining eigenvectors loaded from a text file (consult Computer Code 4.1 to see how to obtain eigenvectors) with an independent variable and the interaction terms for these eigenvectors and this variable. Then, a spatial filter is constructed with stepwise regression using the AIC to select vectors. Results appearing in

Computer Code 6.1. Implementing local spatial autocorrelation statistics, as well as their statistical significance, and spatially varying coefficient estimation.

```
library(spdep)                              Load spdep package.
library(classInt)                           Load classInt package.

pr <- readShapePoly("PuertoRico.shp",       Read Puerto Rico shapefile with its
    proj4string=CRS("+proj=longlat          projection information.
    +ellps=WGS84"))

pr.f <- read.csv(file="PR-farm-data.csv")   Read farm data file.
pr.nb <- read.gal("PuertoRico.GAL")         Create a neighbors list from a GAL file.
pr.listw <- nb2listw(pr.nb, style="W")      Create row standardized spatial weights.
pr.listb <- nb2listw(pr.nb, style="B")      Create binary spatial weights.

# 6.2
f.den02 <- pr.f$cuerdas_02/pr.f$area        Calculate farmland density in 2002.
f.d.sar <- errorsarlm(f.den02 ~ 1,          Run an SAR model.
    listw=pr.listw)
f.d.sar$lambda                              Evaluate the estimated rho value.

z <- c(1.65, 1.96)                          Set threshold values for z-scores:
zc <- c(2.8284, 3.0471)                     for adjusted z-scores;
fc <- c(3.1845, 3.4920)                     for adjusted t-statistics
bf <- c(3.2009, 3.3955)                     for Bonferroni-type z-scores.

f.Ii <- localmoran(f.den02, pr.listb)       Calculate local Moran's I values.
zIi <- f.Ii[,"Z.Ii"]                        Get z-scores of Moran's I values.
mx <- max(zIi)                              Find a maximum value.
mn <- min(zIi)                              Find a minimum value.
```

```
# Mapping significance for z-scores          Set a palette with three colors.
pal <- c("white", "red1", "red4")            Set class intervals with z-score
z3.Ii <- classIntervals(zIi, n=3,            thresholds, minimum, and maximum values.
  style="fixed", fixedBreaks=c(mn, z, mx))    Find a color for each polygon.
cols.Ii <- findColours(z3.Ii, pal)           Plot a significance map for z-scores.
plot(pr, col=cols.Ii)                        Find breaks of the class intervals.
brks <- round(z3.Ii$brks,4)                  Format legend texts.
leg <- paste(brks[-4], brks[-1], sep=" - ")  Plot a legend at bottom-right corner of
legend("bottomright", fill=pal, legend=leg,  the map without a border line.
  bty="n")

# Mapping significance for adjusted z-
scores                                       Set class intervals with adjusted z-
zc3.Ii <- classIntervals(zIi, n=3,           scores.
  style="fixed", fixedBreaks=c(mn, zc, mx))  Find a color for each polygon.
cols.Ii <- findColours(zc3.Ii, pal)          Plot an adjusted significance map.
plot(pr, col=cols.Ii)                        Find breaks for legend texts.
brks <- round(zc3.Ii$brks,4)                 Format legend texts.
leg <- paste(brks[-4], brks[-1], sep=" - ")  Plot a legend.
legend("bottomright", fill=pal, legend=leg,
bty="n")

# Mapping significance for adjusted t
statistics                                   Set class intervals with adjusted t-
fc3.Ii <- classIntervals(zIi, n=3,           statistics.
  style="fixed", fixedBreaks=c(mn, fc, mx))  Find a color for each polygon.
cols.Ii <- findColours(fc3.Ii, pal)          Plot an adjusted significance map.
plot(pr, col=cols.Ii)                        Find breaks for legend texts.
brks <- round(fc3.Ii$brks,4)                 Format legend texts.
leg <- paste(brks[-4], brks[-1], sep=" - ")  Plot a legend.
legend("bottomright", fill=pal, legend=leg,
  bty="n")

# Mapping significance for Bonferroni
adjustment                                   Set class intervals for Bonferroni
bf3.Ii <- classIntervals(zIi, n=3,           adjustment.
  style="fixed", fixedBreaks=c(mn, bf, mx))  Find a color for each polygon.
cols.Ii <- findColours(bf3.Ii, pal)          Plot an adjusted significance map.
plot(pr, col=cols.Ii)                        Find breaks for legend texts.
brks <- round(bf3.Ii$brks,4)                 Format legend texts.
leg <- paste(brks[-4], brks[-1], sep=" - ")  Plot a legend.
legend("bottomright", fill=pal, legend=leg,
  bty="n")

#6.3
pr.nb.s <- include.self(pr.nb)               Update a neighbors list to include
                                             itself as a spatial neighbor.
pr.listb.s <- nb2listw(pr.nb.s,style="B")    Create binary type spatial weights.
f.Gi <- localG(f.den02, pr.listb.s)          Calculate local G* values.

pal.rb <- c("blue","white","red","red4")     Set four colors for mapping.
z4.Gi <- classIntervals(f.Gi, n=4,           Set class intervals with adjusted z-
  style="fixed", fixedBreaks=c(min(f.Gi),    score threshold values.
  -zc[1], zc[1], zc[2], max(f.Gi)))
cols.Gi <- findColours(z4.Gi, pal.rb)        Find a color for each polygon.
plot(pr, col=cols.Gi)                        Plot an adjusted significance map.
brks <- round(z4.Gi$brks,4)                  Find breaks for legend texts.
leg <- paste(brks[-5], brks[-1], sep=" - ")  Format legend texts.
legend("bottomright", fill= pal.rb,          Plot a legend.
  legend=leg, bty="n")

t3.Gi <- classIntervals(f.Gi, n=3,           Set class intervals with adjusted t-
  style="fixed", fixedBreaks=c(min(f.Gi),    statistic threshold values.
  fc[1], fc[2], max(f.Gi)))
cols.Gi <- findColours(t3.Gi, pal)           Find a color for each polygon.
plot(pr, col=cols.Gi)                        Plot an adjusted significance map.
brks <- round(t3.Gi$brks,4)                  Find breaks for legend texts.
leg <- paste(brks[-4], brks[-1], sep=" - ")  Format legend texts.
```

``` brks <- round(z4.Gi$brks,4) leg <- paste(brks[-5], brks[-1], sep=" - ") legend("bottomright", fill= pal.rb, legend=leg, bty="n") ```	Find breaks for legend texts. Format legend texts. Plot a legend.

``
t3.Gi <- classIntervals(f.Gi, n=3,
  style="fixed", fixedBreaks=c(min(f.Gi),
  fc[1], fc[2], max(f.Gi)))
cols.Gi <- findColours(t3.Gi, pal)
plot(pr, col=cols.Gi)
brks <- round(t3.Gi$brks,4)
leg <- paste(brks[-4], brks[-1], sep=" - ")
legend("bottomright", fill=pal,
  legend=leg, bty="n")
``
	Set class intervals with adjusted t-statistic threshold values.
	
	Find a color for each polygon.
	Plot an adjusted significance map.
	Find breaks for legend texts.
	Format legend texts.
	Plot a legend.

``` #6.4 z.f <- scale(f.den02) ur.c <- ifelse(pr.f$u_r==1,1,-1) ```	Calculate z-score of farmland density. Recode urban/rural variable with 1 & -1.
``` evec <- read.table("pr_evecs.txt",header=T) EV <- evec[,-(1:2)] sEV <- cbind(EV, ur.c * EV) ```	Read eigenvectors from a text file. Remove two ID columns. Prepare eigenvectors and interactions of eigenvectors and independent variable.
``` colnames(sEV) <- c(colnames(EV), paste("xEV", 1:NCOL(EV), sep="")) ```	Then set column names.

``
sv.full <- lm(z.f ~ ur.c + ., data=sEV)
sv.sf <- stepAIC(lm(z.f ~ ur.c, data=sEV),
        scope=list(upper=sv.full),
        direction="forward")
summary(sv.sf)
``
	Set a full model for forward method.
	Run a stepwise regression with AIC value as a selection criterion.
	
	Summarize the results.

``
# The selected model in the text 	
sv.sf <- lm(z.f ~ ur.c + EV10 + xEV8 + EV1
+ xEV1 + EV3 + EV12 + EV9, data=sEV)
summary(sv.sf)
``
	Run the regression with the selected eigenvectors in the text.
	Summarize the results.

``` attach(EV) sv.int <- 0.0052 + 3.0909*EV1 - 1.4900*EV3 - 1.2975*EV9 + 3.0649*EV10 + 1.4365*EV12 sv.slp <- -0.2579 + 2.3006*EV1 + 2.4197*EV8 ```	Attach the EV object (i.e. the eigen vector input file without the first two colouns) in the search space. Calculate spatially varying intercept. Calculate spatially varying slope.
``` detach(EV) ```	Remove EV in the search space.
``` summary(sv.int) summary(sv.slp) ```	Summary of spatially varying intercept. Summary of spatially varying slope.

``
pal.rb3 <- c("blue","white","red")
f3.int <- classIntervals(sv.int, n=3,
  style="fixed", fixedBreaks=c(min(sv.int),
  -0.6, 0.6, max(sv.int)))
cols.int <- findColours(f3.int, pal.rb3)
plot(pr, col=cols.int)
brks <- round(f3.int$brks,4)
leg <- paste(brks[-4], brks[-1], sep=" - ")
legend("bottomright", fill= pal.rb3,
legend=leg, bty="n")
``
	Set a color palette.
	Set class intervals for spatially varying intercept.
	
	Find a color for each polygon.
	Plot an adjusted significance map.
	Find breaks for legend texts.
	Format legend texts.
	Locate a legend.

``
f3.slp <- classIntervals(sv.slp, n=3,
  style="fixed", fixedBreaks=c(min(sv.slp),
  -0.4, 0.4, max(sv.slp)))
cols.slp <- findColours(f3.slp, pal.rb3)
plot(pr, col=cols.slp)
brks <- round(f3.slp$brks,4)
leg <- paste(brks[-4], brks[-1], sep=" - ")
legend("bottomright", fill= pal.rb3,
  legend=leg ,bty="n")
``
	Set class intervals for spatially varying slope.
	
	Find a color for each polygon.
	Plot an adjusted significance map.
	Find breaks for legend texts.
	Format legend texts.
	Locate a legend.

``` plot(sv.slp, sv.int, pch=20) cor(sv.slp,sv.int) ```	Plot a scatterplot. Examine the correlation coefficient.

7

Analyzing Spatial Variance and Covariance with Geostatistics and Related Techniques

LEARNING OBJECTIVES:

- To quantify spatial variance
- To quantify spatial covariance
- To differentiate between spatial and aspatial variance
- To differentiate between spatial and aspatial covariance

Chapters 4 and 6 present discussions differentiating between geographic homogeneity and geographic heterogeneity of means, variances, and spatial autocorrelation. But mechanisms generating homogeneous spatial data still result in geographic variability. Spatial sampling (Chapter 3) addresses this natural variation for design-based inference. Chapters 2 and 5 discuss patterned spatial variability. Various geostatistical semi-variogram models describe the trend lines for spatial autocorrelation embedded in this variability (definitions of their parameters – the sill, range, and nugget – appear in Section 2.2). And results of multivariate analyses may well be quite different when spatial auto-correlation is taken into account.

7.1. Semi-variogram models

A semi-variogram is a plot (e.g., Figures 2.5 and 4.14) portraying the magnitude of variance across a geographic landscape (sill), the distance extent of spatial dependency (range), and the magnitude of spatially unstructured variability in a geographic landscape. Two specifications in the set of valid semi-variogram models can be distinguished (Griffith and Layne, 1997). The exponential model relates to the conditional autoregressive (CAR) model of spatial statistics. This semi-variogram model describing the isotropic semi-variance at distance d from locations, $\gamma(d)$, is of the following form:

$$\gamma(d) = \begin{cases} 0, & \text{if } |d| = 0, \\ C_0 + C_1(1 - e^{-d/r}), & \text{if } |d| > 0, \end{cases} \qquad (7.1)$$

where C_0 is the nugget, $C_0 + C_1$ is the total sill (C_1 is frequently equated with the sill), and r is the range parameter ($3r$ is the effective range reaching 95% of the total sill). The Bessel function model relates to the simultaneous autoregressive (SAR) model of spatial statistics. This semi-variogram model is of the following form:

$$\gamma(d) = \begin{cases} 0, & \text{if } |d| = 0, \\ C_0 + C_1[1 - \frac{d}{r} K_1(\frac{d}{r})], & \text{if } |d| > 0, \end{cases} \qquad (7.2)$$

where K_1 is the modified Bessel function of the first-order and second kind (the K-Bessel function in ArcGIS); here the effective range is $4r$. A principal difference between these two trend descriptions is their effective range.

The "Geostatistical Analyst" module in ESRI™ ArcGIS supports the following additional semi-variogram models: circular, spherical, tetraspherical, pentaspherical, Gaussian, rational quadratic, (wave) hole effect, J-Bessel, and stable (special cases are the exponential and the Gaussian). Johnston et al. (2001) furnish the equations for these model specifications. Additional semi-variogram models exist, too, including the power (the linear is a special case), cubic, and Cauchy specifications (Griffith and Layne, 1999).

Rainfall across Puerto Rico can be portrayed on the basis of an expanded set of 112 weather stations (Figure 3.4d presents a selected subset of 90 of these stations). The Manly exponential transformation (Section 4.1) $e^{-0.0125Y}$, where Y denotes rainfall, improves the Shapiro–Wilk normality diagnostic statistic probability from less than 0.0001 to 0.0289 (Figure 7.1). In other

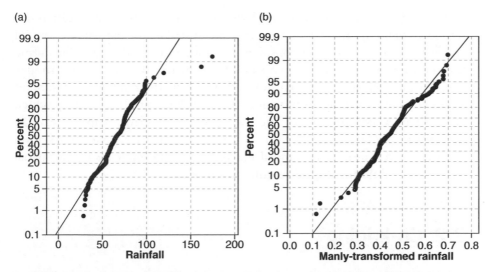

Figure 7.1   Normal quantile plots. (a) Rainfall. (b) Manly-transformed rainfall.

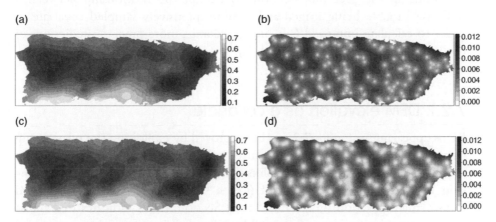

Figure 7.2   Increasing darkness of the gray scale is directly proportional to the transformed rainfall value, or its amount of prediction error. (a) Exponential model interpolation. (b) Exponential model prediction error map. (c) Bessel function model interpolation. (d) Bessel function model prediction error map.

words, this transformation (which inverts the original measurement scale) improves symmetry, but especially the upper-tail values remain arguably too extreme to conform to a normal frequency distribution.

Figure 7.2 presents ordinary kriging interpolation results. Figure 7.2a was constructed with the exponential semi-variogram model, whereas Figure 7.2c was constructed with the Bessel semi-variogram model.

A comparison of the two interpolated maps reveals both little difference between them in the general geographic distribution pattern of rainfall across the island, and some conspicuous spots on both of them illustrating the increase in the spatial dependency field for the Bessel function model. Four of the high spots (the transformation inverts the rainfall measurement scale) coincide with the mountainous areas of the island (Figure 3.3), which is sensible. A comparison of the two prediction error maps reveals an increase in prediction error with increasing distance from weather station locations and a more pronounced illustration of the increase in the spatial dependency field for the Bessel function model.

7.2. Co-kriging

Co-kriging is an interpolation technique that extends univariate kriging, as was done in the preceding section, to exploit the relationship between a response variable being kriged and a more intensively sampled covariate in order to calculate improved (e.g., more accurate, more precise) predictions of the response variable (e.g., Figure 4.7a).

7.2.1. DEM elevation as a covariate

Maps appearing in Figure 7.2 can be improved by exploiting the relationship between rainfall and elevation, the latter being based upon a digital elevation model (DEM) containing 9,181 points that cover the island. The linear relationship between transformed rainfall (i.e., $e^{-0.0125 \times \text{rainfall}}$; see Section 7.1) and transformed elevation (i.e., $\text{DEM}^{0.35}$; see Section 4.3.2) indicates that transformed elevation accounts for roughly 25% of the variation in transformed rainfall (Figure 7.3a); this relationship is negative because of the inverse transformation applied to rainfall. This relationship allows the additional 9,069 DEM elevation points to be employed with co-kriging to improve the maps appearing in Figure 7.2.

A comparison of Figures 7.2 and 7.4 further reveals some fine tuning of the interpolated maps, and improved precision (i.e., reduction in prediction error). The persistence of the interpolated rainfall map patterns suggests that the spatial autocorrelation captured in the univariate maps also characterizes the geographic distribution of DEM elevation. The Bessel function results may be preferable, in part because that specification best characterizes the geographic distribution of transformed elevation (Figure 4.14).

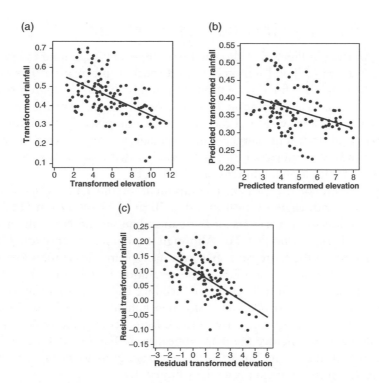

Figure 7.3 Transformed DEM elevation and transformed rainfall scatterplot.
(a) Raw data. (b) Spatial autocorrelation components. (c) Spatial linear
operator filtered data.

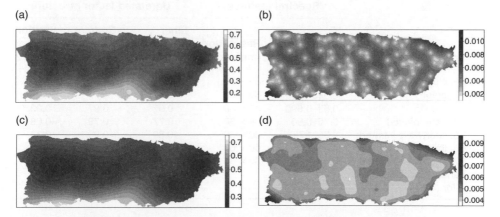

Figure 7.4 Increasing darkness of the gray scale is directly proportional to the transformed
rainfall value, or its amount of prediction error. (a) Exponential model
transformed DEM co-kriged interpolation. (b) Exponential model co-kriged
prediction error map. (c) Bessel function model transformed DEM co-kriged
interpolation. (d) Bessel function model co-kriged prediction error map.

7.2.2. Landsat 7 ETM+ data as a covariate

Maps appearing in Figure 7.2 also can be improved by exploiting the relationship between rainfall and remotely sensed spectral information. The latter is
based on 8,987,017 finer resolution (30 × 30 m) pixels aggregated into
110,863 270^2 coarser resolution (270 × 270 m) pixels, covering the island,
whose values are the average of the finer resolution pixels. The original pixels
were extracted from four merged Landsat images of Puerto Rico.[1] The seven
spectral bands were subjected to a factor analysis without rotation to summarize the data with a single dimension (Table 7.1).

The structure of the principal component of the Landsat spectral data
changes little with aggregation from 30 × 30 m to 270 × 270 m (Table 7.1).
This dimension summarizes six of the bands. The second component essentially is the thermal band (band 6). Although it accounts for only roughly 13%
of the variance in the aggregated spectral data, it primarily captures the underlying terrain (Figures 3.3 and 7.5a). The resolution here is finer than that for
the DEM, allowing more detailed co-kriging. Factor 2 scores account for
roughly 36% of the variance in transformed rainfall (Figure 7.5b). This relationship allows an additional nearly 111,000 factor score points to be employed
with co-kriging to improve the maps appearing in Figure 7.2. One difference
is a southward shift of the impact of the central mountain chain. Overall, the
Bessel function interpolation resembles Figure 4.7.

Table 7.1 Puerto Rico Landsat 7 ETM+ image aggregated pixel characteristics

| | Spectral features | | Unrotated factor structure | | |
| | Range | Resolution | Finer resolution: | Coarser resolution | |
Spectral band	(micrometers)	(meters)	Factor 1	Factor 1	Factor 2
B1: blue	0.45–0.515	30 × 30	0.95	0.95	−0.08
B2: green	0.525–0.605	30 × 30	0.97	0.97	−0.04
B3: red	0.63–0.690	30 × 30	0.97	0.97	0.03
B4: near infrared	0.75–0.90	30 × 30	0.77	0.79	−0.08
B5: shortwave infrared	1.55–1.75	30 × 30	0.89	0.90	0.34
B6: thermal band	10.40–12.5	60 × 60	−0.49	−0.53	0.83
B7: shortwave infrared	2.09–2.35	30 × 30	0.91	0.92	0.31
Variance accounted for (%)			74.8	76.1	13.1

[1] We thank Marco Millones, College of William and Mary, for furnishing us with these
data. The complete image is constructed as follows: the bulk of the island is from January
22, 2003; the northeast part of the island from March 4, 2003; the southeast part of the
island from March 20, 2003; and the southwest part of the island from October 18, 2002.

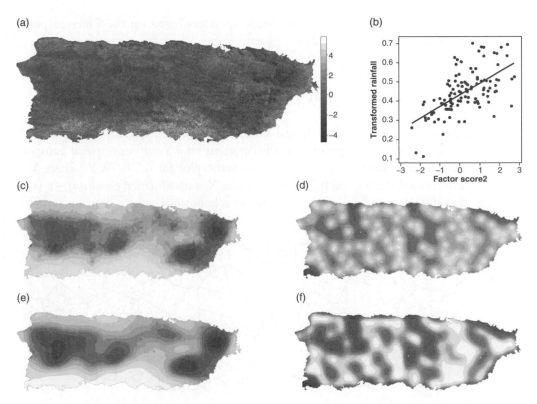

Figure 7.5   Increasing darkness of the gray scale is directly proportional to Factor 2 score, or its amount of prediction error. (a) Factor 2 score map. (b) Scatterplot of Factor 2 versus transformed rainfall. (c) Exponential model co-kriged interpolation. (d) Exponential model co-kriged prediction error map. (e) Bessel function model co-kriged interpolation. (f) Bessel function model co-kriged prediction error map.

7.3. Spatial linear operators

Spatial linear operator construction via spatial autoregression supports a Cochrane–Orcutt type of pre–whitening of georeferenced data (see Section 5.1). It allows an exploration of the preceding notion that common spatial autocorrelation patterns relate rainfall and elevation. Thiessen polygons permit the 112 weather station locations to be spatially related (Figure 7.6). The Moran Coefficient (MC) values for the spatial structure appearing in Figure 7.6 are: 0.4954 (GR = 0.4473) for transformed rainfall, and 0.4947 [Geary Ratio (GR = 0.5193)] for transformed elevation. These values are consistent with the notion that the spatial relationship structure for both geographic distributions is very similar.

The following are the spatial linear operators based on the Thiessen polygons portrayed in Figure 7.6:

transformed rainfall: $(\mathbf{I} - 0.7950\mathbf{W})$

transformed elevation: $(\mathbf{I} - 0.7923\mathbf{W})$

Again, the similarity of the spatial autocorrelation parameters is consistent with the notion that both geographic distributions have a common spatial autocorrelation component. Figure 7.3b – the scatterplot for $0.7950\mathbf{WY}$, where $\mathbf{Y}$ is transformed rainfall, and $0.7923\mathbf{WX}$, where $\mathbf{X}$ is transformed elevation – reveals that the degree of commonality is noticeable but not great.

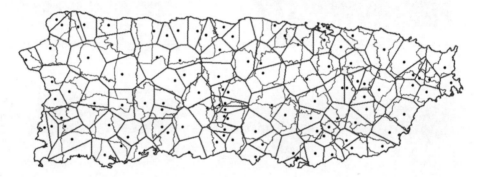

Figure 7.6 A Thiessen polygon partitioning of Puerto Rico for 112 weather station locations.

Transformed variable	s^2	r	$\hat{\rho}$	s_{adj}^2	r_{adj}
Rainfall	0.1120^2		0.7950	0.0752^2	
		−0.5203			−0.6395
Elevation	2.5797^2		0.7923	1.7970^2	

Here positive spatial autocorrelation is suppressing the true relationship between these two variables. In addition, it inflates the variance of transformed rainfall by a factor of $(0.1120/0.0752)^2 = 2.22$, and that of transformed elevation by a factor of $(2.5797/1.7970)^2 = 2.06$. The respective corresponding effective sample sizes are 8.9 and 8.8, which moves any analysis of the original data from a reasonable (over 100) to a quite small (about 9) sample size.

The filtered variables more closely conform with a normal frequency distribution (Figure 7.7). Their respective Shapiro–Wilk statistic probabilities increase to 0.2729 (transformed rainfall) and 0.1313 (transformed elevation). In comparison with Figure 7.1b, the plot in Figure 7.7a is straighter and has better-behaved tails (see Chapter 2).

(a)

(b)

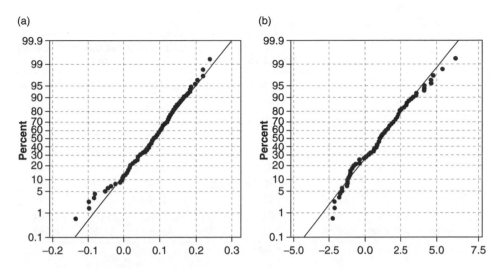

Figure 7.7 Linear operator filtered transformed variable normal quantile plots. (a) Rainfall. (b) Elevation.

7.3.1. Multivariate geographic data

Multivariate data analysis furnishes a number of techniques that handle the simultaneities and complexities in multiple variable analyses (see Johnson and Wichern, 2002). Multiple regression is the extension of autoregressive models such as those appearing in Chapter 5. Discriminant function analysis extends results appearing in Section 5.1 for a two-group problem to three or more groups. Cluster analysis relates to topics discussed in Chapter 6. Principal components analysis (PCA) and factor analysis (FA) address multicollinearity latent in a battery of variables. Eigenvector spatial filtering directly relates to PCA (see Sections 4.2.1 and 5.2). Multivariate ANOVA (MANOVA) addresses the difference-of-means problem involving a battery of variables. Canonical correlation analysis (CCA) addresses a pair of variable sets.

Consider the following eight variables measured for the municipalities of Puerto Rico: Y_1, density of farms in 2002; Y_2, density of farms in 2007; Y_3, density of farmland in 2002; Y_4, density of farmland in 2007; Y_5, mean DEM pixel rainfall; Y_6, standard deviation of DEM pixel rainfall; Y_7, mean DEM pixel elevation; Y_8, standard deviation of DEM pixel elevation. The analysis here involves linear combinations of these variables, rather than transformed versions of them (see Chapter 4).

An FA of these data can begin with a PCA of them. The PCA indicates that only three dimensions span these data. Therefore, the FA involves only three dimensions, whose factor structure appears in Table 7.2. The selected variables illustrate the common finding that most socio-economic and demographic

Table 7.2 Rotated factor structure matrices

Variable	ρ	Raw data			Spatial linear operator filtered data		
		Factor 1	Factor 2	Factor 3	Factor 1	Factor 2	Factor 3
Y_1	0.6420	<u>0.64</u>	<u>0.69</u>	−0.02	<u>0.85</u>	0.38	−0.14
Y_2	0.5411	<u>0.62</u>	<u>0.66</u>	−0.12	<u>0.75</u>	0.40	−0.19
Y_3	0.5055	<u>0.89</u>	0.12	−0.01	0.23	<u>0.88</u>	−0.01
Y_4	0.3317	<u>0.90</u>	−0.05	−0.11	0.13	<u>0.89</u>	−0.22
Y_5	0.8239	−0.19	<u>0.83</u>	−0.05	<u>0.87</u>	−0.05	0.02
Y_6	0.5806	−0.19	−0.29	<u>0.85</u>	−0.37	−0.14	<u>0.85</u>
Y_7	0.7631	0.46	<u>0.65</u>	0.30	<u>0.86</u>	0.18	0.11
Y_8	0.6795	0.05	0.27	<u>0.91</u>	0.24	−0.10	<u>0.90</u>
% variance accounted		33.64	27.30	20.90	38.06	24.24	20.79

Note: Prominent correlation coefficients are underlined.

variables exhibit moderate positive spatial autocorrelation at a meso-scale geographic resolution. A comparison of the spatial and aspatial structure matrix results exemplifies impacts of spatial autocorrelation on covariation: accounting for spatial autocorrelation renders a better simplified rotated structure. Although the standard deviation dimensions persist, factors 1 and 2 are more clearly articulated (e.g., no overlapping variables), with substantive interpretations switched (farm size, and farm number coupled with rain and elevation). In addition, the total generalized variance (i.e., the determinant of the covariance matrix) decreases from 53,572 for the raw data to 34,569 for the spatial linear operator filtered data; in other words, variance inflation due to spatial autocorrelation increases overall variance by a factor of 1.55.

The geographic distributions of the factor scores appear in Figure 7.8. The correlation between factor 1 and adjusted factor 2 is 0.91. The correlation between factor 2 and adjusted factor 1 is 0.94. The correlation between factor 3 and adjusted factor 3 is 0.89. One dimension highlights the mountainous part of the island. Another factor contrasts the south coast with the remaining part of the island. The factor scores adjusted for spatial autocorrelation contain less map pattern.

A MANOVA for the island's five agricultural administrative regions illustrates a similar type of spatial autocorrelation impact (Table 7.3). The original geographic data imply that marked differences between regions exist. The spatial autocorrelation adjusted data indicate otherwise, with Pillai's traces resulting in a change of statistical inference at the 1% level of significance. In terms of variance redistribution, the second discriminating dimension accounts for a third less of the sums-of-squares-and-cross-products (SSCP) variance. In both cases, a diagnostic analysis indicates inequality of regional

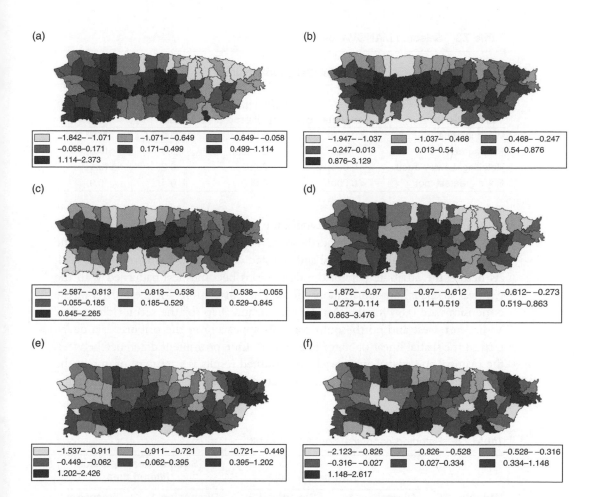

Figure 7.8 Geographic distributions of factor scores; magnitude of score is directly related to darkness of gray scale. (a) Original data factor 1. (b) Spatial linear operator filtered data factor 1. (c) Original data factor 2. (d) Spatial linear operator filtered data factor 2. (e) Original data factor 3. (f) Spatial linear operator filtered data factor 3.

SSCP matrices, with the chi-square statistic decreasing from 269 to 246 by adjusting for spatial autocorrelation effects.

One interesting CCA application explores the dimensions that span a pair of georeferencing coordinate axes and a set of locational attributes (Bailey and Gatrell, 1995). For the Puerto Rico example, which has the geocode set containing two variables (Universal Transverse Mercator versions of latitude and longitude) and the attribute set containing eight variables $(Y_1, \ldots, Y_8)$, results obtained after adjusting for spatial autocorrelation are dramatically different from those obtained with the original georeferenced data, both in significance of dimensions and dimension

Table 7.3   Selected MANOVA results

| Test statistic | Test statistic probabilities | | % SSCP variance accounted | |
	Raw data	Spatial linear operator filtered data	Raw data	Spatial linear operator filtered data
Wilk's lambda	< 0.0001	0.0079	71.6	74.2
Pillai's trace	< 0.0001	0.0205	21.9	14.8
Hotelling–Lawley trace	< 0.0001	0.0025	6.2	10.1
Roy's greatest root	< 0.0001	< 0.0001	0.4	0.9

structure (Table 7.4). Not surprisingly, the two dimensions for the pair of geo-codes are an east–west and a north–south trend (Figure 7.9). Here both of the correlations between the original and adjusted data for these dimensions are 0.91. As before, the attribute part of the dimensions becomes less patterned with the removal of spatial autocorrelation effects. The correlations for these parts of the dimensions are 0.80 for the first dimension, and 0.76 for the second dimension. Visual east–west and north–south contrasts appearing in the original data disappear in the spatial linear operator filtered data. One prominent difference between the original and spatial autocorrelation adjusted results is a removal of one of the global components of spatial autocorrelation, namely a linear trend across the island.

Table 7.4   Selected canonical correlation results

| Variable | Raw data | | Spatial linear operator filtered data | |
	Dimension 1	Dimension 2	Dimension 1	Dimension 2
Canonical correlation	0.77	0.61	0.55	0.25
probability	< 0.001	< 0.001	0.03	0.75
U	0.84	−0.55	0.54	−0.84
V	0.53	0.85	0.83	0.56
Y_1	−0.46	0.23	−0.18	0.36
Y_2	−0.37	0.15	−0.20	0.26
Y_3	−0.54	0.14	−0.41	0.56
Y_4	−0.58	−0.07	−0.63	0.26
Y_5	0.57	0.26	0.44	−0.02
Y_6	0.00	−0.47	−0.08	−0.41
Y_7	−0.17	−0.30	−0.06	−0.07
Y_8	−0.06	−0.72	−0.20	−0.66

Note: Prominent correlation coefficients are underlined.

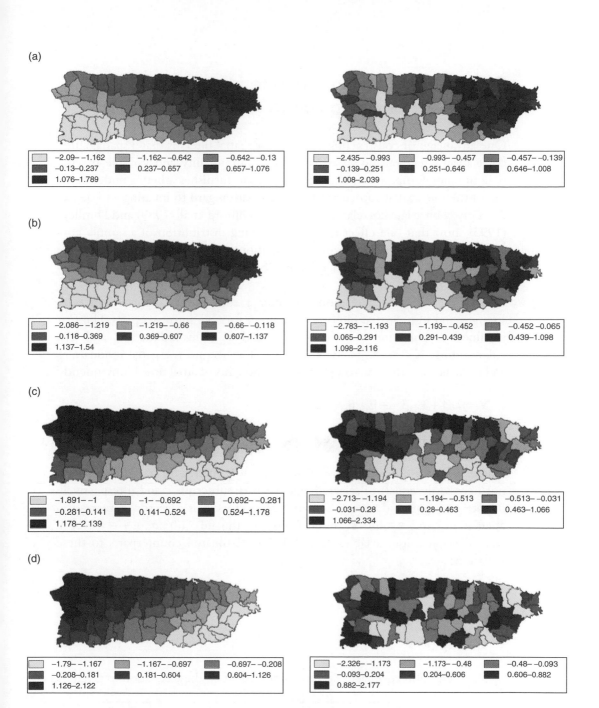

Figure 7.9 Geographic distributions of canonical correlation scores; magnitude of score is directly related to darkness of gray scale. (a) Geocode and attribute parts of dimension 1. (b) Geocode and attribute parts of adjusted dimension 1. (c) Geocode and attribute parts of dimension 2. (d) Geocode and attribute parts of adjusted dimension 2.

7.4. Eigenvector spatial filtering: correlation coefficient decomposition

One advantage of constructing eigenvector spatial filters is that a spatial auto-correlation effect can be separated into a commonality and variable-specific (i.e., unique) components. This decomposition furnishes a better understanding of the role spatial autocorrelation plays with regard to inflating and deflating a given bivariate correlation coefficient. Clifford et al. (1989) and Dutilleul (1993) show that one effect is on the sampling distribution of a sample correlation coefficient. Haining (1991) demonstrates that their findings are equivalent to those obtained by the Cochrane–Orcutt autoregressive pre-whitening method.

Latent spatial autocorrelation can alter a correlation coefficient in both strength and sign. Spatial filtering separates a variable into two parts. The first is a linear combination of common ($\hat{\mathbf{X}}_C$ and $\hat{\mathbf{Y}}_C$) plus unique ($\hat{\mathbf{X}}_U$ and $\hat{\mathbf{Y}}_U$) eigenvectors: $\hat{\mathbf{X}}_C + \hat{\mathbf{X}}_U$ and $\hat{\mathbf{Y}}_C + \hat{\mathbf{Y}}_U$. The second is aspatial residuals, e_X and e_Y, which are the non-geographic components of attributes. Consequently,

$$\mathbf{Y} = \mu_Y \mathbf{1} + \mathbf{E}_C \boldsymbol{\beta}_{C_Y} + \mathbf{E}_{U_Y} \boldsymbol{\beta}_{U_Y} + \boldsymbol{\varepsilon}_Y,$$

$$\mathbf{X} = \mu_X \mathbf{1} + \mathbf{E}_C \boldsymbol{\beta}_{C_X} + \mathbf{E}_{U_X} \boldsymbol{\beta}_{U_X} + \boldsymbol{\varepsilon}_X,$$

where $\mathbf{E}$ is an $n \times H$ matrix for $\mathbf{X}$ and an $n \times K$ matrix for $\mathbf{Y}$ (with H and K not necessarily equal) of selected eigenvectors; subscripts c and u respectively denote common and unique sets of eigenvectors; $\boldsymbol{\beta}$ is a vector of regression coefficients; and $\boldsymbol{\varepsilon}_Y$ and $\boldsymbol{\varepsilon}_X$ respectively are the iid N(0, $\sigma_{\varepsilon_j}^2$), j = X or Y, aspatial variates for variables $\mathbf{X}$ and $\mathbf{Y}$. The estimated counterparts to these equations are

$$\mathbf{X} = \hat{\mathbf{X}}_C + \hat{\mathbf{X}}_U + \mathbf{e}_X,$$

and

$$\mathbf{Y} = \hat{\mathbf{Y}}_C + \hat{\mathbf{Y}}_U + \mathbf{e}_Y.$$

The correlation coefficient decomposition based on these equations is given by

$$r_{XY} = r_{e_{\hat{X}} e_{\hat{Y}}} \sqrt{(1 - R_{\hat{X}}^2)(1 - R_{\hat{Y}}^2)} + r_{\hat{X}_C \hat{Y}_C} \sqrt{R_{\hat{X}_C}^2 R_{\hat{Y}_C}^2} + 0 \sqrt{R_{\hat{X}_U}^2 R_{\hat{Y}_U}^2}$$

$$+ r_{\hat{X}_C e_{\hat{Y}}} \sqrt{R_{\hat{X}_U}^2 (1 - R_{\hat{Y}}^2)} + r_{e_{\hat{X}} \hat{Y}_C} \sqrt{(1 - R_{\hat{X}}^2) R_{\hat{Y}_U}^2} .$$

The third coefficient on the right-hand side is 0 because the correlation between unique eigenvectors, $r_{\hat{X}_U \hat{Y}_U}$, is 0.

The correlation between the two residuals, e_X and e_Y, estimates the relationship between the corresponding attributes outside of their geographic context. The eigenvector spatial filter properties of uncorrelatedness and orthogonality enable general descriptions of spatial autocorrelation effects to be exposed in the bivariate correlation coefficient for two variables: If the spatial filters:

1   are identical linear combinations of eigenvectors and reduce each variable's residual term to 0, then the bivariate correlation is 1.
2   have no eigenvectors in common, and reduce each variable's residual term to 0 (or the pair of residuals has a correlation of 0), then the bivariate correlation is 0.
3   have some eigenvectors in common, and some not in common (i.e., unique to each variable), and their corresponding residual terms are non-zero, then the common ones tend to inflate (and the unique one tend to deflate) the observed correlation coefficient for the pair of residual terms.

A decomposition of this type furnishes detailed information about the way spatial autocorrelation alters a given bivariate correlation coefficient.

A decomposition of the correlation coefficient appearing in Section 5.1 is as follows (the numerical entries appear in Tables 7.5 and 7.6):

$$-0.3719 = -0.2807\sqrt{(1-0.7660) \times (1-0.5713)} - 0.5413\sqrt{0.4545 \times 0.5091}$$
$$+ 0\sqrt{0.3115 \times 0.0622} - 0.0649\sqrt{0.0622 \times (1-0.7660)}$$
$$+ 0.0092\sqrt{(1-0.5713) \times 0.3115}.$$

The common spatial autocorrelation component inflates the correlation coefficient from −0.2807 toward −0.5413, whereas the two unique spatial autocorrelation components respectively deflate the correlation coefficient toward −0.0649 and 0.0092. The net effect is an increase in the correlation coefficient from −0.2807, the aspatial relationship, to −0.3719.

Noteworthy features of this empirical illustration include: (1) the adjusted correlation coefficient is −0.28 with spatial filtering, rather than −0.24 with the spatial linear operator; and (2) spatial filtering furnishes details about common and unique spatial autocorrelation components. This first feature is attributable, in part, to the spatial linear operator employing, by default, all 73 eigenvectors in its computations (i.e., it uses the entire geographic weights matrix), whereas spatial filtering selects a substantially smaller subset of the eigenvectors − 14 for transformed mean rainfall, and 7 for transformed irrigated farm density.

A decomposition of the correlation coefficient appearing in Section 7.3 is as follows (the numerical entries appear in Tables 7.5 and 7.6):

$$-0.5203 = -0.6199\sqrt{(1-0.6840)\times(1-0.7047)} - 0.5831\sqrt{0.4968\times0.6519}$$
$$+0\sqrt{0.1872\times0.0528} - 0.0158\sqrt{0.1872\times(1-0.7047)}$$
$$+0.0360\sqrt{(1-0.6840)\times0.0528}.$$

Table 7.5 Correlation coefficient decomposition summary statistics

Component	Transformed mean rainfall	Transformed irrigated farm density	Transformed rainfall	Transformed elevation
R^2 for common eigenvectors	0.4545	0.5091	0.4968	0.6519
R^2 for unique eigenvectors	0.3115	0.0622	0.1872	0.0528
R^2 for all selected eigenvectors	0.7660	0.5713	0.6840	0.7047
Stepwise level of significance	0.10	0.10	0.10	0.10
Residual MC z-score	2.1616	0.5364	1.5566	0.3590
Shapiro–Wilk (S-W) probability	0.8625	0.4848	0.1426	0.0992
ESF MC	0.6333	0.5523	0.7486	0.7392

The common spatial autocorrelation component deflates the correlation coefficient from −0.6199 toward −0.5831, and the two unique spatial autocorrelation components respectively further deflate the correlation coefficient toward −0.0158 and 0.0360. The net effect is a decrease in the correlation coefficient from −0.6199, the aspatial relationship, to −0.5203.

Noteworthy features of this empirical illustration include: (1) the adjusted correlation coefficient is −0.62 with spatial filtering, rather than −0.64 with the spatial linear operator; (2) spatial filtering furnishes details about common and unique spatial autocorrelation components. This first feature is attributable, in part, to the spatial linear operator employing, by default, all 112 eigenvectors in its computations (i.e., it uses the entire geographic weight matrix), whereas spatial filtering selects a substantially smaller subset of the eigenvectors: 13 for transformed elevation, and 14 for transformed rain.

7.5. R code for concept implementations

Computer Code 7.1 replicates the data analyses in Chapter 7. R packages used include *gstat* for geostatistics, *psych* for principal component analysis, and *CCA* for canonical correlation analysis. This computer code utilizes selected simple predefined functions for mapping, stepwise regression, and the decomposition of a correlation coefficient.

Table 7.6   Bivariate correlations between rainfall and selected covariate components

Component	Transformed mean rainfall and transformed irrigated farm density	Transformed rainfall and transformed elevation
r_{e_X, e_Y}: underlying attribute	−0.2807	−0.6199
$r_{\hat{X}_C, \hat{Y}_C}$: spatial autocorrelation	−0.5413	−0.5831
$r_{e_X, \hat{Y}_U}$: cross-correlation	0.0092	−0.0158
$r_{\hat{X}_U, e_Y}$: cross-correlation	−0.0649	0.0360
$r_{\hat{X}_U, \hat{Y}_U}$: unique, uncorrelated	0	0
Observed	−0.3719	−0.5203

Kriging procedures in R require a grid as an input argument for locations at which kriging predictions are made. In the following computer code, a grid is created via regular spatial sampling with the *spsample( )* function. When a large number of samples are drawn, this function's output is large. Hence, the kriging procedure takes more time, and the resulting prediction surface has a better spatial resolution. Figures 7.5c–f were created with ESRI's ArcGIS Geostatistical Analyst extension. The corresponding R code in Computer Code 7.1 produces similar, but not exactly identical, output; discrepancies are attributable to the use of slightly different geographic neighborhoods. Figure 7.10 displays the R code output. Furthermore, Figures 7.5c and 7.5e are symbolized differently with the 'Filled Contours' option, which is the default in ArcGIS Geostatistical Analysis.

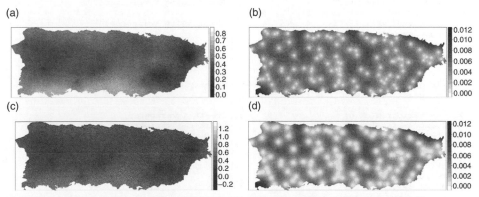

Figure 7.10   Equivalent R output for Figures 7.5c–f. (a) Exponential model co-kriged interpolation. (b) Exponential model co-kriged prediction error map. (c) Bessel function model co-kriged interpolation. (d) Bessel function model co-kriged prediction error map.

Computer Code 7.1. Implementing semi-variogram model estimation, kriging, co-kriging, and selected spatially adjusted multivariate techniques.

| ```
library(car)
library(spdep)
``` | Load *car* package.<br>Load *spdep* package. |
| `# 7.1: variogram and kriging` | |
| `prec <-readShapePoints("prec_stations.shp")` | Read station shapefile. |
| ```
qqnorm(prec$Rainfall)
qqline(prec$Rainfall)
shapiro.test(prec$Rainfall)
``` | Create a normal-quantile plot for original rainfall variable.<br>Conduct a normality test. |
| ```
qqnorm(prec$rain_tr)
qqline(prec$rain_tr)
shapiro.test(prec$rain_tr)
``` | Create a normal-quantile plot for transformed rainfall variable.<br>Conduct a normality test. |
| ```
library(gstat)
pr.v <- variogram(rain_tr ~ 1, prec)
pr.vf.exp <- fit.variogram(pr.v,
   vgm(0.013,"Exp", 0.35, 0))
plot(pr.v, pr.vf.exp)
``` | Load *gstat* package for kriging.<br>Create a variogram.<br>Fit the variogram with an exponential model.<br>Plot the fitted variogram. |
| ```
pr <- readShapePoly("PuertoRico.shp")
pr.reg <- spsample(pr, 100000,
   type="regular")
pr.grid <- SpatialPixels(pr.reg)
``` | Read municipalities polygon shapefile.<br>Draw locations at which kriging predictions are created.<br>Convert the object as a SpatialPixel class. |
| ```
ok.exp <- krige(rain_tr ~ 1, prec, pr.grid,
pr.vf.exp)
color.pal <- colorRampPalette(c("dark
red","orange","light Yellow"))
color.palr <- colorRampPalette(c("light
yellow","orange","dark red"))
spplot(ok.exp["var1.pred"],
col.regions=color.pal)
spplot(ok.exp["var1.var"],
col.regions=color.palr)
``` | Conduct kriging with the exponential model.<br>Create two color ramps to be used in mapping kriging results.<br><br>Map kriging predictions.<br><br>Map kriging variances. |
| ```
pr.vf.bes <- fit.variogram(pr.v,
vgm(0.01,"Bes", 0.35, 0.002))
plot(pr.v, pr.vf.bes)
``` | Fit the variogram with a Bessel model.<br><br>Plot the fitted variogram. |
| ```
ok.bes <- krige(rain_tr ~ 1, prec, pr.grid,
pr.vf.bes)
spplot(ok.bes["var1.pred"],
col.regions=color.pal)
spplot(ok.bes["var1.var"],
col.regions=color.palr)
``` | Conduct kriging with the Bessel model.<br><br>Map kriging predictions.<br><br>Map kriging variances. |
| `# 7.2: co-kriging` | |
| ```
# 7.2.1
ck.g <- gstat(NULL,"rain",rain_tr ~ 1,prec)
ck.g <- gstat(ck.g,"dem",dem_tr ~ 1,prec)
``` | Specify a model with two variables. |
| ```
ck.v <- variogram(ck.g)
ck.vf.exp <- fit.lmc(ck.v, ck.g,
vgm(0.013,"Exp", 0.35, 0))
``` | Create a variogram.<br>  Fit the variogram with an exponential function. |
| ```
ck.exp <- predict(ck.vf.exp, pr.grid)
spplot(ck.exp["rain.pred"],
col.regions=color.pal)
spplot(ck.exp["rain.var"],
``` | Conduct kriging.<br>Map the kriging predictions.<br><br>Map the kriging variances. |
```

`col.regions=color.palr)`	

`ck.vf.bes <- fit.lmc(ck.v, ck.g,`
`vgm(0.01,"Bes", 0.35, 0.002))`
`ck.bes <- predict(ck.vf.bes, pr.grid)`
`spplot(ck.bes["rain.pred"],`
`col.regions=color.pal)`
`spplot(ck.bes["rain.var"],`
`col.regions=color.palr)`
	Fit the variogram with a Bessel
	function.
	Conduct kriging.
	Map the Kriging predictions.
	
	Map the kriging variances.

`# 7.2.2`	

`library(psych)`
`lsat <- read.csv("landsat_tm.csv",`
`header=T)`
`tm.pca <- principal(lsat[,4:10], 2,`
`rotate="none", scores=T)`
`print(tm.pca$loadings, cutoff=0.001)`
	Load *psych* package for PCA.
	Read a Landsat TM image data.
	
	Conduct PCA.
	
	Display loadings.

`factors <- cbind(lsat[,1:3], tm.pca$scores)`
`coordinates(factors) <- c("x","y")`
`fact.grid <- factors`
`gridded(fact.grid) <- T`
`spplot(fact.grid,"PC2",`
`col.regions=color.pal)`
	Store factor scores with *x*, *y*
	coordinates; convert it as a grid.
	
	Map the second factor.

`pts <- overlay(fact.grid, prec)`
 	
`plot(factors$PC2[pts], prec$rain_tr,`
`pch=20)`
`tm.cor <- cor(factors$PC2[pts],`
`prec$rain_tr)`
`print(tm.cor)`
	Conduct overlay to find grid pixels
	where the stations are located.
	Plot a scatterplot with rainfall and
	the second factor on the stations.
	Calculate correlation.

`# co-kriging with tm: exponential`
`ck.tm <- gstat(NULL, "rain", rain_tr ~ 1,`
`prec, model=pr.vf.exp)`
`vov <- var(factors$PC2)/var(prec$rain_tr)`
`tm.vf.exp <- pr.vf.exp`
`tm.vf.exp$psill <- pr.vf.exp$psill * vov`
`ck.tm <- gstat(ck.tm, "tm", PC2 ~ 1,`
`factors, nmax=8, model=tm.vf.exp)`
`co.vf.exp <- pr.vf.exp`
`co.vf.exp$psill <- sqrt(pr.vf.exp$psill *`
`tm.vf.exp$psill) * tm.cor`
`ck.tm <- gstat(ck.tm, c("rain","tm"),`
`model=co.vf.exp)`
`ck.tm.exp <- predict(ck.tm, pr.grid)`
`spplot(ck.tm.exp["rain.pred"],`
`col.regions=color.pal)`
`spplot(ck.tm.exp["rain.var"],`
`col.regions=color.palr)`
	Specify a model with the previous
	exponential model.
	Calculate a ratio of variance.
	Adjust the partial sill with the
	variance ratio for the second factor.
	Add the variogram.
	
	Adjust the partial sill for cross-
	variogram with the correlation.
	
	Add the co-variogram.
	
	Conduct co-kriging.
	Map co-kriging predictions.
	
	Map co-kriging variances.

`# co-kriging with tm: Bessel`
`ck.tm.m <- gstat(NULL, "rain", rain_tr ~ 1,`
`prec, model=pr.vf.bes)`
`tm.vf.bes <- pr.vf.bes`
`tm.vf.bes$psill <- pr.vf.bes$psill * vov`
`ck.tm.m <- gstat(ck.tm.m, "tm", PC2 ~ 1,`
`factors, nmax=4, model=tm.vf.bes)`
`co.vf.bes <- pr.vf.bes`
`co.vf.bes$psill <- sqrt(pr.vf.bes$psill *`
`tm.vf.bes$psill) * tm.cor`
	Similarly conduct co-kriging with a
	Bessel function.

```ck.tm.m <- gstat(ck.tm.m, c("rain","tm"), model=co.vf.bes) ck.tm.bes <- predict(ck.tm.m, pr.grid) spplot(ck.tm.bes["rain.pred"], col.regions=color.pal) spplot(ck.tm.bes["rain.var"], col.regions=color.palr)```	Map the co-kriging prediction.

Map the co-kriging variances. |
| ```# 7.3: spatial linear operator``` | |
| ```pr.thiess <- readShapePoly("pr_thiessen.shp") plot(pr.thiess) plot(prec, add=T, pch=20) thiess.nb <- read.gal("pr_thiessen.gal") th.listw <- nb2listw(thiess.nb, style="W") th.listb <- nb2listw(thiess.nb, style="B")``` | Read a shapefile of Thiessen polygons.

Map the Thiessen polygons with stations. Read spatial neighbor structure. Create a *listw* object with W style and B style. |
| ```moran.test(prec$rain_tr, th.listb) geary.test(prec$rain_tr, th.listb) rain.sar <- errorsarlm(prec$rain_tr ~ 1, listw=th.listw) rain.sar$lambda rain.lf <- prec$rain_tr - rain.sar$lambda * lag.listw(th.listw, prec$rain_tr)``` | Conduct spatial autocorrelation tests.

Estimate a spatial autocorrelation parameter for linear operator filtering. Calculate linear operator filtered variable. |
| ```moran.test(prec$dem_tr, th.listb) geary.test(prec$dem_tr, th.listb) elev.sar <- errorsarlm(prec$dem_tr ~ 1, listw=th.listw)

elev.sar$lambda elev.lf <- prec$dem_tr - elev.sar$lambda * lag.listw(th.listw, prec$dem_tr)``` | Conduct spatial autocorrelation tests.

Estimate a spatial autocorrelation. parameter for linear operator filtering.

Calculate linear operator filtered variable. |
```sd(cbind(prec$rain_tr, prec$dem_tr)) cor(prec$rain_tr, prec$dem_tr) sd(cbind(rain.lf, elev.lf)) cor(rain.lf, elev.lf)```	Calculate standard deviations and correlations for the variables and linear operator filtered variables.
```(sd(prec$rain_tr)/sd(rain.lf))^2 (sd(prec$dem_tr)/sd(elev.lf))^2```	Inflated variances.
```qqnorm(rain.lf);qqline(rain.lf) qqnorm(elev.lf);qqline(elev.lf)```	Create normal-quantile plots.
```shapiro.test(rain.lf) shapiro.test(elev.lf)```	Conduct normality tests.
```# 7.3.1: Multivariate```	
``pr.farm <- read.csv("PR-farm-data.csv") pr.nb <- read.gal("PuertoRico.gal") pr.listw <- nb2listw(pr.nb, style="W") pr.listb <- nb2listw(pr.nb, style="B")

y1 <- pr.farm$nofarms_02/pr.farm$area y2 <- pr.farm$nofarms_07/pr.farm$area y3 <- pr.farm$cuerdas_02/pr.farm$area y4 <- pr.farm$cuerdas_07/pr.farm$area y5 <- pr.farm$rain_mean y6 <- pr.farm$rain_std y7 <- pr.farm$elev_mean``` | Read Puerto Rico farm data.

Read a spatial neighbor information. Create *listw* objects with W and B styles. Construct a data object with 8 variables. |

`y8 <- pr.farm$elev_std`	
`y <- cbind(y1,y2,y3,y4,y5,y6,y7,y8)`	
`y1.sar <- errorsarlm(y1 ~ 1,` `listw=pr.listw)`	Estimate a spatial autocorrelation parameter for the first variable.

`y.rho <- apply(y, 2, function(x, listw)`
`{errorsarlm(x~1, listw=listw)$lambda},`
`listw=pr.listw)`
`print(y.rho)`
	Estimate spatial autocorrelation parameters for the other 7 variables using apply function.

`y.fa <- principal(y, 3, rotate="varimax",`
`scores=T)`
`print(y.fa$loadings, cutoff=0.001)`
	Conduct PCA with varimax rotation.
	
	Print the factor loadings.

`f.lf <- function(x, listw, rho) {x -`
`rho*lag.listw(listw, x)}`
`y.lf <- mapply(f.lf, as.data.frame(y),`
`rho=y.rho, MoreArgs=list(listw=pr.listw))`
`y.lf.fa <- principal(y.lf, 3,`
`rotate="varimax", scores=T)`
`print(y.lf.fa$loadings, cutoff=0.001)`
	Generate linear operator filtered variables for the 8 variables.
	
	Conduct PCA with the linear operator filtered variables.

`sum(diag(cov(y)))` `sum(diag(cov(y.lf)))`	Examine total variances.
`library(RColorBrewer)` `library(classInt)`	Load RColorBrewer and classInt packages.

`windows(w=14,h=7)`
`pal.red <- brewer.pal(7,"Reds")`
`q7 <- classIntervals(y.fa$scores[,1],7,`
`style="quantile")`
`cols.red <- findColours(q7, pal.red)`
`plot(pr, col=cols.red)`
`brks <- round(q7$brks,3)`
`leg <- paste(brks[-8], brks[-1], sep="-")`
`legend("bottomright", fill=pal.red,`
`legend=leg, bty="n")`
`title("Original Factor 1")`
	Create a new window.
	Create a color palette.
	Find classes.
	
	Assign colors to each record.
	Map the factor score with the colors.
	Get class break information.
	Format legend texts.
	Add a legend and a title.

`source("all_functions.R")`	Load functions to map the other factors. You need to set a correct folder.

`mapping.seq(pr, y.lf.fa$scores[,1], 7,`
`main="Spatial liner operator filtered`
`Factor 1")`
`mapping.seq(pr, y.fa$scores[,2], 7,`
`main="Original Factor 2")`
`mapping.seq(pr, y.lf.fa$scores[,2], 7,`
`main="Spatial liner operator filtered`
`Factor 2")`
`mapping.seq(pr, y.fa$scores[,3], 7,`
`main="Original Factor 3")`
`mapping.seq(pr, y.lf.fa$scores[,3], 7,`
`main="Spatial liner operator filtered`
`Factor 3")`
	Map the other factors and linear operator filtered factors.

`# MANOVA`	
`y.m <- manova(y ~ as.factor(pr.farm$ADM))`	Conduct MANOVA for 5 administrative districts.
`y.m.s <- summary(y.m, test="Wilks")` `m.test <- c("Wilks", "Pillai", "Hotelling-`	Get a summary of the MANOVA results with four different tests.

```Lawley", "Roy")```
```lapply(m.test, function(x, m)```
```{summary(m,test=x)}, m=y.m)```
```round(y.m.s$Eigenvalues/sum(y.m.s$Eigenvalu```
```es)*100,2)```
	Calculate SSCP variance percentages.

```y.lf.m <- manova(y.lf ~```
```as.factor(pr.farm$ADM))```
```lapply(m.test, function(x, m)```
```{summary(m,test=x)}, m=y.lf.m)```
```y.lf.meig <- summary(y.lf.m,```
```test="Wilks")$Eigenvalues```
	Conduct MANOVA with linear operator filtered variables and summarize the results.

```round(y.lf.meig /sum(y.lf.meig)*100,2)```	Calculate SSCP variance percentages.

```# cononical correlation```
```library(CCA)```
```uv <- pr.farm[,c("u","v")]```
```y.cc <- cc(uv, y)```
```y.cc[1]```
```round(y.cc$scores$corr.X.xscores,2)```
```round(y.cc$scores$corr.Y.yscores,2)```
	Load CCA package.
	Get x, y coordinates.
	Conduct canonical correlation analysis for the Canonical correlation.
	Display the dimensions.

```y.lf.cc <- cc(uv, y.lf)```
```y.lf.cc[1]```
```round(y.lf.cc$scores$corr.X.xscores,2)```
```round(y.lf.cc$scores$corr.Y.yscores,2)```
	Conduct canonical correlation for the x, y coordinates with the linear operator filtered variables.

```mapping.seq(pr, y.cc$scores$xscores[,1], 7,```
```main="Raw: Dimension 1")```
```mapping.seq(pr, y.cc$scores$yscores[,1], 7,```
```main="Raw: Dimension 1")```
```mapping.seq(pr, y.lf.cc$scores$xscores[,1],```
```7, main="SLOP: Dimension 1")```
```mapping.seq(pr, y.lf.cc$scores$yscores[,1],```
```7, main="SLOP: Dimension 1")```
```mapping.seq(pr, y.cc$scores$xscores[,2]*1,```
```7, main="Raw: Dimension 2")```
```mapping.seq(pr, y.cc$scores$yscores[,2]*1,```
```7, main="Raw: Dimension 2")```
```mapping.seq(pr,```
```y.lf.cc$scores$xscores[,2]*1, 7,```
```main="SLOP: Dimension 1")```
```mapping.seq(pr,```
```y.lf.cc$scores$yscores[,2]*1, 7,```
```main="SLOP: Dimension 1")```
	Map the canonical correlation scores.

```# 7.4 Eigenvector spatial filtering```	
```evec <- read.table("pr_evecs.txt",``` ```header=T)```	Read a file for eigenvectors.
```EV <- evec[,-(1:2)]```	Extract only eigenvectors.

```rain <- pr.farm$rain_mean```
```lm.full <- lm(rain ~ ., data=EV)```
```rain.sf <- stepwise.forward(lm.full,```
```lm(rain ~ 1, data=EV), 0.1, verbose=F)```
```rain.sf.sum <- summary(rain.sf)```
	Conduct eigenvector spatial filtering and save the summary of the eigenvector spatial filtering.

```irr.tr <- log(pr.farm$irr_farms_07/``` ```pr.farm$area + 0.04)```	Transform irrigated farm density.

```lm.full <- lm(irr.tr ~ ., data=EV)```
```irr.sf <- stepwise.forward(lm.full,```
```lm(irr.tr ~ 1, data=EV), 0.1, verbose=F)```
	Conduct eigenvector spatial filtering and save the summary of the eigenvector spatial filtering.

```irr.sf.sum <- summary(irr.sf)```	

```rain.selev <- names(rain.sf$coefficient)[-1]```
```irr.selev <- names(irr.sf$coefficient)[-1]```
```evc <- rain.selev[rain.selev %in% irr.selev]```
	Get selected eigenvectors for rainfall and irrigated farm density.
	Find commonly selected eigenvectors.

```lm.rain.c <- lm(rain ~ ., data=EV[,evc])```
```lm.rc.sum <- summary(lm.rain.c)```
```lm.irr.c <- lm(irr.tr ~ ., data=EV[,evc])```
```lm.ic.sum <- summary(lm.irr.c)```
	Run linear regression of rainfall with commonly selected eigenvectors for rainfall and irrigated farm density.

```eu.r <- rain.selev[!(rain.selev %in% evc)]```
```lm.rain.u <- lm(rain ~ ., data=EV[,eu.r])```
```lm.ru.sum <- summary(lm.rain.u)```
	Run linear regression with eigenvectors selected only for rainfall or irrigated farm density, respectively.

```eu.i <- irr.selev[!(irr.selev %in% evc)]```
```lm.irr.u <- lm(irr.tr ~ ., data=EV[,eu.i])```
```lm.iu.sum <- summary(lm.irr.u)```	

```r1 <- cor(rain.sf$residuals, irr.sf$residuals)```	Calculate correlation of the variables.
```r2.x <- rain.sf.sum$r.squared``` ```r2.y <- irr.sf.sum$r.squared```	Calculate R^2 values with all eigenvectors.

```r2 <- cor(lm.rain.c$fitted.values, lm.irr.c$fitted.values)```
```r2.xc <- lm.rc.sum$r.squared```
```r2.yc <- lm.ic.sum$r.squared```
	Calculate correlation of spatial autocorrelation components.
	Calculate R^2 values with common eigenvectors.

```r3 <- cor(lm.rain.u$fitted.values, irr.sf$residuals)```
```r4 <- cor(rain.sf$residuals, lm.irr.u$fitted.values)```
```r2.xu <- lm.ru.sum$r.squared```
```r2.yu <- lm.iu.sum$r.squared```
	Calculate correlations of cross-correlation components.
	
	Calculate R^2 values with unique eigenvectors.

```r5 <- round(cor(lm.rain.u$fitted.values, lm.irr.u$fitted.values), 6)```	Examine the uncorrelation.
```r.xy <- r1*sqrt((1-r2.x)*(1-r2.y)) + r2*sqrt(r2.xc*r2.yc) + r3*sqrt(r2.xu*(1-r2.y)) + r4*sqrt((1-r2.x)*r2.yu)```	Examine the linear combination of the components.

```lm.morantest(rain.sf, listw=pr.listb)$statistic```
```shapiro.test(rain.sf$residuals)$p.value```
```moran.test(rain.sf$fitted.values, listw=pr.listb)$estimate[1]```
	Conduct spatial autocorrelation and normality tests for rainfall and its eigenvector spatial filter model.

```lm.morantest(irr.sf, listw=pr.listb)$statistic```
```shapiro.test(irr.sf$residuals)$p.value```
```moran.test(irr.sf$fitted.values, listw=pr.listb)$estimate[1]```
	Conduct spatial autocorrelation and normality tests for irrigated farm density and its eigenvector spatial filter model.

```evec.th <- read.table("pr_thiessen_evecs.txt", header=T)```
 	
```decomp.prec <- cor.decomp(prec$rain_tr, prec$dem_tr, evec.th[,-1])```
	Conduct the same analysis with transformed rainfall and elevation variables based on the Thiessen polygons.
	Cor.decomp function is defined in all_functions.R file.

| ```
decomp.prec$r.sq
decomp.prec$bi.cor
lm.morantest(decomp.prec$x.sf,
listw=th.listb)$statistic
lm.morantest(decomp.prec$y.sf,
listw=th.listb)$statistic
shapiro.test(residuals(decomp.prec$x.sf))$p
.value
shapiro.test(residuals(decomp.prec$y.sf))$p
.value
moran.test(decomp.prec$x.sf$fitted.values,
listw=th.listb)$estimate[1]
moran.test(decomp.prec$y.sf$fitted.values,
listw=th.listb)$estimate[1]
``` | Examine $R^2$ components.<br>Examine correlation components.<br>Conduct spatial autocorrelation and normality tests. |
```

8

Methods for Spatial Interpolation in Two Dimensions

LEARNING OBJECTIVES:

- To generalize a map from a small sample of locationally tagged values (i.e., a massive number of imputations)
- To calculate imputations for missing values
- To calculate uncertainty for missing-value imputations
- To estimate parameters in the presence of missing values

Spatial scientists wish to proceed with empirical analyses even when faced with incomplete data. Data may be incomplete in two different ways: the absence of values in a dataset; or the absence of values for locations in a geographic landscape. Missingness may arise because of deliberate data suppression (e.g., for confidentiality reasons), measurement equipment malfunctions (e.g., rain gauge overflow, remotely sensed image striping), data retrieval failure (e.g., survey non-response), or sparse sampling of a region (e.g., collecting soil samples), to name a few reasons. Imputation methodologies furnish tools that yield geographic interpolations/extrapolations in order to complete maps with missing-value holes in them.

Kriging is perhaps the most common, statistically sound method (see Section 7.1). It exploits the spatial autocorrelation latent in georeferenced data in order to interpolate. Co-kriging combines this exploitation with the borrowing of information from a covariate in order to interpolate (see

Section 7.2). The resulting imputations are the best linear unbiased predictors, and their uncertainty can be portrayed with a prediction error map. Spatial autoregression model specifications also can be used to produce imputations (see Griffith et al., 1989). These relate to maximum likelihood solutions when datasets are incomplete with data values missing at random (MAR) or completely at random (MCAR), and hence relate to the expectation–maximization (EM) algorithm (i.e., they exploit the sufficient spatial statistics). Griffith (1993a), extending Bennett et al. (1984), connects this solution to the kriging solution. More recently, LeSage and Pace (2004) rediscovered this particular solution. Analysis of covariance (ANCOVA) allows an extension of this solution to eigenvector spatial filtering (after Yates, 1933). The latter formulations enable their solutions to be expressed in terms of new observation predictions and their variances.

8.1. Kriging: an algebraic basis

Semi-variogram modeling (see Section 7.1) deals with the following $n \times n$ partitioned spatial covariance matrix, which captures spatial autocorrelation (Cliff and Ord, 1981) effects:

$$\Sigma \begin{pmatrix} \Sigma_{oo} & \Sigma_{om} \\ \Sigma_{mo} & \Sigma_{mm} \end{pmatrix} = \begin{pmatrix} \mathbf{V}_{oo} & \mathbf{V}_{oo} \\ \mathbf{V}_{oo} & \mathbf{V}_{oo} \end{pmatrix}^{-1} \sigma^2, \tag{8.1}$$

where the subscript o denotes observed data, the subscript m denotes missing data, and σ^2 is the error variance for response variable Y. The covariance matrix Σ_{oo} is estimated from sample data, with its structure described by a semi-variogram model. Weighted least squares furnishes parameter estimates for this model, and these yield a trend curve when substituted into the model specification (see Figure 2.5). Next, this structure description is borrowed for locations without observed values to construct and estimate Σ_{mo}, which in turn allows the calculation of imputations for a vector of missing values, $\mathbf{Y}_m$. Locational coordinates for the imputations relative to those for the observed values $\mathbf{Y}_o$ are the only ancillary information needed, given an assumption of stationarity across the geographic landscape under study. The resulting general kriging equation is (Christensen, 1991, p. 268)

$$\hat{\mathbf{Y}}_m = \mathbf{X}_m \boldsymbol{\beta} + \Sigma_{mo} \Sigma_{oo}^{-1} (\mathbf{Y}_o - \mathbf{X}_o \boldsymbol{\beta}), \tag{8.2}$$

where $\mathbf{X} = \mathbf{1}$ for ordinary kriging, and contains a covariate for co-kriging. For the case of no covariates, $\boldsymbol{\beta}_0 = \boldsymbol{\mu}$, and the geographic interpolation spreads deviations from a sample mean across a map. If spatial autocorrelation is zero, then $\Sigma_{oo}^{-1} = \mathbf{I}$ and $\Sigma_{mo} = \mathbf{0}$, and hence the interpolated value is the sample mean. This particular solution is the default one for many aspatial statistical software packages.

The continuous geographic distribution of temperature over a landscape lends itself to spatial interpolation (see Willmott and Matsuura, 1995). Its spatial interaction is one of mixing, implying that it should be described with a semi-variogram model having a range parameter, rather than a specific range. The exponential and Bessel function specifications (see Section 4.3.2) have this specific property. Puerto Rico has 84 weather stations currently operating (Figure 8.1a). Of these, 46 have sufficient data for calculating average annual maximum temperature (Figure 8.1c). Figure 8.2 portrays semi-variogram plots, with superimposed semi-variogram model trend lines, for this temperature. As with precipitation (see Figure 4.8), an inverse relationship exists between this temperature and elevation (Figure 8.1b): as elevation increases, temperature tends to decrease.

Figures 8.3a and 8.4a portray ordinary kriging interpolations for the sparse and non-randomly located currently operating climate stations (Figure 8.1c). These visualizations are sensible; both models imply decreasing temperature in the mountainous areas, and increasing temperatures in the southwest desert

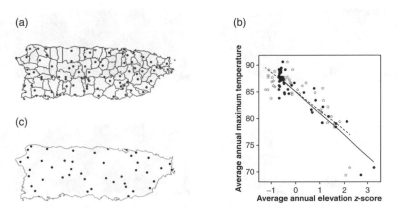

Figure 8.1 Eighty-four 2011 climate data gathering stations. (a) Full set of stations (http://www.sercc.com/climateinfo/historical/historical_pr.html). (b) Scatterplots of temperature versus elevation (solid dot, raw data; asterisk, transformed data). (c) Forty-six stations with recorded average annual maximum temperature.

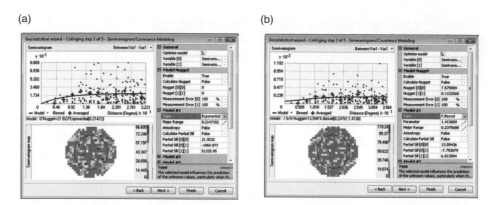

Figure 8.2 Co-kriging semi-variogram model estimation. (a) Exponential with
elevation covariate. (b) Bessel function with transformed elevation (i.e.,
DEM$^{0.35}$) covariate.

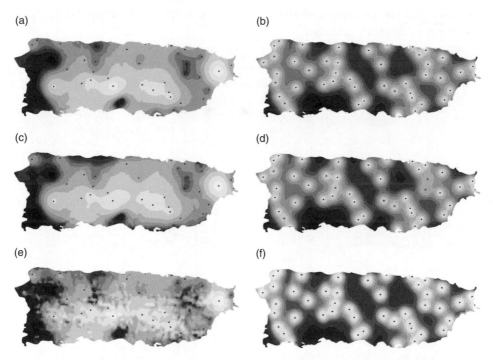

Figure 8.3 Exponential semi-variogram model interpolation of average annual
maximum temperature; from bright yellow to dark brown denotes
increasing temperature. (a) Kriged temperature. (b) Prediction error in
(a). (c) Kriged temperature exploiting a quadratic trend surface.
(d) Prediction error in (c). (e) Co-kriged temperature exploiting an elevation
covariate. (f) Prediction error in (e).

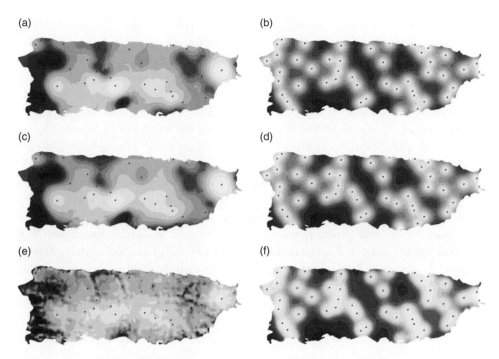

Figure 8.4 Bessel function semi-variogram model interpolation of average annual maximum temperature; from bright yellow to dark brown denotes increasing temperature. (a) Kriged temperature. (b) Prediction error in (a). (c) Kriged temperature exploiting a quadratic trend surface. (d) Prediction error in (c). (e) Co-kriged temperature exploiting a transformed elevation covariate. (f) Prediction error in (e).

region. The accompanying prediction error maps portray the typical higher levels of uncertainty for parts of the island without stations.

Given the nature of the physical landscape depicted in Figure 3.3, namely a mountain chain traversing the island from east to west, a quadratic trend surface could be employed to capture this physical feature (and the inverse relationship between temperature and elevation; see Figure 8.1b). Figures 8.3c and 8.4c furnish a slightly more sensible kriging interpolation of the temperature. Both the mountain range traversing much of the island and El Yunque (the mountain that dominates 28,000 acres of tropical forest on the eastern side of the island), become visible. This specification also results in the more traditional prediction error map pattern, with each operating climate station location surrounded by concentric rings of distance decaying precision.

Because a digital elevation model (DEM) exists for Puerto Rico, elevation can be used as a covariate for co-kriging. Although the preceding quadratic trend surface term may be used as an approximation of this elevation, a DEM removes much of the measurement error introduced by employing the quadratic approximation. Figures 8.3e and 8.4e furnish even more sensible depictions of the geographic distribution of average annual maximum temperature across the island; they contain far more detail than their Figure 8.3c and 8.4c counterparts. Moreover Figures 8.3c and 8.4c look like, and are, smoothed versions of Figures 8.3e and 8.4e. Because of the relationship between temperature and elevation (Figure 8.1b), the distance decay of precision is slower (Figures 8.3f and 8.4f).

One moral of this example is that additional information may not alter a krigged surface in a substantial way. Figures 8.3a and 8.4a represent the geographic distribution of temperature across Puerto Rico nearly as well as Figures 8.3e and 8.4e. Figures 8.3c and 8.4c mostly reflect the $X_m\beta$ term where matrix X contains the given first- and second-order polynomial terms of the imputation locational coordinates. Finally, Figures 8.3e and 8.4e mostly reflect the $X_m\beta$ term, where the matrix X contains either the DEM elevation values or their transformed values as a single covariate.

8.2. The EM algorithm[1]

Essentially the same imputation principles apply when a polygon surface partitioning is superimposed on geographic landscape (e.g., administrative areal units), data are post-stratified by these polygons, and some polygon values are missing (which is distinct from values of 0). The EM algorithm (Dempster et al., 1977), an iterative procedure for computing maximum likelihood estimates when datasets are incomplete, with data values being either MAR or MCAR, is a useful device for calculating the necessary imputations. Flury and Zoppè (2000, p. 209) emphasize "that the E-step does not simply involve replacing missing data by their conditional expectations (although this is true for many important applications of the algorithm)."

But, frequently, model-based estimation problems desire just this type of imputation output from the algorithm, especially for small geographic area estimation problems. Fortunately, traditional regression techniques render conditional expectations for missing values in a dataset that are equivalent to EM algorithm results when values are missing only in the response variable, Y.

---

[1] This section is based on Giffith (2010a).

Extending the notation used for equation (8.2), let $\mathbf{X}_o$ denote the matrix of covariate values for the set of observed response values, and $\mathbf{X}_m$ denote the matrix of covariate values for the set of missing response values (this problem specification is analogous to that for co-kriging). Furthermore, let $\mathbf{1}$ denote an $n \times 1$ vector of ones that can be partitioned into $\mathbf{1}_o$, denoting the vector of ones for the set of observed response values, and $\mathbf{1}_m$, denoting the vector of ones for the set of missing response values. Then the ANCOVA specification of the multiple regression model may be written in partitioned matrix form as

$$\begin{pmatrix} \mathbf{Y}_o \\ \mathbf{0}_m \end{pmatrix} = \begin{pmatrix} \mathbf{1}_o & \mathbf{X}_o \\ \mathbf{1}_m & \mathbf{X}_m \end{pmatrix} \begin{pmatrix} \beta_0 \\ \beta_X \end{pmatrix} + \begin{pmatrix} \mathbf{0}_{om} \\ -\mathbf{I}_{mm} \end{pmatrix} (\boldsymbol{\beta}_m) + \begin{pmatrix} \boldsymbol{\varepsilon}_o \\ \mathbf{0}_m \end{pmatrix}, \tag{8.3}$$

where $\mathbf{0}_j$ ($j = $ o, m) is an $n_j \times 1$ vector of zeroes, $\mathbf{0}_{om}$ is an $n_o \times n_m$ matrix of zeros, β_0 and β_X respectively are the intercept and slope multiple regression parameters, $\boldsymbol{\beta}_m$ is an $n_m \times 1$ vector of conditional expectations expressed as regression parameters, $\mathbf{I}_{mm}$ is an $n_m \times n_m$ identity matrix, and $\boldsymbol{\varepsilon}_o$ is an $n_o \times 1$ vector of random error terms. The ordinary least squares – as well as maximum likelihood – regression coefficient estimates, b_0 and $\mathbf{b}_X$, of β_0 and β_X, respectively, for this ANCOVA specification are given by

$$\begin{pmatrix} b_0 \\ \mathbf{b}_X \end{pmatrix} = \begin{pmatrix} n - n_m & \mathbf{1}_o^T \mathbf{X}_o \\ \mathbf{X}_o^T \mathbf{1}_o & \mathbf{X}_o^T \mathbf{X}_o \end{pmatrix}^{-1} \begin{pmatrix} \mathbf{1}_o^T \mathbf{Y}_o \\ \mathbf{X}_o^T \mathbf{Y}_o \end{pmatrix}, \tag{8.4}$$

where T denotes matrix transpose, which is the regression result for the observed data only. In addition, the regression coefficients, $\mathbf{b}_m$, for the indicator variables are given by

$$\mathbf{b}_m = b_0 \mathbf{1}_m + \mathbf{X}_m \mathbf{b}_X = \hat{\mathbf{Y}}_m, \tag{8.5}$$

which is the vector of point estimates for additional observations (i.e., the prediction of new observations) that practitioners recommend should have Y values within the interval defined by the extreme values contained in the vector $\mathbf{Y}_o$. In addition, the matrix

$$\begin{pmatrix} n_o & \mathbf{1}_o^T \mathbf{X}_o \\ \mathbf{X}_o^T \mathbf{1}_o & \mathbf{X}_o^T \mathbf{X}_o \end{pmatrix}$$

can become singular (seeGriffith, 2010a).

The standard error of the coefficients produced by equation (8.5) is given by

$$\mathbf{s}_{\mathbf{b}_m} = \sqrt{\langle [\mathbf{I}_{mm} + \mathbf{X}_m (\mathbf{X}_o^T \mathbf{X}_o)^{-1} \mathbf{X}_m^T] \rangle_{\text{diag}} \, \hat{\sigma}_{\varepsilon}^2}, \tag{8.6}$$

which is the well-known vector of standard errors for the point estimate prediction equation for new observations. The following is the bivariate regression equation upon which the EM solution is based:

predicted temperature $= 87.93526 - 0.00401 \times$ elevation, $R^2 = 0.8454.$

Equation (8.5) indicates that equation (8.2) uses this relationship between 46 pairs of data to impute 9,181 map values to compute 9,000+ imputations. A bivariate regression analysis of the relationship between predictions from these two equations indicates that EM imputations based upon elevation account for roughly 50% of the variation in the kriged values (Figure 8.5a). The prediction error is roughly equivalent on average; accounting for spatial autocorrelation introduces considerably more variability into the kriging prediction error than equation (8.6) produces (Figure 8.5b).

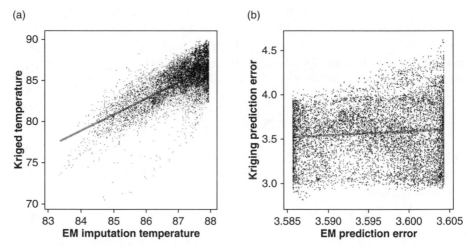

Figure 8.5   Scatterplots between kriging and EM results. (a) Imputations. (b) Prediction errors.

8.3. Spatial autoregression: a spatial EM algorithm

The preceding results can be extended to the simultaneous autoregressive (SAR) model specification (see Section 5.1) based upon the row standardized matrix $\mathbf{W}$:

$$\begin{pmatrix} \mathbf{Y}_o \\ \mathbf{0}_m \end{pmatrix} = \rho \mathbf{W} \begin{pmatrix} \mathbf{Y}_o \\ \mathbf{0}_m \end{pmatrix} + (\mathbf{I} - \rho \mathbf{W}) \mathbf{X} \boldsymbol{\beta} + \sum_{j=1}^{M} \gamma_j (-\mathbf{I}_m + \rho \mathbf{W}_{oj}^{\star}) + \boldsymbol{\varepsilon}, \qquad (8.7)$$

where $\mathbf{W}_{oj}^{\star}$ is the column of the geographic weights matrix $\mathbf{W}$ associated with the jth missing value, and M is the number of missing values. The particular solution equations are given by:

$$\hat{\mathbf{Y}}_m = \mathbf{X}_m \hat{\boldsymbol{\beta}}_o - \hat{\mathbf{V}}_{mm}^{-1} \hat{\mathbf{V}}_{mo} (\mathbf{Y}_o - \mathbf{X}_o \hat{\boldsymbol{\beta}}_o), \quad \text{where } \mathbf{V} = (\mathbf{I} - \rho \mathbf{W})^{\mathrm{T}} (\mathbf{I} - \rho \mathbf{W}),$$

and

$$s_{\hat{y}_m}^2 = \hat{\sigma}^2 \hat{\mathbf{V}}_{mm}^{-1} \{ \mathbf{I}_{mm} + \mathbf{A} \, [\mathbf{X}_o^{\mathrm{T}} \hat{\mathbf{V}}_{oo}^{-1} \mathbf{X}_o - \mathbf{X}_o^{\mathrm{T}} \hat{\mathbf{V}}_{mo} \hat{\mathbf{V}}_{mm}^{-1} \hat{\mathbf{V}}_{mo} \mathbf{X}_o]^{-1} \mathbf{A}^{\mathrm{T}} \}_{\text{diag}},$$

where $\mathbf{A} = \hat{\mathbf{V}}_{mo} \mathbf{X}_o + \hat{\mathbf{V}}_{mm} \mathbf{X}_m$. These are the predicted values and the predicted variances for new georeferenced observations. These variances reduce to those for the conventional prediction of new observations when zero SA is present. One of the differences between equations (8.3) and (8.7) is that the former yields a zero residual for imputed values, whereas the latter may well have non-zero residuals.

A cross-validation/jackknifing demonstration with a single suppressed value and employing equation (8.7) illustrates the utility of this specification in a way that enables an assessment of imputations. The DEM for Puerto Rico (Figures 3.3b and 4.12a) can be post-stratified into the island's 73 municipalities (Figure 8.6). Figure 8.6a portrays the transformed mean elevation[2] by municipality; Figure 8.6b portrays the Box–Cox transformed standard deviation of elevation by municipality. The SAR spatial autocorrelation parameter estimate is $\hat{\rho} = 0.7654$.

Figure 8.7a is the transformed mean elevation values scatterplot of observed versus equation (8.7) imputations. Calculation of these imputations included a single covariate, the transformed elevation standard deviation, which accounts for roughly 48% of the variation in the transformed mean elevation. The imputed values account for roughly 79% of the variation in their observed counterparts. Their regression equation is

predicted transformed elevation
   $= -0.3829 + 1.0732$ (imputed transformed elevation).

---

[2] The transformed elevation is given by $\ln(\text{mean elevation} + 17.5)$, and the standard deviation by $\sqrt{s_{\text{elevation}}} - 25$.

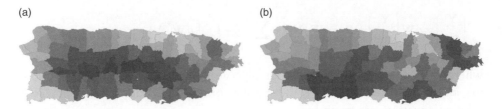

Figure 8.6   Box–Cox transformed geographically aggregated DEM elevation values. (a) Mean. (b) Standard deviation.

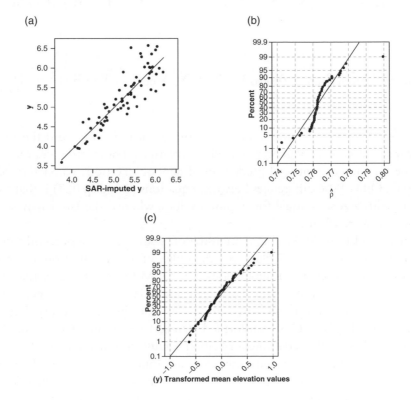

Figure 8.7   Transformed aggregated mean elevation (y). (a) Transformed mean elevation values scatterplot of observed versus equation (8.7 imputations. (b) Normal quantile plot for the 73 values of $\hat{\rho}$. (c) Normal quantile plot for the residuals (i.e., observed minus imputation).

Consequently, the imputations borrow strength from both a covariate and spatial autocorrelation.

The distribution of $\hat{\rho}$ deviates from a bell-shaped curve in both of its tails (Figure 8.7b). Its mean is 0.7633, which is slightly less than the estimate for the complete dataset (i.e., 0.7654), and its standard deviation is 0.0075, which is very small. The residuals essentially conform to a bell-shaped curve (Figure 8.7c). These results corroborate the usefulness of equation (8.7).

8.4. Eigenvector spatial filtering: another spatial EM algorithm

Here the particular solution equations are a special case of equation (8.5), and are given by

$$\hat{\mathbf{Y}}_m = \mathbf{X}_m \mathbf{b}_X + \mathbf{E}_{m,K} \mathbf{b}_{\mathbf{E}_K}, \tag{8.8}$$

$$\mathbf{s}^2_{Y_m} = \hat{\sigma}^2 \{ \mathbf{I}_m + \left(\mathbf{X}_m \quad \mathbf{E}_{mK} \right) \left[\left(\mathbf{X}_m \quad \mathbf{E}_{mK} \right)^{\mathrm{T}} \left(\mathbf{X}_m \quad \mathbf{E}_{mK} \right) \right]^{-1} \left(\mathbf{X}_m \quad \mathbf{E}_{mK} \right)^{\mathrm{T}} \}_{\mathrm{diag}} .$$

In terms of equation (8.3), equation (8.7) becomes

$$\begin{pmatrix} \mathbf{Y}_o \\ \mathbf{0}_m \end{pmatrix} = \alpha \mathbf{1} + \begin{pmatrix} \mathbf{X}_o \\ \mathbf{X}_m \end{pmatrix} \boldsymbol{\beta}_X - \sum_{j=1}^{M} y_j \begin{pmatrix} \mathbf{0}_o \\ \mathbf{I}_m \end{pmatrix} + \sum_{k=1}^{K} \begin{pmatrix} \mathbf{E}_{ok} \\ \mathbf{E}_{mk} \end{pmatrix} \boldsymbol{\beta}_{\mathbf{E}_k} + \boldsymbol{\varepsilon}. \tag{8.9}$$

As mentioned previously, these are the predicted values and the predicted variances for new georeferenced observations. The spatial filter can be constructed using stepwise regression procedures.

The Puerto Rican data analysis in Section 8.3 may be redone with the eigenvector spatial filtering technique. Figure 8.8a is the transformed mean elevation values scatterplot of observed versus equation (8.9) imputations. Calculation of these imputations included a single covariate, the transformed elevation standard deviation, which accounts for roughly 48% of the variation in the transformed mean elevation. The imputed values account for roughly 75% of the variation in their observed counterparts. Their regression equation is

   predicted transformed elevation
      = −0.4471 + 0.9123 (imputed transformed elevation).

Again, the imputations borrow strength from both a covariate and spatial autocorrelation.

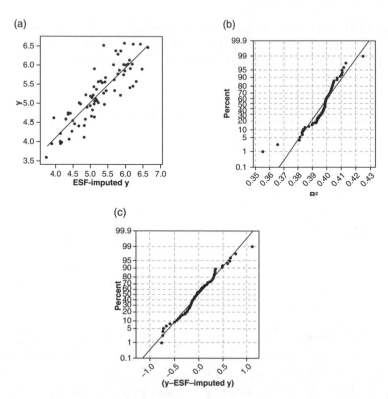

Figure 8.8   Transformed aggregated mean elevation (y). (a) Transformed mean elevation values scatterplot of observed versus equation (8.9) imputations. (b) Normal quantile plot for the 73 values of the R^2 increase attributable to each constructed spatial filter. (c) Normal quantile plot for the residuals (i.e., observed minus imputation).

    Twelve eigenvectors are selected by the complete dataset to account for spatial autocorrelation. Sixty-three of the 73 suppressed observation cases select all 12 when estimating their missing values. Two observations select 2 additional eigenvectors while selecting 8 of the 12 appearing in the complete data regression model. Three cases select only 11, another three select only 10, and yet another two select only 9 of the 12 eigenvectors appearing in the complete data regression model. The distribution of the resulting increase in the R^2 attributable to spatial autocorrelation deviates from a bell–shaped curve in its lower tail (Figure 8.8b), paralleling the finding for $\hat{\rho}$. Its mean is 0.3979, which is slightly less than the estimate for the complete dataset, and its standard deviation is 0.0101, which is very small. The residuals do conform to a bell–shaped curve (Figure 8.8c). These results corroborate the usefulness of equation (8.9).

One advantage of this spatial filter specification is that it supports a simple extension of this imputation methodology to the generalized linear model for spatial data. The appropriate stepwise binomial, Poisson, or negative binomial regression selects the appropriate eigenvectors to construct a spatial filter. Consider the 2007 percentage of farms utilizing irrigation, with mean rainfall as a covariate. The complete data logistic regression model results indicate that mean rainfall accounts for roughly 38% of the variance in this percentage, with eight eigenvectors indicating that spatial autocorrelation accounts for an additional 41%. Maximum pseudo-likelihood estimation[3] (see Huang and Ogata, 1999) reveals that spatial autocorrelation accounts for only an additional 10% of the variation with the auto-binomial model specification. Treating the eigenvector spatial filter imputations as new observation predictions produces missing-value estimates that account for roughly 56% of the variation in a percentage whose range is 0 to 0.400 (Figure 8.9b). They also can be estimated by setting the missing-value numerator to its denominator divided by 2 (i.e., the missing-value probability becomes 0.5, and hence the logit value becomes 0), and including the missing-value indicator variable.[4] Substituting a missing-value indicator variable regression coefficient into the logistic equation renders its missing-value percentage imputation. Of note is that, overall, the eigenvector spatial filter imputations are superior to the auto-binomial imputations (Figure 8.9a); the latter imputations account for roughly 38% of the variation in the observed percentages.

Next, consider the 2007 density of farms utilizing irrigation, with mean rainfall as a covariate. This density is a count, a Poisson random variable, divided by area, whose logarithm can be included in a generalized linear model as an offset variable. The complete-data Poisson regression model results indicate that mean rainfall and offset variable account for roughly 17% of the variance in this density, with seven eigenvectors indicating that positive spatial autocorrelation accounts for an additional 63%. The auto-Poisson cannot be employed for imputation purposes here because it cannot account for positive spatial autocorrelation. Treating the imputations as new observation predictions produces missing-value estimates that account for roughly 60% of the variation in a density whose rather narrow range is 0 to 1.78 (Figure 8.9c). They also can be estimated by setting the

---

[3] Maximum pseudo-likelihood estimation involves including the spatial lag term in a generalized linear model (GLM) to estimate the spatial autocorrelation parameter, without adjusting the normalizing factor. It is practical because the maximum likelihood estimates require Markov chain Monte Carlo (MCMC) techniques. It is flawed because its standard errors are statistically inefficient.

[4] This specification resulted in one of the 73 estimations failing to converge without modifying the default optimization technique.

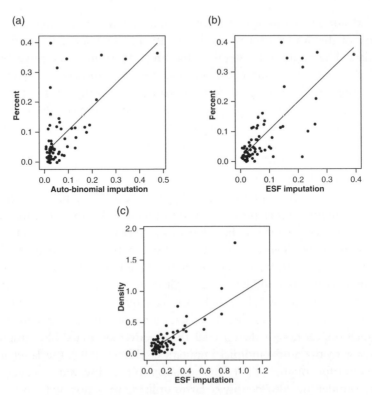

Figure 8.9 Generalized linear model imputations for farms utilizing irrigation.
(a) Auto-binomial random variable. (b) Eigenvector spatial filter and
binomial random variable. (c) Eigenvector spatial filter and Poisson
random variable.

missing value to 1 (i.e., its logarithm is 0), and including the missing-value indicator variable.[5] Taking the antilogarithm of a missing-value indicator variable
regression coefficient renders its missing-value count imputation.

8.5. R code for concept implementations

Computer Code 8.1 demonstrates the EM imputations for various distributions based upon normal, binomial, and Poisson regressions. For the normal
cases, the imputations have been calculated with different model specifications: a conventional non-spatial linear regression, an SAR model, and an

---

[5] This problem was simplified here by calculating imputations using only the eigenvectors
selected in the complete data analysis.

eigenvector spatial filter specification. For each of these specifications, imputations are computed 73 times, once for each observed value at a time being suppressed. For the binomial and Poisson cases, this computer code illustrates just one imputation, which is a typical situation encountered with empirical datasets. Regarding the eigenvector spatial filter EM specification for the binomial and Poisson regression cases, output was created with eigenvectors selected on the basis of statistical significance. As mentioned in Chapter 5, stepwise regression procedures using the AIC criterion tend to select more eigenvectors. The R code presented here generates results for both an AIC and a statistical significance selection criterion.

Kriging and co-kriging output reported in Section 8.1 was created with the ArcGIS Geostatistical Analyst extension (Figures 8.2–8.5). The corresponding R code in Computer Code 8.1 does not produce exactly the same results because the two software packages employ slightly different modeling assumptions and/or specifications (e.g., the number of neighbors used for interpolation, and the directional search for neighbors). Because the kriging results produced with R code are different from the ArcGIS results, the kriging versus EM imputation scatterplots (Figures 8.5 and 8.10) differ. In addition, the default mapping methods differ between ArcGIS Geostatistical Analyst and R. While the former creates kriged maps with a 'Filled Contours' option as its default, typically the latter creates levelplot kriged maps (similar to the ArcMap stretch option) with the *spplot()* function. This difference can be conspicuous for co-kriging prediction maps: Figures 8.3e and 8.4e (ArcGIS output) differ visually from Figure 8.11 (R output).

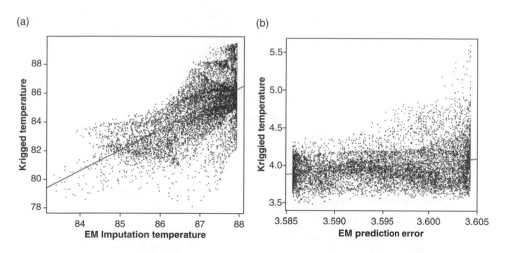

(a) (b)

Figure 8.10 Scatterplots between kriging and EM results obtained with R.
(a) Imputations. (b) Prediction errors.

(a)   (b)

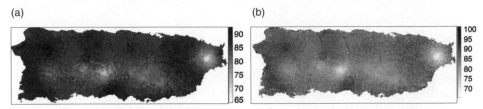

Figure 8.11   R output for co-kriging exploiting an elevation covariate (i.e., Figures 8.3e and 8.4e). (a) Exponential semi-variogram model co-kriged interpolation with elevation covariate. (b) Bessel function semi-variogram model co-kriged interpolation with transformed elevation covariate.

Computer Code 8.1. Implementing EM imputations in R.

```
library(spdep)                                   Load spdep and gstat packages.
library(gstat)

# 8.1
pr.outline <-                                    Read Puerto Rico outline shapefile.
readShapePoly("pr_outline.shp")
station <-                                        Read a shapefile of 46 weather stations
readShapePoints("stations46.shp")                in Puerto Rico.
plot(pr.outline)                                 Map the Puerto Rico outline and weather
plot(station, add=T, pch=20)                     stations.
plot(scale(station$elevation),                   Create a scatterplot of elevation vs.
station$temperatur, pch=20)                       temperature.
stn.df <- as.data.frame(station)                 Store the attributes of the station
                                                 shapefile in a data frame.

# kriging out grid
pr <- readShapePoly("PuertoRico.shp")            Read Puerto Rico shapefile.
pr.reg <- coordinates(spsample(pr, 100000,       Draw regular random sample points for x,
type="regular"))                                 y coordinates for kriging predictions.
colnames(pr.reg) <- c("x", "y")                  Set column names.
pr.grid <-                                        Convert spatial points into spatial
SpatialPixels(SpatialPoints(pr.reg))             pixel.

# kriging (exponential model)
t.v <- variogram(temperatur ~ 1, station)        Create a variogram.
t.vf.exp <- fit.variogram(t.v,                   Fit the variogram with an exponential
vgm(20,"Exp", 0.25, 3))                           model.
ok.t.exp <- krige(temperatur ~ 1, station,       Conduct kriging with the exponential
pr.grid, t.vf.exp)                               model.
color.pal <- colorRampPalette(c("dark            Set color ramps to be used for mapping
red","orange","light Yellow"))                   kriging predictions and errors.
color.palr <- colorRampPalette(c("light
yellow","orange","dark red"))
spplot(ok.t.exp["var1.pred"],                    Map the kriging predictions.
col.regions=color.pal)
spplot(ok.t.exp["var1.var"],                     Map the kriging variances.
col.regions=color.palr)

# kriging with quadratic trend (exponential
model)
t.v.tr <- gstat(NULL, "temp", temperatur ~       Specify a model quadratic trend.
x^2 + x*y + y^2, station)
t.vm.tr <- variogram(t.v.tr)                      Create a variogram.
t.vf.tr.exp <- fit.lmc(t.vm.tr , t.v.tr,         Fit the variogram with an exponential
vgm(15,"Exp", 0.25, 4))                           model.
t.tr.exp <- predict(t.vf.tr.exp, pr.grid)
spplot(t.tr.exp["temp.pred"],                    Map kriging predictions.
col.regions=color.pal)
spplot(t.tr.exp["temp.var"],                     Map kriging variances.
col.regions=color.palr)

# co-kriging with elevation (exponential
model)
rs.temp <- read.csv("pr_elev_rs.csv")            Read elevation data file (from a raster).
rs.pts <- SpatialPoints(                          Create spatial points with x, y
cbind(rs.temp[,c("x","y")]))                      coordinates in the elevation data file.
rs.spf <- SpatialPointsDataFrame(rs.pts,         Create a SpatialPointsDataFrame object.
rs.temp)

t.ck.v <- gstat(NULL, "temp", temperatur ~       Specify a model with the previous
1, station, model=t.vf.exp)                       exponential model.
vov <- var(rs.temp$elevation) /                  Calculate a ratio of variance.
var(station$temperatur)
```

| ```r
rs.vf.exp <- t.vf.exp
rs.vf.exp$psill <- t.vf.exp$psill * vov
t.ck.v <- gstat(t.ck.v, "elev", elevation ~
1, rs.spf, nmax=8, model=rs.vf.exp)
co.vf.exp <- t.vf.exp
co.vf.exp$psill <- sqrt(t.vf.exp$psill *
rs.vf.exp$psill) * cor(station$elevation,
station$temperatur)
t.ck.v <- gstat(t.ck.v, c("temp", "elev"),
model=co.vf.exp)
ck.x.exp <- predict(t.ck.v, pr.grid)
spplot(ck.x.exp["temp.pred"],
col.regions=color.pal)
spplot(ck.x.exp["temp.var"],
col.regions=color.palr)
``` | Adjust the partial sill with the variance ratio for the second factor. Add the variogram.<br><br>Adjust the partial sill for cross-variogram with the correlation.<br><br>Add the co-variogram.<br><br>Conduct co-kriging.<br>Map co-kriging predictions.<br><br>Map co-kriging variances. |
| ```r
# kriging (bessel model)
t.v <- variogram(temperatur ~ 1, station)
t.vf.bes <- fit.variogram(t.v,
vgm(10,"Bes", 0.18, 5))
ok.t.bes <- krige(temperatur ~ 1, station,
pr.grid, t.vf.bes)
spplot(ok.t.bes["var1.pred"],
col.regions=color.pal)
spplot(ok.t.bes["var1.var"],
col.regions=color.palr)
``` | Similarly conduct kriging with a Bessel function.<br><br><br><br>Map the kriging prediction.<br><br>Map the kriging variances. |
| ```r
# kriging with quadratic trend (bessel
model)
t.v.tr <- gstat(NULL, "temp", temperatur ~
x^2 + x*y + y^2, station)
t.vm.tr <- variogram(t.v.tr)
t.vf.tr.bes <- fit.lmc(t.vm.tr , t.v.tr,
vgm(10,"Bes", 0.18, 5))
t.tr.bes <- predict(t.vf.tr.exp, pr.grid)
spplot(t.tr.bes["temp.pred"],
col.regions=color.pal)
spplot(t.tr.bes["temp.var"],
col.regions=color.palr)
``` | Similarly conduct kriging with a quadratic trend and a Bessel function.<br><br><br><br><br><br>Map the kriging prediction.<br><br>Map the kriging variances. |
| ```r
# co-kriging with elevation (bessel model)
t.ck.v <- gstat(NULL, "temp", temperatur ~
1, station, model=t.vf.bes)
rs.vf.bes <- t.vf.bes
vov <-
var(rs.temp$elevation^0.35)/var(station$tem
peratur)
rs.vf.bes$psill <- t.vf.bes$psill * vov
t.ck.v <- gstat(t.ck.v, "elev",
elevation^0.35 ~ 1, rs.spf, nmax=8,
model=rs.vf.bes)
co.vf.bes <- t.vf.bes
co.vf.bes$psill <- sqrt(t.vf.bes$psill *
rs.vf.bes$psill)*cor(station$elevation^0.35
, station$temperatur)
t.ck.v <- gstat(t.ck.v, c("temp", "elev"),
model=co.vf.bes)
ck.x.bes <- predict(t.ck.v, pr.grid)
spplot(ck.x.bes["temp.pred"],
col.regions=color.pal)
spplot(ck.x.bes["temp.var"],
col.regions=color.palr)
``` | Similarly conduct co-kriging with a Bessel function.<br><br><br><br><br><br><br><br><br><br><br><br><br><br><br><br>Map co-kriging predictions.<br><br>Map co-kriging variances. |

```# 8.2: EM Linear model specification```	
```em.lm <- lm(temperatur ~ elevation,```	Conduct linear regression model between
```data=station)```	temperature and elevation.
```summary(em.lm)```	Report the regression results.
```elev.obs <-```	Store elevation data in a data frame.
```data.frame(elevation=rs.temp$elevation)```	
```em.lm.pred <- predict(em.lm, elev.obs,```	Conduct predictions.
```interval="prediction")```	
```# predicted values```	
```kr.pts <- overlay(t.tr.exp["temp.pred"],```	Find overlapped locations with 'rs.pts'
```rs.pts)```	spatial points among kriging predictions.
```kr.pred <- as.data.frame(```	Get values of the overlapped locations.
```t.tr.exp["temp.pred"])[kr.pts,]```	
```plot(em.lm.pred[,"fit"], kr.pred$temp.pred,```	Create a scatterplot of kriging
```pch=20, cex=0.5, xlab="EM Imputation```	predictions vs. EM imputations.
```temperature", ylab="krigged temperature")```	
```abline(lm(kr.pred$temp.pred~em.lm.pred[,"fi```	Add a trend line.
```t"]),col=4, lwd=2)```	
```# errors```	
```kr.var <-```	Similarly create a scatterplot of kriging
```as.data.frame(t.tr.exp["temp.var"])[kr.pts,```	variance vs. EM prediction errors.
```]```	
```der <- em.lm.pred[,"upr"] -```	
```em.lm.pred[,"fit"]```	
```plot(der, sqrt(kr.var$temp.var), pch=20,```	
```cex=0.5, xlab="EM prediction error",```	
```ylab="krigged prediction error")```	
```abline(lm(sqrt(kr.var$temp.var)~der),col=4,```	
```lwd=2)```	
```# 8.3 spatial EM```	
```pr.farm <- read.csv("PR-farm-data.csv")```	Read Puerto Rico farm data.
```elev.mean.tr <- log(pr.farm$elev_mean +```	Transform two variables: means and
```17.5)```	standard deviations of elevations.
```elev.std.tr <- sqrt(pr.farm$elev_std - 25)```	
```source("all_functions.R")```	Load functions.
```mapping.seq(pr, elev.mean.tr, 9, main="Mean```	Map the transformed means of elevation.
```Elevation")```	
```mapping.seq(pr, elev.std.tr, 9,```	Map the transformed standard deviations
```main="Eelvation Standard Deviation")```	of elevations.
```pr.nb <- read.gal("PuertoRico.gal")```	Load a GAL file.
```pr.listw <- nb2listw(pr.nb, style="W")```	Create a *listw* object.
```errorsarlm(elev.mean.tr ~ elev.std.tr,```	Get an estimate for the spatial
```listw=pr.listw)$lambda```	autocorrelation parameter.
```n <- length(pr.nb)```	Get the number of observations.
```x <- elev.std.tr```	Make 'x' variable from 'elev.std.tr.'
```wx <- lag.listw(pr.listw, x)```	Create a spatially lagged variable.
```eig.values <- eigenw(pr.listw)```	Get eigenvalues of a spatial weight
```rho.range <- 1/range(eig.values)```	matrix and set the parameter space for
	rho.
```em.sar.out <- matrix(0,n,4)```	Create an object to store outputs.
```colnames(em.sar.out) <- c("rho","b0","b1",```	Set column names.
```"ymp")```	
```fr <- function(pars, y, wy, x, wx,```	Define a function to be optimized.
```eig.values, imp, cimp) {```	
``` rho <- pars[1]```	Get four parameters passed in pars

```
  b0 <- pars[2]
  b1 <- pars[3]
  ymp <- pars[4]
  jacob <- sum(log(1 - rho*eig.values))
  j <- exp(jacob/72)
  sum(((rho*wy + b0*(1-rho) + b1*(x -
rho*wx) + ymp*(imp + rho*cimp)-y)/j)^2)
}
```

object.

Calculate a Jacobian term.

Set a model to be minimized.

```
grr <- function(pars, y, wy, x, wx,
eig.values, imp, cimp) {
  rho <- pars[1]
  b0 <- pars[2]
  b1 <- pars[3]
  ymp <- pars[4]

  jacob <- sum(log(1 - rho*eig.values))
  j <- exp(jacob/72)
  derj <-  sum(eig.values/(1 - rho *
eig.values))/72

  expr1 <- 1 - rho
  expr2 <- x - rho * wx
  expr3 <- imp + rho * cimp
  expr4 <- rho * wy + b0 * expr1 + b1 *
expr2 + ymp * expr3 - y

  g.rho <- sum(2 * ((wy - b0 - b1*wx + ymp
* cimp)/j + expr4 * j* derj/j^2) * expr4/j)
  g.b0 <-   sum(2 * expr1/j * expr4/j)
  g.b1 <-   sum(2 * expr2/j * expr4/j)
  g.ymp <- sum(2 * expr3/j * expr4/j)
  c(g.rho, g.b0, g.b1, g.ymp)
}
```

Define derivatives for the parameters.

Set equations to be used in the
derivatives.

Derivative for rho, b0, b1, and ymp
parameters, respectively.

Return the derivatives.

```
get.cimp <- function(x, listw){
  n <- length(listw$neighbours)
  cimp <- rep(0,n)
  nbs <- pr.listw$neighbours[[i]]
  for (j in 1:length(nbs)) {
    c.nb <- nbs[j]
    c.nb.i <-
    pr.listw$neighbours[[c.nb]]==i
    cimp[c.nb] <-
    pr.listw$weights[[c.nb]][c.nb.i]
  }
  return(cimp)
}
```

Define a function to create W_{oj}^{*} in
equation (8.7).

```
for (i in 1:n) {
  y <- elev.mean.tr
  y[i] <- 0
  wy <- lag.listw(pr.listw, y)

  cimp <- get.cimp(i, pr.listw)
  imp <- rep(0,n)
  imp[i] <- -1
  opt <- nlminb(c(rho=0.5, b0=0, b1=0,
  ymp=0), fr, grr, y=y, wy=wy, x=x, wx=wx,
  eig.values=eig.values, imp=imp,
  cimp=cimp, lower=c(rho.range[1], rep(-
  Inf,3)), upper=c(rho.range[2],
  rep(Inf,3)), control=list(iter.max=1000))
```

Repeat imputations setting one
observation missing (replacing an
observation with zero).
Get spatially lagged dependent variable.

Calculate W_{oj}^{*} in equation (8.7).

Imp with -1 for the missing observation
and 0 for the other observations.
Fit the nonlinear model optimizing *fr()*
function.

```
   em.sar.out[i,] <- opt$par                Store the results.
}

lm.em.sar <-
lm(elev.mean.tr~em.sar.out[,4])             Examine the model fit.
summary(lm.em.sar)
plot(em.sar.out[,4], elev.mean.tr, pch=20)
abline(lm.em.sar)                           Scatterplot of SAR imputations vs.
                                            observations.
qqnorm(em.sar.out[,1],pch=20)
qqline(em.sar.out[,1])                       Normal-quantile plot.
mean(em.sar.out[,1])
sd(em.sar.out[,1])                          Mean and standard deviations of estimated
                                            rho parameters.
resids <- elev.mean.tr - em.sar.out[,4]
qqnorm(resids, pch=20)                       Get residuals
qqline(resids)                               Create a normal-quantile plot.


# 8.4: Eigenvector spatial filtering EM

# normal
evec <- read.table("pr_evecs.txt",
header=T)                                    Read eigenvectors from a file.
EV <- evec[,-(1:2)]

elev.base <- lm(elev.mean.tr ~ elev.std.tr)
summary(elev.base)$r.squared
elev.full <- lm(elev.mean.tr ~ elev.std.tr
+ ., data=EV)                                Run a stepwise linear regression model
elev.sf <- stepwise.forward(elev.full,       with the candidate set of eigenvectors.
lm(elev.mean.tr ~ elev.std.tr, data=EV),
0.1, verbose=F)                              Relation between means and standard
                                             deviations of elevations.
n <- length(elev.mean.tr)
esf.em.out <- matrix(NA, n, 2)
colnames(esf.em.out) <- c("imputed", "# of   Set up an output object and its column
EVs")                                        names.
for (i in 1:n){
  y <- elev.mean.tr                          Repeat the ESF EM estimation replacing
  y[i] <- 0                                  one observation with zero at a time.
  iv <- rep(0,n)
  iv[i] <- -1                                A variable with -1 for missing
                                             observation and 0 for the others.
  xyEV <- as.data.frame(cbind(y,
x=elev.std.tr, EV, iv))
  elev.base <- lm(y ~ x, data=xyEV)
  elev.full <- lm(y ~ iv + ., data=xyEV)     Stepwise regression.
  elev.sf <- stepwise.forward(elev.full,
lm(y ~ iv + x, data=xyEV), 0.1,
verbose=FALSE)
  esf.em.out[i,1] <-
elev.sf$coefficients[2]                      Save the imputations and the number of
  esf.em.out[i,2] <- elev.sf$rank-1          selected eigenvectors.
}

imp.lm <- lm(elev.mean.tr~esf.em.out[,1])
plot(esf.em.out[,1], elev.mean.tr, pch=20)   Examine the imputation results.
abline(lm(elev.mean.tr~esf.em.out[,1]))      Create a scatterplot of imputations vs.
                                             observations.
resids <- elev.mean.tr - esf.em.out[,1]
qqnorm(resids, pch=20)                        Get residuals and create a normal-
qqline(resids)                                quantile plot.
```

Code	Comment

`r.sqs <- matrix(NA, n, 2)`
`colnames(r.sqs) <- c("r.sq", "base.sq")`
`for (i in 1:n){`
`  yx <- elev.mean.tr`
`  iv <- rep(0,n)`
`  yx[i] <- NA`
 	
`  xyEV <- as.data.frame(cbind(yx,`
`x=elev.std.tr, EV))`
`  elev.full <- lm(yx ~ ., data=xyEV)`
`  elev.sf <- stepwise.forward(elev.full,`
`lm(yx ~ x, data=xyEV), 0.1, verbose=FALSE)`
`  elev.base <- lm(yx ~ x, data=xyEV)`
`  r.sqs[i,1] <- summary(elev.sf)$r.squared`
`  r.sqs[i,2] <-`
`summary(elev.base)$r.squared`
`}`
	Calculate increases of R2 by the selected eigenvectors (in order to create Figure 8.8c).

`r.sq.inc <- r.sqs[,1] - r.sqs[,2]`
`qqnorm(r.sq.inc, pch=20)`
`qqline(r.sq.inc)`
`mean(r.sq.inc)`
	Normal-quantile plot (Figure 8.8c)

`# Auto-binomial`
`fp <-`
`pr.farm$irr_farms_07/pr.farm$nofarms_07`
`fp.col <- cbind(pr.farm$irr_farms_07,`
`pr.farm$nofarms_07-pr.farm$irr_farms_07)`
`rain <- pr.farm$rain_mean`
	Get the rates of irrigated farms
	
	Combine numbers of irrigated farms and irrigated farms into one object.
	Get mean rainfalls.

`i <- 1`
`y.i <- pr.farm$irr_farms_07`
`y.i[i] <- 0`
`wy <- lag.listw(pr.listw, y.i)`
`y <- fp.col`
`y[i,] <- pr.farm$nofarms_07[i]/2`
	Set ith observation missing.
	
	Calculate spatial lagged variable.
	
	The ith observation is set to the half of the total number of farms.

`iv <- rep(0,n)`
`iv[i] <- -1`
`cimp <- get.cimp(i, pr.listw)`
	A variable with -1 for missing observation and 0 for the others.
	Calculate W_{oj}^* in equation (8.7).

`ab.s1 <- glm(y ~ wy + rain + iv + cimp,`
`family=binomial)`
`appimp <- iv + ab.s1$coefficient["wy"]*cimp`
`ab.s2 <- glm(y ~ wy + rain + appimp,`
`family=binomial)`
	Get approximate estimation of rho at the first step.
	And then the imputation at the second step using the estimate of rho.

`inv.logit(ab.s2$coefficient["appimp"])`	Calculate inverse of logit.
`# ESF binomial`	Similarly, conduct ESF binomial EM.

`eb.base <- glm(fp.col ~ rain,`
`family=binomial)`
`summary(lm(fp~eb.base$fitted.values))$r.squared`
	Binomial regression only with means of rain.

`i <- 1` `y[i,] <- pr.farm$nofarms_07[i]/2`	The 1st observation is set missing. Replace its value with the half of total number of farms.
`iv <- rep(0,n)` `iv[i] <- -1`	A variable with -1 for missing observation and 0 for the others.

| ```
fp.full <- glm(y ~ rain + iv + ., data=EV,
family=quasibinomial)
disp <- summary(fp.full)$dispersion
fp.sf <- stepAIC(glm(y ~ rain + iv,
data=EV, family=binomial), scale=disp,
scope=list(upper=fp.full),
direction="forward", trace=0)
summary(fp.sf)
``` | Eigenvector spatial filtering with AIC criterion. |
| ```
sel.ev <- c(2,4,9,10,12,14,16,17)
sel <- as.matrix(EV[,sel.ev])
fp.sf <- glm(fp.col ~ rain + iv + sel,
family=binomial)
``` | Read the result in the textbook (i.e., the selected eigenvectors). Eigenvector spatial filter model with the selected eigenvectors. |
| ```
library(dispmod)
fp.sf.w <- glm.binomial.disp(fp.sf)
``` | Logistic regression following Williams's procedure to control overdispersion. |
| ```
inv.logit(fp.sf.w$coefficient[3])
fp[i]
``` | Compare imputation and observation. |
| ```
# ESF Poisson
irr.07 <- pr.farm$irr_farms_07
irr.base <- glm(irr.07 ~ rain,
offset=log(pr.farm$area),
family=quasipoisson)
``` | Similarly conduct eigenvector spatial filtering for Poisson case. |
| ```
i <- 1
iv <- rep(0,n)
irr.07[i] <- 1
iv[i] <- -1
xyEV <- as.data.frame(cbind(irr.07, rain,
EV))
``` | Replace the observation with 1. |
| ```
irr.full <- glm(irr.07 ~ rain + iv + .,
data=EV, offset=log(pr.farm$area),
family=quasipoisson)
irr.sf <- stepAIC(glm(irr.07 ~ rain + iv,
data=EV, offset=log(pr.farm$area),
family=poisson),
           scope=list(upper=irr.full),
direction="forward", trace=0)
``` | |
| ```
sel.ev <- names(irr.sf$coefficients)[4:10]
sel <- as.matrix(EV[,sel.ev])
irr.sf <- glm(irr.07  ~ rain + iv + sel,
offset=log(pr.farm$area), family=poisson)
pr.farm$irr_farms_07[i]/pr.farm$area[i]
exp(irr.sf$coefficients[3])/pr.farm$area[i]
``` | Read the result in the textbook (i.e., the selected eigenvectors). |

9

More Advanced Topics in
Spatial Statistics

LEARNING OBJECTIVES:

- To introduce additional, selected advanced topics in spatial statistics
- To highlight Bayesian map analysis
- To outline and demonstrate the designing of Monte Carlo spatial simulation experiments
- To raise awareness about spatial error and uncertainty

Chapters 2–8 address the standard range of conventional topics in spatial statistics. Spatial autocorrelation is the unifying concept spanning these chapters. But other more advanced themes merit comment, too. Three such topics are noteworthy, and hence are discussed in this chapter.

The frequently used statistical methods of Chapters 2–8 are known as frequentist methods, which assume that unknown parameters are fixed constants; and affiliated probability distributions consist of relative frequencies. A competing view, known as Bayesian methods, assumes that unknown parameters are random variables having distributions, and affiliated probability distributions reflect degrees of belief. Bayes's theorem furnishes the basis for this latter perspective, and more recent developments in computing have made widespread Bayesian analysis feasible. Table 9.1 furnishes a selected comparison between the two statistical approaches. Of note is that for many (but not all) simple statistical problems where frequentist methodology appears to yield satisfying answers, with relatively non-subjective assumptions, the Bayesian approach yields basically the same answers.

Chapter 3 presents the bootstrap and jackknife resampling techniques. It alludes to the more general technique of Monte Carlo simulation. Bayesian numerical estimation techniques also employ Monte Carlo simulation. As with the bootstrap, pseudo-random number generators play critical roles in the execution of a Monte Carlo simulation experiment. Such experiments exploit two crucial statistical theorems: the central limit theorem and the law of large numbers. Monte Carlo spatial simulation experiments furnish an invaluable tool for spatial statistics because this branch of statistics often deals with mathematically intractable statistical problems, and has a paucity of analytical solutions.

Finally, Chapter 8 emphasizes the utility of prediction error maps: in kriging, for example, mean response maps always should be accompanied by prediction error maps. Researchers need to be aware of sources of error in spatial data, as well as how spatial autocorrelation impacts these sources.

9.1. Bayesian methods for spatial data

This section discusses two closely linked features of spatial analysis: Bayesian methods and mixed models. Bayesian methods involve positing prior statistical distributions governing parameters (see Kass and Wasserman, 1996, for some selection guidelines). These distributions combine with the likelihood function for a sample of data, resulting in complex normalizing factors (see the discussion of weighting functions in Section 5.1). The resulting combination is a posterior distribution constituting the basis for statistical decisions (Gelman, 2002). Figure 9.1 illustrates that posited prior distributions dominate for very small samples, whereas a likelihood function dominates for very large samples. The differentiation between the likelihood and the prior distributions results in this specification being called a hierarchical Bayes model. WinBUGS (Cowles, 2004) is one software package supporting both – its GeoBUGS module supports Bayesian map analysis – while SAS is another software package starting to support both.

Mixed models introduce an additional random component, a random effects term ξ, (i.e., n effects, one for each observation) into a model specification such as equation (5.2):

$$\mathbf{Y} = \mathbf{X}\boldsymbol{\beta} + \boldsymbol{\xi} + \boldsymbol{\varepsilon}. \tag{9.1}$$

Table 9.1 Some comparisons between frequentist and Bayesian perspectives

Feature	Frequentist	Bayesian
Definition of probability	Long-run expected frequency in repeated (actual or hypothetical) experiments (law of large numbers)	Relative degree of belief in the state of the world
Point estimate	Maximum likelihood estimate	Mean, mode, or median of the posterior probability distribution
Confidence intervals for parameters	Based on the likelihood ratio test (LRT); i.e., the expected probability distribution of the maximum likelihood estimate over many experiments	"Credible intervals" based on the posterior probability distribution
Confidence intervals for non-parameters	Based on likelihood profile/LRT, or by resampling from the sampling distribution of the parameter	Calculated directly from the distribution of parameters
Model selection	Discard terms that are not significantly different from a nested (null) model at a previously set confidence level	Retain terms in models, on the argument that processes are not absent simply because they are not statistically significant
Difficulties	Confidence intervals are confusing (range that will contain the true value in a proportion α of repeated experiments); rejection of model terms for "non-significance"	Subjectivity; need to specify priors

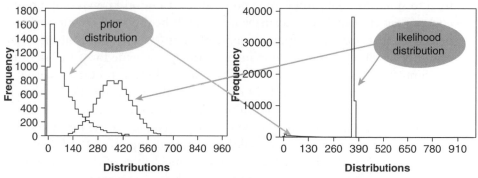

Figure 9.1 A contrast of relative importance of a prior distribution and its accompanying likelihood function.

A critical estimation problem here involves the ability to differentiate between ξ and ε, rather than specifying a single composite error term. A frequentist solution is to include repeated measures. In spatial statistics, these often are measures through time at each location in a sample. Although it also may include repeated measures, a Bayesian solution may be to posit a prior distribution for each term. Regardless, the random effects term frequently has both a spatially structured and a spatially unstructured component. The spatially structured component becomes a property of parameters, and, as such, directly relates to an eigenvector spatial filter. Furthermore, because of complexity, implementation of a random effects term often involves only the intercept of a model specification. The accompanying assumption is that the intercept is a random outcome variable that is a function of a mean value (the conventional constant intercept term) plus a random error. The frequentist approach integrates this term out via, say, empirical Bayes techniques; the Bayesian approach uses prior distributions to construct a separate distribution for each of the n random effects in the term.

9.1.1. Markov chain Monte Carlo techniques

Historically, the complexity of normalizing factors in Bayesian analysis restricted implementations to those cases having analytical solutions (i.e., the conjugate prior cases). Today, the combination of Markov chain theory and Monte Carlo simulation techniques enables implementation for a much wider range of prior–likelihood pairings. Markov chain Monte Carlo (MCMC) is used to simulate values from some posterior distribution known only up to a constant factor, namely the normalizing factor. It begins with conditional (i.e., prior) distributions, and outputs a sample of parameters drawn from the target posterior distribution. Gibbs sampling is a principal scheme for spatial statistics for simulating from the posterior distribution, where a transition kernel is formed by the full conditional distributions of the posterior distribution in question. The Gibbs sampling algorithm takes each location in turn, simulates a result for it, and substitutes that result into the sample for the location's previous value before moving to another location. In doing this, MCMC exploits the sufficient statistics. Figure 9.2 portrays the mechanics of this procedure.

One serious consideration in this type of analysis is convergence of a generated Markov chain. Each iteration can be treated as a point in time, allowing employment of time series techniques for diagnostic purposes. An analyst must discard the beginning set of simulated results (i.e., the burn-in period) to avoid arbitrary initial parameter estimates corrupting the final estimates. Next, assessment of a time-series correlogram reveals whether or not sequential iterations contain serial correlation. In cases where substantial serial correlation exists, a chain should be weeded (i.e., only every *k*th output is retained). The trade-off here is the need to generate considerably more iterations in order to obtain uncorrelated outcomes. Fitting a trend line to the resulting sample values (i.e., bivariate regression of simulated values on iteration number) should yield a trend-line slope of essentially zero. Finally, a comparison of multiple chains, say with ANOVA techniques, furnishes information regarding convergence: within-chains variance should dominate between–chains variance.

Incorporation of spatial structure conventionally involves a conditional autoregressive (CAR) model specification for the random effects term. This specification employs a smaller geographic field and captures a weaker level of spatial correlation than the SAR model described in Section 5.1. Because of difficulties in estimating the spatial autocorrelation parameter for this specification, analysts frequently include an improper CAR (ICAR) model, where the spatial autocorrelation parameter is set to its maximum value, followed by estimation of a spatially unstructured random effects term (see Lavine and Hodges, 2012). The final terms are the relative variances for these two terms.

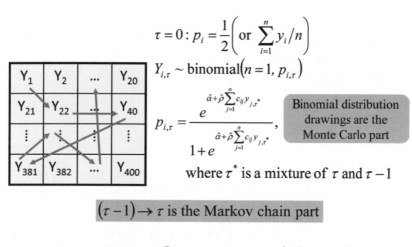

$$\tau = 0 : p_i = \frac{1}{2}\left(\text{or} \ \sum_{i=1}^{n} y_i / n \right)$$

$$Y_{i,\tau} \sim \text{binomial}\left(n = 1, p_{i,\tau}\right)$$

$$p_{i,\tau} = \frac{e^{\hat{\alpha} + \hat{\rho}\sum_{j=1}^{n} c_{ij} y_{j,\tau^*}}}{1 + e^{\hat{\alpha} + \hat{\rho}\sum_{j=1}^{n} c_{ij} y_{j,\tau^*}}},$$

Binomial distribution drawings are the Monte Carlo part

where τ^* is a mixture of τ and $\tau - 1$

$(\tau - 1) \rightarrow \tau$ is the Markov chain part

$$\text{Sufficient statistics} : T_{1,\tau} = \sum_{i=1}^{n} y_{i,\tau} \times 1 \quad \& \quad T_{2,\tau} = \frac{1}{2}\sum_{i=1}^{n} y_{i,\tau} \times \sum_{j=1}^{n} c_{ij} y_{j,\tau}$$

Figure 9.2 Features of an MCMC iteration.

9.1.2. Selected Puerto Rico examples

Consider the percentage of urban population across Puerto Rico in 2000. Computer Code 9.1 reports the code for implementing this analysis in WinBUGS. The prior distribution for the binomial regression intercept parameter is uniform; *dflat* is a special WinBUGS version of this distribution, because the intercept can range between plus and minus infinity. WinBUGS results obtained for this problem were replicated with the Bayes option in SAS PROC GENMOD. (Both used a seed of 362309067.)

Figure 9.3 displays the WinBUGS output. The intercept estimate is 2.834, with a standard error estimate of 0.002; corresponding frequentist estimates are identical. The burn-in period used is 1,000. The effective number of parameters estimated (pD) is 1. The correlogram exhibits only trace serial correlation. The 95% credibility interval is (2.380, 2.389). The posterior distribution appears to be approximately normal. More specifically, the bivariate regression slope coefficient estimate for the chain is 1.1×10^{-8}, $P(|t| > 1.41) = 0.160$. Figure 9.4 shows how well the posterior distribution corresponds to a bell-shaped curve.

Computer Code 9.1. WinBUGS code for simple binomial regression analysis.

```
#MODEL
model
{
for (i in 1 : N) {
    U[i]   ~ dbin(p[i], T[i])
    p[i] <- 1/(1+exp(-alpha))
}
# Other priors:
alpha ~ dflat()
}
#DATA
list(N = 73,
U = c(42527, 64685, 36201, 30886, 59572,24196, 36971, 33421,
37713, 185703, 50242, 63929, 38583, 18664, 75728,27605, 35270,
25584, 29709, 25387, 35476, 27305, 11048, 3792, 16800,95880,
11062, 2839, 23077, 23364, 34650, 178792, 40875, 16472,
23848,21330, 94085, 91593, 41997, 434374, 99850, 42042, 14767,
14262, 23852,139445, 21499, 40457, 35130, 43707, 46236, 20682,
17200, 32126, 35859, 27850, 58848, 29802, 21087, 23829, 37238,
11787, 40919, 14688, 40395,18346, 39958, 16671, 28462, 17412,
32281, 254115, 74856),
```

```
T = c(44444, 64685, 38925, 35244, 61929, 25450, 37910, 34017,
39697, 186076, 52362, 63929, 44204, 19817, 75728, 29965, 36867,
34415, 29709, 28348, 36743, 29032, 17318, 11061, 20002, 98434,
19143, 6449, 26493, 27913, 37105, 186475, 46911, 16614, 25935,
26261, 94085, 100131, 45409, 434374, 100053, 42042, 14767,
19811, 35336, 140502, 23753, 42753, 40997, 47370, 50531, 21888,
23844, 34485, 36452, 28909, 59035, 37597, 23072, 26719, 39246,
12741, 46384, 20152, 44301, 19117, 40712, 18004, 31113, 21665,
34689, 254115, 75872)
)
#INITIAL VALUES
list(alpha=0)
```

One possible next step in an analysis is to account for spatial autocorrelation, which involves introducing a random effects term. Importing an ArcGIS shapefile into WinBUGS enables the software to generate the necessary spatial weights matrix; it employs the queen's adjacency criterion. Computer Code 9.2 furnishes the code for implementing an ICAR model specification. The resulting Markov chains require a thinning factor of 100 (i.e., weeding such that only every 100th simulated value is retained). The result is an increase in the intercept estimate to 3.764 as well as an increase in its standard error to 0.018. Estimating the spatial autocorrelation parameter: reduces the thinning factor to 5; yields an estimate of 0.1713 (i.e., 0.1713/0.1814 = 0.944, which is close to the assumed maximum value for the ICAR specification); and increases the intercept estimate to 5.058, with a standard error of 1.098. Maps of the ICAR and CAR random effects terms appear in Figure 9.5.

A spatial filter allows estimation of a spatially structured term without resorting to simultaneous estimation of a spatially unstructured random effects term. Here estimation of the eigenvector spatial filter is a pre-processing step, and the thinning factor is 3. The resulting intercept estimate is 2.995, and the standard error 0.003; the spatial filter coefficient estimate is 1. Computer Code 9.3 furnishes the code for implementing this model specification. Extending this specification to include a spatially unstructured random effects term results in a thinning factor of 1, and increases the intercept term estimate to 6.704, with a standard deviation of 0.064. Results maps for each of these specifications appear in Figure 9.6.

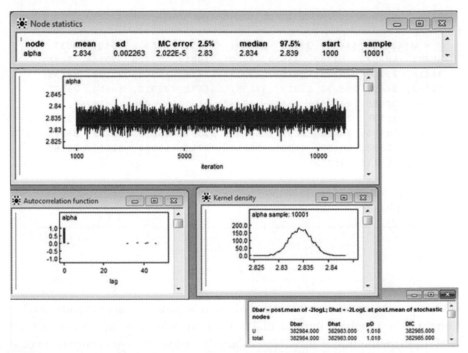

Figure 9.3 WinBUGS compiled screenshot for selected output.

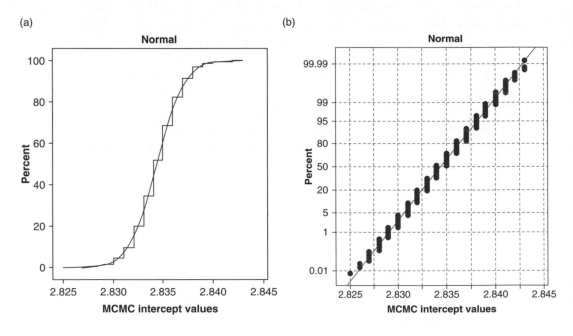

Figure 9.4 Correspondence between the sample posterior distribution in Figure 9.3 and a normal distribution. (a) Cumulative distribution function. (b) Normal quantile plot.

Computer Code 9.2. WinBUGS code for ICAR binomial regression analysis.

```
#MODEL
model
{
for (i in 1 : N) {
    U[i]   ~ dbin(p[i], T[i])
    p[i] <- exp(alpha+SS[i])/(1+exp(alpha+SS[i]))
}
# improper CAR prior distribution for random effects:
SS[1:N] ~ car.normal(adj[], weights[], num[], precSS)
for(k in 1:sumNumNeigh) {weights[k] <- 1}
# Other priors:
alpha  ~ dflat()
precSS ~ dgamma(0.5, 0.0005)    # prior on SS precision
varSS <- 1 / precSS            # SS variance
}
#DATA
list(N = 73,
U = c(42527, 64685, 36201, 30886, 59572,24196, 36971, 33421,
37713, 185703, 50242, 63929, 38583, 18664, 75728,27605, 35270,
25584, 29709, 25387, 35476, 27305, 11048, 3792, 16800, 95880,
11062, 2839, 23077, 23364, 34650, 178792, 40875, 16472,
23848,21330, 94085, 91593, 41997, 434374, 99850, 42042, 14767,
14262, 23852,139445, 21499, 40457, 35130, 43707, 46236, 20682,
17200, 32126, 35859, 27850, 58848, 29802, 21087, 23829, 37238,
11787, 40919, 14688, 40395,18346, 39958, 16671, 28462, 17412,
32281, 254115, 74856),
T = c(44444, 64685, 38925, 35244, 61929, 25450, 37910, 34017,
39697, 186076, 52362, 63929, 44204, 19817, 75728, 29965, 36867,
34415, 29709, 28348, 36743, 29032, 17318, 11061, 20002, 98434,
19143, 6449, 26493, 27913, 37105, 186475, 46911, 16614, 25935,
26261, 94085, 100131, 45409, 434374, 100053, 42042, 14767,
19811, 35336, 140502, 23753, 42753, 40997, 47370, 50531, 21888,
23844, 34485, 36452, 28909, 59035, 37597, 23072, 26719, 39246,
12741, 46384, 20152, 44301, 19117, 40712, 18004, 31113, 21665,
34689, 254115, 75872),
num = c(4, 3, 4, 4, 3, 3, 5, 3, 5, 5, 5, 6, 7, 3, 4, 6, 6, 8,
5, 6, 5, 6, 5, 5, 5, 6, 6, 6, 5, 3, 6, 5, 4, 3, 5, 4, 3, 4, 4,
5, 3, 4, 2, 7, 7, 7, 4, 6, 7, 7, 6, 3, 8, 7, 5, 7, 3, 7, 3, 3,
5, 2, 6, 6, 4, 2, 2, 4, 5, 3, 3, 6, 4),
adj = c(
2, 6, 9, 13,
1, 9, 42,
4, 18, 38, 45,
3, 6, 13, 18,
7, 16, 39,
```

```
1, 4, 13,
5, 8, 12, 16, 17,
7, 12, 37,
1, 2, 13, 20, 42,
15, 21, 40, 55, 73,
14, 47, 54, 68, 73,
7, 8, 17, 19, 37, 72,
1, 4, 6, 9, 18, 20, 24,
11, 67, 68,
10, 21, 40, 46,
5, 7, 17, 39, 44, 53,
7, 12, 16, 19, 53, 56,
3, 4, 13, 24, 27, 28, 45, 63,
12, 17, 25, 56, 72,
9, 13, 24, 26, 42, 43,
10, 15, 46, 49, 55,
25, 40, 41, 46, 48, 72,
32, 44, 45, 51, 53,
13, 18, 20, 26, 28,
19, 22, 48, 56, 72,
20, 24, 28, 31, 33, 34,
18, 32, 45, 59, 60, 63,
18, 24, 26, 31, 35, 63,
48, 50, 56, 58, 69,
51, 53, 58,
26, 28, 33, 34, 35, 36,
23, 27, 45, 51, 60,
26, 31, 34, 36,
26, 31, 33,
28, 31, 36, 52, 63,
31, 33, 35, 52,
8, 12, 72,
3, 44, 45, 71,
5, 16, 44, 71,
10, 15, 22, 41, 46,
22, 40, 72,
2, 9, 20, 43,
20, 42,
16, 23, 38, 39, 45, 53, 71,
3, 18, 23, 27, 32, 38, 44,
15, 21, 22, 40, 48, 49, 50,
11, 54, 57, 68,
22, 25, 29, 46, 50, 56,
21, 46, 50, 54, 55, 61, 64,
29, 46, 48, 49, 64, 65, 69,
```

```
23, 30, 32, 53, 58, 70,
35, 36, 63,
16, 17, 23, 30, 44, 51, 56, 58,
11, 47, 49, 55, 57, 61, 73,
10, 21, 49, 54, 73,
17, 19, 25, 29, 48, 53, 58,
47, 54, 61,
29, 30, 51, 53, 56, 69, 70,
27, 60, 63,
27, 32, 59,
49, 54, 57, 62, 64,
61, 64,
18, 27, 28, 35, 52, 59,
49, 50, 61, 62, 65, 66,
50, 64, 66, 69,
64, 65,
14, 68,
11, 14, 47, 67,
29, 50, 58, 65, 70,
51, 58, 69,
38, 39, 44,
12, 19, 22, 25, 37, 41,
10, 11, 54, 55
),
sumNumNeigh = 348)
#INITIAL VALUES
list(alpha=0, precSS=1,
SS=c(0,0,0,0,0,0,0,0,0,0,0,0,0,0,0,0,0,0,0,0,0,0,0,0,0,0,0,0,0,0,
0,0,0,0,0,0,0,0,0,0,0,0,0,0,0,0,0,0,0,0,0,0,0,0,0,0,0,0,0,0,0,0,0,
0,0,0,0,0,0,0,0,0,0)
)
```

(a)   (b)

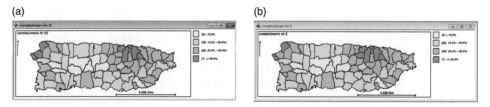

Figure 9.5 WinBUGS random effects terms. (a) Obtained with an ICAR specification.
(b) Obtained with a CAR specification.

Computer Code 9.3. WinBUGS code for eigenvector spatial filter binomial regression analysis.

```
#MODEL
model
{for (i in 1 : N) {
    U[i]  ~ dbin(p[i], T[i])
    p[i] <- 1/(1+exp(-alpha - b*SF[i]))}
# Other priors:
alpha ~ dflat()
b ~ dnorm(1,1.0E-5)
}
#DATA
list(N = 73,
U = c(42527, 64685, 36201, 30886, 59572,24196, 36971, 33421,
37713, 185703, 50242, 63929, 38583, 18664, 75728,27605, 35270,
25584, 29709, 25387, 35476, 27305, 11048, 3792, 16800,95880,
11062, 2839, 23077, 23364, 34650, 178792, 40875, 16472,
23848,21330, 94085, 91593, 41997, 434374, 99850, 42042, 14767,
14262, 23852,139445, 21499, 40457, 35130, 43707, 46236, 20682,
17200, 32126, 35859, 27850, 58848, 29802, 21087, 23829, 37238,
11787, 40919, 14688, 40395,18346, 39958, 16671, 28462, 17412,
32281, 254115, 74856),
T = c(44444, 64685, 38925, 35244, 61929, 25450, 37910, 34017,
39697, 186076, 52362, 63929, 44204, 19817, 75728, 29965, 36867,
34415, 29709, 28348, 36743, 29032, 17318, 11061, 20002, 98434,
19143, 6449, 26493, 27913, 37105, 186475, 46911, 16614, 25935,
26261, 94085, 100131, 45409, 434374, 100053, 42042, 14767,
19811, 35336, 140502, 23753, 42753, 40997, 47370, 50531, 21888,
23844, 34485, 36452, 28909, 59035, 37597, 23072, 26719, 39246,
12741, 46384, 20152, 44301, 19117, 40712, 18004, 31113, 21665,
34689, 254115, 75872),
SF = c(-1.137518, 1.491700, 1.069692, 1.662677, -0.748245,
0.262096, -0.402159, -0.017504, -0.164057, 0.409578, 2.613552,
0.304349, 0.341998, -1.310238, 0.466386, -0.957026, 0.362092,
-0.889712, 0.164100, -1.232902, 1.451166, 1.630955, 1.673424,
0.299560, -0.322737, -0.484777, -0.209917, 1.505092, 0.001573,
-0.953810, 0.230846, 0.340325, 0.054938, -1.335408, -1.410285,
-0.394615, 0.086024, -2.688523, -1.730705, -0.183643, -0.139794,
0.280239, -0.018101, -1.971644, 0.284003, -0.599356, 0.799498,
0.479685, 0.310890, 2.101611, -0.919954, -0.322202, -0.072132,
-0.955641, -0.713250, 0.981736, 0.121009, -0.832610, -0.958571,
-0.350464, 1.379148, -0.657765, -1.397524, -0.706984, 2.837594,
1.746381, 0.747843, -1.527760, 1.852185, 0.608635, -0.818181,
0.103756, -1.520626))
#INITIAL VALUES
list(alpha=0, b=1)
```

(a)   (b)

Figure 9.6   WinBUGS random effects terms. (a) Eigenvector spatial filter.
(b) Spatially unstructured random effects obtained with an eigenvector
spatial filter model specification.

9.2. Designing Monte Carlo simulation experiments

Monte Carlo simulation is named for the city in the principality of Monaco, famous for the roulette wheel, a simple random number generator. The Monte Carlo method is a brute-force way of providing approximate solutions to a variety of mathematical problems by performing statistical sampling experiments with a computer using pseudo–random numbers. MCMC makes heavy use of Monte Carlo simulation. Other parts of spatial statistics also employ this tool. The following steps are critical in designing an appropriate Monte Carlo experiment:

1 Properly specify the spatial statistical model of interest (e.g., an auto–logistic model).
2 Determine what properties of the model need to vary (e.g., size of geographic landscape, level of spatial autocorrelation); control for other sources of variation.
3 Select the set of population parameter values to study (e.g., values commonly reported in the literature, error levels frequently encountered in practice, proper Type I and Type II error controls, controlling the degree of bias when model misspecification is of interest).
4 Perform checks based upon standard statistical theory to verify the trustworthiness of the simulated output (e.g., assume spatial autocorrelation is 0).
5 Execute a sufficient number of replications (e.g., 10,000).

Step 5 needs to ensure that the law of large numbers is operating. This allows summary statistics across a Monte Carlo simulation to exploit the central limit theorem.

9.2.1. A Monte Carlo experiment investigating eigenvector selection when constructing a spatial filter

One concern with eigenvector spatial filtering arises from the controversy surrounding the use of stepwise regression techniques (e.g., Derksen and Keselman, 1992; Steyerberg et al., 1999). Well-recognized stepwise multiple regression limitations include: model selection bias, spurious inflation of R^2 values (i.e., Freedman's paradox), severe problems in the presence of multicollinearity, and the size of a candidate eigenvector set – which may well affect the number of noise (i.e., merely by chance) eigenvectors selected. Model selection bias arises when chance inclusion of meaningless eigenvectors produces an underestimate of the variance, and a corresponding exaggeration of the precision of the resulting model. However, restricting attention to a candidate set of eigenvectors (much less than n) dictated by a minimal level of spatial autocorrelation helps minimize this bias. Meanwhile, one index for assessing R^2 inflation is comparison with the pseudo-R^2 for a corresponding autoregressive model. Experience to date indicates that the eigenvector spatial filter specification often renders a slightly higher (albeit comparable) value than the pseudo-R^2 value associated with an SAR specification. Furthermore, the eigenvectors extracted from a modified spatial weights matrix are orthogonal and uncorrelated by construction, minimizing or eliminating parameter estimation bias. Finally, a test of residuals for the presence of spatial autocorrelation allows amelioration of this situation. For example, if overcorrection for spatial autocorrelation occurs, then the appropriate marginal selections can be classified as noise eigenvectors and then removed.

An informative but simple Monte Carlo simulation experiment lets spatial autocorrelation be 0 for a random variable, and then varies the size of the landscape as well as the type of random variable. The design used here includes a 5 × 5 and a 25 × 25 lattice, and the normal ($\mu = 0$, $\sigma^2 = 1$), Poisson ($\mu = 11$), and binomial ($N_{tr} = 10$, $p = 0.4$) random variables (Figure 9.7). It explores only the most observed positive spatial autocorrelation case; the number of replications is 10,000, and the stepwise regression selection criterion is $\alpha = 0.01$. Table 9.2 reports selected summary results from this experiment. One implication of these results is that sample size matters with eigenvector spatial filtering: as the number of locations increases, although stepwise regression selects relatively few vectors having spurious relationships with the response variable, the percentage of variance they account for tends to decrease substantially. When an analysis involves at least a moderate number of locations, even if numerous eigenvectors are selected by the stepwise regression procedure,

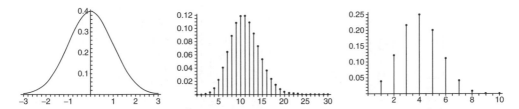

Figure 9.7 Theoretical random variable distributions from which samples were drawn for the Monte Carlo simulation experiments.

these vectors describe only trace levels of spatial autocorrelation – the spurious spatial autocorrelation contained in random data.

One implication of this experiment is that the use of stepwise regression for constructing spatial filters benefits from increased sample size. Another is that relatively small sample sizes, which have a more pronounced tendency to select too many eigenvectors, may well yield residuals displaying negative spatial autocorrelation (i.e., overcorrection has occurred; see Section 2.5). In these instances, residual spatial autocorrelation distribution theory furnishes a tool for removing the noise eigenvectors.

These results are consistent with those reported in Tiefelsdorf and Griffith (2007, Appendix A) for non-random data that are based on initial random variables constructed with near-zero spatial autocorrelation.

9.2.2. A Monte Carlo experiment investigating eigenvector selection from a restricted candidate set of vectors

Table-9.2- type results are poorer when $\alpha = 0.05$ or $\alpha = 0.15$. However, a second simulation experiment involving these stepwise selection levels, as well as a 35 × 35 lattice, but only for a normal random variable, suggests that rather than using an arbitrary relative Moran Coefficient (MC) MC_{max}, where MC_{max} denotes the maximum MC value of 0.25 for positive spatial autocorrelation cases to establish a candidate set of eigenvectors from which to select, only vectors having an MC value exceeding the threshold

$$2.9970 - \frac{2.8805}{1 + e^{-0.6606 - 0.2525 z_{MC}}} \tag{9.2}$$

Table 9.2 Summary simulation experiment statistics for the specimen simulation experiment

Lattice	n	# MC/MC$_{max}$ > 0.25 eigenvectors	Normal			Poisson			Binomial		
			# vectors		Max R^2	# vectors		Max psuedo-R^2	# vectors		Max pseudo-R^2
			% 0	Max		% 0	Max		% 0	Max	
5 × 5	25	9	90.8	3	0.31	91.6	2	0.62	91.8	3	0.61
25 × 25	625	191	14.0	10	0.05	14.7	9	0.11	14.3	9	0.12

Table 9.3 Summary simulation experiment statistics for normal random variables based on equation-(9.1)-determined candidate sets of eigenvectors

Stepwise selection criterion	5 × 5 (n = 25)				25 × 25 (n = 625)				35 × 35 (n = 1,225)			
	# vectors			Max R^2	# vectors			Max R^2	# vectors			Max R^2
	Total	% 0	Max		Total	% 0	Max		Total	% 0	Max	
1%	2	98.2	1	0.286	19	82.0	3	0.024	38	67.2	4	0.014
5%	2	90.2	2	0.309	29	73.7	4	0.024	59	48.6	13	0.024
10%	2	80.3	2	0.300	49	60.4	5	0.033	97	0[a]	23	0.039[b]

[a] 58.6% of the constructed spatial filters contained between 8 and 12 eigenvectors.
[b] The minimum variance accounted for by a constructed spatial filter is 0.1%.

should be included in this candidate set (Griffith and Chun, 2009). For a 10% level of significance, this threshold value becomes 0.90. For a 5% level of significance, it becomes 0.85. And for a 1% level of significance, it becomes 0.76. All three of these values are substantially greater than 0.25.

Results reported in Table 9.3 further support benefits from increased sample size. In all but one instance, large percentages of attempted spatial filter construction fail (i.e., selection of 0 vectors) with random data. This tendency is weaker with generalized linear models (Table 9.2), most likely because the weightings involved in their parameter estimation corrupt the orthogonality and uncorrelatedness properties of the eigenvectors. This second experiment further supports the use of stepwise regression for eigenvector spatial filter construction in practice, because most empirical georeferenced datasets involve sample sizes that are not small (e.g., less than 30). Even when numerous noise vectors are selected, the constructed spatial filter for larger sample sizes would be dismissed because it accounts for almost no variation in its response variable (e.g., in the worst-case scenario, for which a spatial filter construction occurs for every simulated variable, 23 vectors account for a mere 3.9% of the variation). Results from simulations, with 1,000 replications, for 50×50 ($n = 2,500$) and 75×75 ($n = 5,625$) square tessellation landscapes corroborate these findings, including convergence of the percentage of zeros to 0. This latter outcome most likely is attributable to the curse of very large sample sizes, for which almost everything becomes significant.

9.3. Spatial error: a contributor to uncertainty

Arbia et al. (1999) suggest that principal sources of spatial error are: random variable variation, location error, and interaction between the spatial autocorrelation in both of these sources of error. Griffith et al. (2007) find that location error makes a difference, but moderate amounts still may result in parameter estimates falling within the correct confidence intervals. They also confirm that most location error for polygon-based geographic data is a displacement to adjacent polygons. These are contributors to uncertainty, or the margin of error of geographic measurements.

Chapters 2 and 5 address this topic by recognizing variance inflation attributable to the presence of spatial autocorrelation in georeferenced data. Even simple histograms can be dramatically distorted (Chapter 2). Adjustments accounting for spatial autocorrelation help minimize uncertainty (Chapter 5). Spatial sampling (Chapter 3) impacts directly on margins of error. The tessellated random sampling design helps guarantee improved geographic coverage of a landscape, but fails to help with the problem of small sample size. Small sample sizes produce very large margins of error. Chapter 4 alludes to the modifiable areal unit problem, which introduces considerable uncertainty into geographic data analyses. Chapter 4 also emphasizes the role of model assumptions, which are crucial to model-based inference (i.e., assumptions must mirror the real world in order for model-based inference to be sound). Chapter 6 emphasizes that in many cases a global analysis fails to be sufficiently informative, and a local analysis becomes necessary. Even when the average level of pollution for a toxic dump site is below a target threshold for remediation action, parts of the site may well be far above this threshold, and hence in need of remediation. Chapter 7 addresses the issues of accuracy and precision. Simple analyses can be improved by including a few judiciously selected covariates (e.g., co-kriging). Finally, Chapter 8 summarizes imputation methods. Spatial analysts need to keep in mind that these ways of filling gaps in maps also result in suppression of variance. Imputations are smoothing exercises; they produce conditional means. Consequently, the residuals accompanying them are zero or near-zero.

Discussions especially in Chapter 3 highlight sampling error, in Chapter 5 specification error, and in Chapter 7 prediction errors. Other sources of error include measurement, stochastic noise, and calculation. Modern computing technology has all but eliminated this latter source. Mixed models (Section 9.1) address stochastic noise, partitioning it into spatially structured and spatially unstructured components.

9.4. R code for concept implementations

Computer Code 9.4 implements the simulation experiments summarized in Section 9.2, but only for the normal distribution cases. As indicated earlier, R stepwise regression functions, especially in the *MASS* package, employ AIC as a selection criterion. Resulting stepwise selections tend to include more eigenvectors than a procedure based upon statistical significance. In this exercise, the conventional stepwise regression based on model significance is implemented, as in earlier chapters of this book, with *stepwise.forward* and the all_functions.R file. This function enables duplication of the Monte Carlo experiments summarized in Section 9.2, although specific results will differ because the pseudo-random number generators employ a different seed with each execution. Note that a simulation experiment comprising a large number of replications and a large spatial tessellation, such as the 25×25 and 35×35 square tessellations, may take a long time to execute.

The Bayesian data analyses in this chapter have been done with the WinBUGS software. The *R2WinBUGS* and *BRugs* packages in R allow WinBUGS to interface with R. These packages have functions to call WinBUGS with a model, data, and initial values in R, and to store Bayesian simulation results as R objects. Accordingly, procedures such as data preparation, visualization of MCMC results, and post-processing can be integrated into the single R environment.

Computer Code 9.4. Implementing Monte Carlo experiments for eigenvector selection.

```
# 9.2.1
source("all_functions.R")

# Normal 5x5 case
n <- 5
n.sim <- 10000
EV <- gen.ev.square(n, 0.25)

r.norm <- sapply(1:n.sim, function(x, n)
{rnorm(n^2)}, n=n)

sim.n.5 <- matrix(NA, n.sim, 2)
colnames(sim.n.5) <- c("# of EV", "r.sq")
for (i in 1:n.sim){
  y <- r.norm[,i]
  lm.full <- lm(y ~ ., data=EV)
  lm.i <- stepwise.forward(lm.full,
    lm(y ~ 1, data=EV), 0.01, verbose=F)
  sim.n.5[i,] <- c(lm.i$rank-1,
    summary(lm.i)$r.squared)
}
summary(sim.n.5)
sum(sim.n.5[,1]==0)/n.sim


# Normal 25x25 case
n <- 25
n.sim <- 10000
EV <- gen.ev.square(n, 0.25)
r.norm <- sapply(1:n.sim, function(x, n)
{rnorm(n^2)}, n=n)

sim.n.25 <- matrix(NA, n.sim, 2)
colnames(sim.n.25) <- c("# of EV","r.sq")
for (i in 1:n.sim){
  y <- r.norm[,i]
  lm.full <- lm(y ~ ., data=EV)
  lm.i <- stepwise.forward(lm.full,
    lm(y ~ 1, data=EV), 0.01, verbose=F)
  sim.n.25[i,] <- c(lm.i$rank-1,
    summary(lm.i)$r.squared)
}
summary(sim.n.25)
sum(sim.n.25[,1]==0)/n.sim
```

Load functions to be used including *gen.ev.square()*.

Set a square tessellation size.
Set a number of simulations.
Generate eigenvectors with 0.25 of Moran's *I*.
Generate random numbers from the standard normal distribution.

Create an output object with n.xim by 2 dimension and set its column names.

Conduct spatial filtering for each random set.

Store the number of selected eigenvectors and R^2.

Summary statistics of the output.

Conduct the same simulation with a 25x25 square tessellation.

```# 9.2.2```
```n.sim <- 10000```
```# Normal 5x5 case 1%```
```sim.n.5.1p <- sim.sf.norm (n=5, n.sim,```
```mc=0.76)```
```summary(sim.n.5.1p)```
```sum(sim.n.5.1p[,1]==0)/n.sim```
	Conduct the same simulation with a 5x5 square tessellation for 1% level, using the *sim.sf.norm()* function which is defined in the all_functions.R file:

```# Normal 5x5 case 5%```
```sim.n.5.5p <- sim.sf.norm (n=5, n.sim,```
```mc=0.85)```
```summary(sim.n.5.5p)```
```sum(sim.n.5.5p[,1]==0)/n.sim```
	for 5% level

```# Normal 5x5 case 10%```
 	
```summary(sim.n.5.10p)```
```sum(sim.n.5.10p[,1]==0)/n.sim```
	for 10% level.

```# Normal 25x25 case 1%```
```sim.n.25.1p <- sim.sf.norm (n=25, n.sim,```
```nc=0.76)```
```summary(sim.n.25.1p)```
```sum(sim.n.25.1p[,1]==0)/n.sim```
	With a 25x25 square tessellation: for 1% level

```# Normal 25x25 case 5%```
```sim.n.25.5p <- sim.sf.norm (n=25, n.sim,```
```nc=0.85)```
```summary(sim.n.25.5p)```
```sum(sim.n.25.5p[,1]==0)/n.sim```
	for 5% level.

```# Normal 25x25 case 10%```
```sim.n.25.5p <- sim.sf.norm (n=25, n.sim,```
```nc=0.90)```
```summary(sim.n.25.10p)```
```sum(sim.n.25.10p[,1]==0)/n.sim```
	for 10% level.

```# Normal 35x35 case 1%```
```sim.n.35.1p <- sim.sf.norm (n=35, n.sim,```
```nc=0.76)```
```summary(sim.n.35.1p)```
```sum(sim.n.35.1p[,1]==0)/n.sim```
	With a 35x35 square tessellation: for 1% level

```# Normal 35x35 case 5%```
```sim.n.35.5p <- sim.sf.norm (n=35, n.sim,```
```nc=0.85)```
```summary(sim.n.35.5p)```
```sum(sim.n.35.5p[,1]==0)/n.sim```
	for 5% level

```# Normal 35x35 case 10%```
```sim.n.35.10p <- sim.sf.norm (n=35, n.sim,```
```nc=0.90)```
```summary(sim.n.35.10p)```
```sum(sim.n.35.10p[,1]==0)/n.sim```
	for 10% level.

References

Abdi, H. and Williams, L. (2010) Jackknife, in N. Salkind (ed.), *Encyclopedia of Research Design*, Vol. 2. Thousand Oaks, CA: Sage, pp. 655–60.

Abramowitz, M. and Stegun, I. (eds) (1972) *Handbook of Mathematical Functions with Formulas, Graphs, and Mathematical Tables*. New York: Dover.

Anselin, L. (1995) Local indicators of spatial association – LISA, *Geographical Analysis*, 27: 93–115.

Anselin, L., Syabri, I. and Kho, Y. (2006) *GeoDa*: an introduction to spatial data analysis, *Geographical Analysis*, 38: 5–22.

Arbia, G., Griffith, D. and Haining, R. (1999) Error propagation modeling in raster GIS: adding and ratioing operations, *Cartography and Geographic Information Science*, 26: 297–315.

Bailey, T. and Gatrell, A. (1995) *Interactive Spatial Data Analysis*. Harlow: Longman.

Bennett, R., Griffith, D. and Haining, R. (1984) The problem of missing data on spatial surfaces, *Annals – Association of American Geographers*, 74: 138–56.

Besag, J. (1974) Spatial interaction and the statistical analysis of lattice systems, *Journal of the Royal Statistical Society B*, 36: 192–225.

Box, G. and Tidwell, P. (1962) Transformation of the independent variables, *Technometrics*, 4: 531–50.

Christensen, R. (1991) *Linear Models for Multivariate, Time Series, and Spatial Data*. Berlin: Springer-Verlag.

Chun, Y. and Griffith, D. (2011) Modeling network autocorrelation in space-time migration flow data: an eigenvector spatial filtering approach, *Annals – Association of American Geographers*, 101: 523–36.

Cliff, A. and Ord, J. (1973) *Spatial Autocorrelation*. London: Pion.

Cliff, A. and Ord, J. (1975) The comparison of means when samples consist of spatially autocorrelated observations, *Environment and Planning A*, 7: 725–34.

Cliff, A. and Ord, J. (1981) *Spatial Processes: Models and Applications*. London: Pion.

Clifford, P., Richardson, S. and Hémon, D. (1989) Assessing the significance of the correlation between two spatial processes, *Biometrics*, 45: 123–34.

Cressie, N. (1981) Transformations and the jackknife, *Journal of the Royal Statistical Society B*, 43: 177–82.

Cressie, N. (1991) *Statistics for Spatial Data*. New York: Wiley.

Cowles, M. (2004) Review of WinBugs 1.4, *American Statistician*, 58: 330–6.

Cuaresma, J.C. and Feldkircher, M. (2012) Spatial filtering, model uncertainty and the speed of income convergence in Europe, *Journal of Applied Econometrics*, forthcoming, doi: 10.1002/jae.2277.

de Castro, M. and Singer, B. (2006) Controlling the false discovery rate: a new application to account for multiple and dependent tests in local statistics of spatial association, *Geographical Analysis*, 38: 180–208.

de Jong, P., Sprenger, C. and van Veen, F. (1984) On extreme values of Moran's *I* and Geary's *c*, *Geographical Analysis*, 16: 17–24.

De Marco, P., Jr., Diniz-Filho, J.A.F. and Bini, L. (2008) Spatial analysis improves species distribution modelling during range expansion, *Biology Letters*, 4: 577–80.

Dempster, A., Laird, N. and Rubin, D. (1977) Maximum likelihood from incomplete data via the EM algorithm, *Journal of the Royal Statistical Society B*, 39: 1–38.

Derksen, S. and Keselman, H. (1992) Backward, forward and stepwise automated subset selection algorithms: frequency of obtaining authentic and noise variables, *British Journal of Mathematical and Statistical Psychology*, 45: 265–82.

Diaconis, P. and Efron, B. (1983) Computer-intensive methods in statistics, *Scientific American*, 248 (5 May): 116–30.

Diniz-Filho, J.A.F. and Bini, L.M. (2005) Modelling geographical patterns in species richness using eigenvector-based spatial filters, *Global Ecology and Biogeography*, 14: 177–85.

Diniz-Filho, J.A.F., Nabout, J.C., Telles, M.P.C., Soares, T.N. and Rangel, T.F. (2009) A review of techniques for spatial modeling in geographical conservation and landscape genetics, *Genetics and Molecular Biology*, 32: 203–11.

Dormann, C.F., McPherson, J., Araújo, M., Bivand, R., Bolliger, J., Carl, G., Davies, R., Hirzel, A., Jetz, W., Kissling, W.D., Kühn, I., Ohlemüller, R., Peres-Neto, P., Reineking, B., Schröder, B., Schurr, F. and Wilson, R. (2007) Methods to account for spatial autocorrelation in the analysis of species distributional data: A review, *Ecography*, 30: 609–28.

Dutilleul, P. (1993) Modifying the *t* test for assessing the correlation between two spatial processes, *Biometrics*, 49: 305–14.

Dutilleul, P., Pelletier, B. and Alpargu, G. (2008) Modified *F* tests for assessing the multiple correlation between one spatial process and several others, *Journal of Statistical Planning and Inference*, 138: 1402–15.

Ficetola, G.F. and Padoa-Schioppa, E. (2009) Human activities alter biogeographical patterns of reptiles on Mediterranean islands, *Global Ecology and Biogeography*, 18: 214–22.

Flury, B. and Zoppè, A. (2000) Exercises in EM, *American Statistician*, 54: 207–9.

Fotheringham, S. (1997) Trends in quantitative methods I: Stressing the local, *Progress in Human Geography*, 21: 88–96.

Geary, R. (1954) The contiguity ratio and statistical mapping, *Incorporated Statistician*, 5: 115–41.

Gelman, A. (2002) Posterior distribution, in A. El-Shaarawi and W. Piegorsch (eds), *Encyclopedia of Environmetrics*, Vol. 3. Chichester: Wiley, pp. 1627–8.

Getis, A. and Ord, J. (1992) The analysis of spatial association by use of distance statistics, *Geographical Analysis*, 24: 189–206.

Griffith, D. (1988) Estimating spatial autoregressive model parameters with commercial statistical packages, *Geographical Analysis*, 20: 176–86.

Griffith, D. (1993a) Advanced spatial statistics for analyzing and visualizing geo-referenced data, *International Journal of Geographical Information Systems*, 7: 107–23.

Griffith, D. (1993b) *Spatial Regression Analysis on the PC: Spatial Statistics Using SAS*, Washington, DC: Association of American Geographers.

Griffith, D. (1996) Spatial autocorrelation and eigenfunctions of the geographic weights matrix accompanying geo-referenced data, *Canadian Geographer*, 40: 351–67.

Griffith, D. (2003) *Spatial Autocorrelation and Spatial Filtering: Gaining Understanding through Theory and Scientific Visualization*. Berlin: Springer-Verlag.

Griffith, D. (2008) Spatial filtering-based contributions to a critique of geographically weighted regression (GWR), *Environment and Planning A*, 40: 2751–69.

Griffith, D. (2010a) Some simplifications for the Expectation-Maximization (EM) algorithm: the linear regression model case, *InterStat*, March article 2 (http://interstat.statjournals.net/YEAR/2010/abstracts/1003002.php, http://interstat.statjournals.net/YEAR/2010/articles/1003002.pdf), 23 pp.

Griffith, D. (2010b) Spatial filtering, in M. Fischer and A. Getis (eds), *Handbook of Applied Spatial Analysis: Software Tools, Methods and Applications*. Berlin: Springer-Verlag, pp. 301–18.

Griffith, D. (2010c) The Moran coefficient for non-normal data, *Journal of Statistical Planning and Inference*, 140: 2980–90.

Griffith, D. (2011) Visualizing analytical spatial autocorrelation components latent in spatial interaction data: an eigenvector spatial filter approach, *Computers, Environment and Urban Systems*, 35: 140–9.

Griffith, D. and Amrhein, C. (1991) *Statistical Analysis for Geographers*. Upper Saddle River, NJ: Prentice Hall.

Griffith, D. and Amrhein, C. (1997) *Multivariate Statistical Analysis for Geographers*. Upper Saddle River, NJ: Prentice Hall.

Griffith, D. and Chun, Y. (2009) Eigenvector selection with stepwise regression techniques to construct spatial filters. Paper presented at the annual Association of American Geographers meeting, Las Vegas, 25 March.

Griffith, D. and Layne, L. (1997) Uncovering relationships between geo-statistical and spatial autoregressive models, in the 1996 *Proceedings on the Section on Statistics and the Environment*, American Statistical Association, pp. 91–96.

Griffith, D. and Layne, L. (1999) *A Casebook for Spatial Statistical Data Analysis*. New York: Oxford University Press.

Griffith, D., Haining, R. and Bennett, R. (1989) Statistical analysis of spatial data in the presence of missing observations: an application to urban census data, *Environment and Planning A*, 21: 1511–23.

Griffith, D., Wong, D. and Whitfield, T. (2003) Exploring relationships between the global and regional measures of spatial autocorrelation, *Journal of Regional Science*, 43: 683–710.

Griffith, D., Millones, M., Vincent, M., Johnson, D. and Hunt, A. (2007) Impacts of positional error on spatial regression analysis: a case study of address locations in Syracuse, New York, *Transactions in GIS*, 11: 655–79.

Grimpe, C. and Patuelli, R. (2011) Regional knowledge production in nanomaterials: a spatial filtering approach. *Annals of Regional Science*, 46 (3): 519–41.

Haining, R. (1991) Bivariate correlation with spatial data, *Geographical Analysis*, 23: 210–27.

Hinkley, D. (2006) Jackknife methods, in S. Kotz, N. Balakrishnan, C. Read and B.Vidakovic (eds), *Encyclopedia of Statistical Sciences*, 2nd edn, Vol. 6. Hoboken, NJ: Wiley, pp. 3727–33.

Huang, F. and Ogata, Y. (1999) Improvements of the maximum pseudo-likelihood estimators in various spatial statistical models, *Journal of Computational and Graphical Statistics*, 8: 510–30.

Jacob, B.G., Muturi, E.J., Caamano, E.X., Gunter, J.T., Mpanga, E., Ayine, R., Okelloonen, J., Nyeko, J.P.M., Shililu, J.I., Githure, J.I., Regens, J.L., Novak, R.J. and Kakoma, I. (2008) Hydrological modeling of geophysical parameters of arboviral and protozoan disease vectors in internally displaced people camps in Gulu, Uganda, *International Journal of Health Geographics*, 7: 11.

Johnson, R. and Wichern, D. (2002) *Applied Multivariate Statistical Analysis*, 5th edn. Upper Saddle River, NJ: Prentice Hall.

Johnston, K., Ver Hoef, J., Krivoruchko, K. and Lucas, N. (2001) *Using ArcGIS^{TM} Geostatistical Analyst*. Redlands, CA: ESRI Press.

Kass, R. and Wasserman, L. (1996) The selection of prior distributions by formal rules, *Journal of the American Statistical Association*, 91: 1343–70.

Lavine, M. and Hodges, J. (2012) On rigorous specification of ICAR models, *American Statistician*, 66: 42–9.

LeSage, J. and Pace, K. (2004) Models for spatially dependent missing data, *Journal of Real Estate Finance and Economics*, 29: 233–54.

LeSage, J. and Pace, K. (2009) *Introduction to Spatial Econometrics*. Boca Raton, FL: Chapman & Hall/CRC.

Lloyd, C. (2007) *Local Models for Spatial Analysis*. Boca Raton, FL: CRC Press.

Manly, B. (1976) Exponential data transformations, *The Statistician*, 25: 37–42.

Matloff, N. (1980) The jackknife: algorithm AS 148, *Applied Statistics*, 61: 115–17.

Möller, J. and Soltwedel, R. (2007) Recent development of regional labor market analysis using spatial econometrics: Introduction, *International Regional Science Review*, 30: 95–9.

Moran, P. (1948) The interpretation of statistical maps, *Journal of the Royal Statistical Society B*, 10: 243–51.

Ord, J.K. and Getis, A. (1995) Local spatial autocorrelation statistics: distribution issues and an application, *Geographical Analysis*, 27: 286–306.

Overton, S. and Stehman, S. (1993) Properties of designs for sampling continuous spatial resources from a triangular grid, *Communications in Statistics*, 22: 251–64.

Patuelli, R., Griffith, D., Tiefelsdorf, M. and Nijkamp, P. (2011) Spatial filtering and eigenvector stability: space-time models for German unemployment data, *International Regional Science Review*, 34: 253–80.

Pecci, F. and Pontarollo, N. (2010) The application of spatial filtering technique to the economic convergence of the European regions between 1995 and 2007, in D. Taniar, O. Gervasi and B. Murg (eds), *ICCSA 2010*, Part I, Lecture Notes in Computer Science 6016. Berlin: Springer-Verlag, pp. 46–61.

Ripley, B. (1990) Gibbsian interaction models, in D. Griffith (ed.), *Spatial Statistics: Past, Present, and Future*. Ann Arbor, MI: Institute of Mathematical Geography, pp. 3–25.

Schott, J. (2005) *Matrix Analysis for Statistics*, 2nd edn. Hoboken, NJ: Wiley.

Sen, A. and Sööt, S. (1977) Rank tests for spatial correlation, *Environment and Planning A*, 9: 897–903.

Shalizi, C. (2010) Computing science: the bootstrap, *American Scientist*, 98: 186–90.

Stehman, S. and Overton, S. (1996) Spatial sampling, in S. Arlinghaus (ed.), *Practical Handbook of Spatial Statistics*. Boca Raton, FL: CRC Press, pp. 31–63.

Steyerberg, E., Eijkemans, M. and Habbema, J. (1999) Stepwise selection in small data sets: a simulation study of bias in logistic regression analysis, *Journal of Clinical Epidemiology*, 52: 935–42.

Tatsuoka, M. (1988) *Multivariate Analysis*, 2nd edn (with contributions by P. Lohnes). New York: Macmillan.

Tiefelsdorf, M. and Boots, B. (1995) The exact distribution of Moran's *I*, *Environment and Planning A*, 27: 985–99.

Tiefelsdorf, M. and Griffith, D. (2007) Semi-parametric filtering of spatial autocorrelation: the eigenvector approach, *Environment and Planning A*, 39: 1193–221.

Tiefelsdorf, M., Griffith, D. and Boots, B. (1999) A variance stabilizing coding scheme for spatial link matrices, *Environment and Planning A*, 31: 165–80.

Welch, B. (1951) On the comparison of several mean values: an alternative approach, *Biometrika*, 38: 330–6.

Willmott, C. and Matsuura, K. (1995) Smart interpolation of annually averaged air temperature in the United States, *Journal of Applied Meteorology*, 34: 2577–86.

Yates, F. (1933) The analysis of replicated experiments when the field results are incomplete, *Empirical Journal of Experimental Agriculture*, 1: 129–42.

Index

Page numbers followed by a letter f refer to figures, by a letter t refer to tables and those in **bold** refer to computer code.